When We Touched the Sk

History and politics titles from New Clarion Press

Lawrence Black *et al.*, *Consensus or Coercion? The State, the People and Social Cohesion in Post-war Britain*

John Carter and Dave Morland, *Anti-Capitalist Britain*

Duncan Hall, *'A Pleasant Change from Politics': Music and the British Labour Movement between the Wars*

Anne Kerr and Tom Shakespeare, *Genetic Politics: From Eugenics to Genome*

David Renton, *Classical Marxism: Socialist Theory and the Second International*

David Renton and Keith Flett (eds), *New Approaches to Socialist History*

David Stack, *The First Darwinian Left: Socialism and Darwinism 1859–1914*

Leo Zeilig (ed.), *Class Struggle and Resistance in Africa*

When We Touched the Sky

The Anti-Nazi League 1977–1981

Dave Renton

New Clarion Press

First published 2006

New Clarion Press
5 Church Row, Gretton
Cheltenham GL54 5HG
England

New Clarion Press is a workers' co-operative.

A catalogue record for this book is available from the British Library.

ISBN   paperback   1 873797 48 6
         hardback   1 873797 49 4

Typeset in Times New Roman by Jean Wilson Typesetting, Coventry
Printed in Great Britain by The Cromwell Press, Trowbridge

Contents

Preface

My motives for writing this book go back decades. As a teenager growing up in 1980s Britain, I found that punk music spoke to me in a way that nothing else could. A small part of the appeal came from the anger of punk lyrics. A much greater part came from the sound itself. Sometimes clean and simple, at other times messy, off-time and elaborate, there was something *different* about the music, which excited my emotions, and left me feeling shocked and alive. It seemed to me then that there must be a history to this sound, some common experience which could explain the four-chord amphetamine buzz of the Buzzcocks or the Sex Pistols, the urban poetry of the Jam, the terrace-chant songs of Sham 69, and the punk-dub mix of the Clash.

Later, as a young adult, I happened to take part in the revived Anti-Nazi League of the early 1990s, a movement outside the scope of this book. This second incarnation was different from the anti-fascism of the 1970s. It was called into being to meet a lesser threat and did not take off in quite the same way as its predecessor. Yet it possessed some of the verve of the ANL, as it had existed the first time around. Hearing Jimmy Pursey's re-formed Sham 69 play the Astoria in central London in 1992, some of the mystery of punk music finally made sense. Later, at the 1994 Anti-Nazi League carnival, I witnessed a coming together of the left with the 'Crusties' of the anti-roadbuilding movement. This carnival brought out 150,000 people, to celebrate the defeat of the British National Party in East London. BNP candidate Derek Beackon had been elected in autumn 1993. The number of racist attacks rose sharply. But one year later, and despite an increase in the BNP vote, the anti-racist movement succeeded in pushing the BNP out. It was a different coalition from that of the 1970s. In place of mohicans and safety pins, the audience wore dreadlocks and combat gear. Instead of Tom Robinson, the Levellers headlined. Despite these surface differences, in essentials it was the same movement.

One activist from the time, Ben Watson, reminds us that the street music of the 1970s contained an energy that has a tendency to step outside the moment of its birth. 'Punk', he writes, 'cannot be understood simply narrating its events in chronological order . . . its determinations can only be unpicked by examining the latest developments in the contradictions it exploited, which means understanding the current relationship of capital and commodification to musical truth.'[1] This history does not follow Ben Watson's advice formally – the narrative will be too neatly chronological for his tastes – but obeys it implicitly and structurally, because he is right, the politics of punk contain layers of contemporary meaning and still stand beyond their time. The account here was written between spring 1998 and autumn 2005. When I began to write, the forces of British fascism were in a condition of atrophy, following their defeat in East London in 1993–4. Since that time, such organizations as the British National Party have enjoyed periods of advance, helped by external conditions, such as the decline of Labour's traditional roots under Blair and the hostility of the tabloids to asylum seekers. A new coalition, Unite Against Fascism, was launched in autumn 2003. I have tried not to change this book too much, avoiding the temptation of rewriting it to reflect recent experiences. Instead, the most basic influences on the writing of the book are the idea that fascism should be challenged, and an interest in the ways in which this has been done before.

Despite that warning, I will quote one article from the *Guardian* in May 2002, published as I was finishing a first draft of this book. The journalist Jackie Ashley complained of the friendly coverage that the British National Party had been awarded in the run-up to that year's local elections. Reflecting on past struggles, she wrote:

> Leon Trotsky has not made a big impact on my life, except for the circles and the arrows. Everyone on the left in my generation probably remembers them: the symbols of the Anti-Nazi League. It may have been kicked off by the Socialist Workers Party, but thousand of Labour activists, trade unionists and students carried the circles and arrows, back in the 1970s as we marched against the National Front. Immigrants were welcome here, we said. No platform for racists and fascists, we shouted. And back then, it seemed to have worked.[2]

Her argument could stand as a summary of this book.

Given that this was one of the largest and most effective campaigns of the postwar British left, it is surprising to observe how little interest historians have shown in 1970s anti-fascism. One of the key participants, Dave Widgery, described the ANL in his superb history of Rock Against Racism, *Beating Time* (1986), while RAR also features briefly in Jon Savage's history of punk rock, *England's Dreaming* (1991), in Pete Alexander's *Racism, Resistance and Revolution* (1987) and in Paul Gilroy's collection, *There Ain't No Black in the Union Jack* (1987). Nigel Copsey discusses the ANL briefly in his book *Anti-Fascism in Twentieth Century Britain* (2000), although the author would be the first to admit that his real interest is in the smaller groups which also played their part. Anthony Messina also discusses the campaign in his *Race and Party Competition* (1989), but Messina's focus is on electoral politics, and this narrows the limits of his analysis. There are also accounts in the literature published by smaller left-wing groups from the period.[3]

The heroes of Jon Savage's narrative are the Situationists, whose

symbolism was copied by Malcolm McLaren, and other members of the
Sex Pistols' entourage. While offering passing thanks to the members of
Rock Against Racism, for liberating punk from the 'miasma of fascism',
Savage goes on to complain of knuckle-headed leftists who failed to understand that when bands like the Sex Pistols wore swastikas, they meant
it as a radical joke. True enough, the members of RAR might have responded, but was the joke ever *funny*?[4]

The two writers who have studied the movement most closely are Dave
Widgery and Paul Gilroy. Widgery describes the anti-fascism of the
1970s as a successful broad alliance between revolutionaries and young
punks. His is a participant's memoir; an honest, favourable history of the
movement. Gilroy's approach is different. While celebrating the positive
relationship between black music and RAR, Paul Gilroy goes on to suggest that there was a radical break between the two stages of the
anti-fascist campaign. RAR fought both fascism and the state. The ANL,
by contrast, subscribed to the 1939–45 legend of British anti-fascism. Its
leaflets criticized the NF as sham patriots. Ultimately, it colluded with the
state. These insights are by no means accidental to Gilroy's work. *There
Ain't No Black* was his first work, and the criticisms there of the ANL
have reappeared in several of his subsequent books.[5] This history will disagree with his claim that there is a break in the history of the movement.
But it will suffice to observe here that neither Gilroy nor Widgery ever
conducted sustained research into the separate activities of the Anti-Nazi
League. For both of these writers, the discussion of the ANL is subsidiary
to their main interest, which is RAR. The account here contains the first
book-length history of the Anti-Nazi League, and of the campaign as a
whole.

Apart from the books mentioned, almost nothing of any length has
been written about the campaign. There are a few web articles, the occasional short book chapter. This book will argue that the campaign should
be studied both because it was an interesting movement and because it
worked. Most of the research for this book is based on published but so
far unused material, including leaflets, fanzines and reports from
left-wing papers such as *Morning Star* and *Socialist Worker* and the Rock
Against Racism fanzine, *Temporary Hoarding*.

This study was shaped by the assistance of many friends and comrades.
All historical work is collaborative, but this book was more so than most.
I should first of all thank those who became friends while campaigning
against the BNP in the early 1990s. They include Rachel Aldred, Mat-
thew Barratt, Jenni Borg, Chris Brooke, Palash Dave, Jake Hotson, Bruce
Howard, Sam James, Dave Pinnock, Robin Sen, Alexis Wearmouth and
Matthew Zepf. I would also like to thank a different generation of
anti-racist activists, including Matt Perry, Nick Seccombe and Maureen
Foster, for their support in Sunderland in 2002 and 2003.

Several debts have been more immediate. I first took the decision to
write about the Anti-Nazi League after the socialist photographer Jess

Hurd gave me a collection of papers from the 1970s, which she had put together while writing a student dissertation on the same subject. Martin Williams loaned me original film of the Lewisham protests; Alan Miles was kind enough to give me a copy of his film retrospective on Rock Against Racism, *Who Shot the Sheriff?* Former Anti-Nazi League organizer Pete Alexander loaned me such files as he still has, and shared ideas as to the structure and content of the book. He also kindly agreed to read through the text, suggesting a number of changes. It was not the first time he has helped me. Instead I have felt his encouragement over many years, and on many different projects. All I can do here is offer him my heartfelt thanks.

Several of the arguments here were first tried out in discussions with Nigel Copsey. Ian Goodyer allowed me to quote from his MA dissertation on 'The Cultural Politics of Rock Against Racism', which deserves publication soon. Many other activists gave me original material to use. These collections included notes, memorabilia and photographs. Often the images of demonstrations would vary from the account recorded in the papers at the time. This private material was enormously suggestive, vital stuff. I have also been fortunate to have access to a range of archives, the British Library and the British Newspaper Library, the National Museum of Labour History and especially the archives at Warwick and Hull universities.

As part of the research for this book, I also interviewed eighty activists who had taken part in the campaign. This generation of activists from the late 1970s have gone on to work within all sorts of different left-wing and anti-racist movements. The interviewees included members and ex-members of a dozen trade unions, Anti-Fascist Action, the Anti-Nazi League, the All-London Campaign Against Racism and Fascism, the Asian Youth Movement, the International Marxist Group, the Jewish Socialist Group, the Labour Party and the Liberal Democrats, Red Action, the Socialist Labour League, the Socialist Workers Party and many other groups. The list is by no means definitive. I hope that other accounts will follow this book, providing their own memories or other perspectives on the time.

Given that many of the people who provided their memories are still active on the political left or in the anti-racist campaigns, it would be inappropriate to give the full names of every one of the interviewees in the text. Allowing the exception of those whose names are already well in the public domain, the surnames of most other interviewees have been left out. I trust that the parties of British fascism are unlikely to grow again to the size they once enjoyed, but in case they do, I have no desire to provide them with details of people who blocked them in the past. More to the point, as I showed drafts of this book to people for comments, several of the interviewees themselves asked for anonymity.

Some readers may complain that I have not interviewed surviving fascists. Similar complaints have been made in reviews of my previous books.[6] This choice reflects my belief that fascism thrives on inequality and racial hatred. I do not think that it is possible to approach the views of surviving, unrepentant fascists as if they constituted some neutral source. Of course, in writing this book, I did attempt to gather information on the mind-set of British fascism, through the newspapers and other materials written by fascists at the time, and through the testimony of individuals who left fascist parties. I am particularly grateful to Gerry Gable and the staff of the anti-fascist magazine *Searchlight*, who interrupted their busy campaigns, allowing me to consult the files in their office and discuss the ideas used in this book.

I should also explain something about the terms used in this history. In the 1970s, most activists used the term 'black' to refer to all people who considered themselves thus. In this book, I tend to follow that language. But all our words are far too broad. I do not hold to the racist myth that there is one or even several 'black communities'. The main purpose of this phrase seems to be to provide the representatives of the state with an excuse for their failure to win the trust of all sections of the urban poor, as in that ghastly sentence, 'We appeal to community leaders to restore order'. In real people's lives, there have been all sorts of conflicts between Africans and Caribbeans, Muslims, Sikhs and Hindus, men and women, black workers and black bosses, old people and young. But the theme of this book is conflict between racism and anti-racists. Internal differences are of less importance here.

One other term may require explanation. At several points I refer to the Socialist Workers Party or SWP, the organization that helped to launch first Rock Against Racism, and then the Anti-Nazi League. Prior to 1 January 1977, this party was known as the International Socialists or IS. Most present-day writers use 'SWP' to refer to the party in all its previous forms, but I also quote from contemporary sources, using the terms from the time. If there is ever any confusion, readers should understand that the IS and the SWP were the same party.

In addition to the interviews that have been mentioned, several people also helped by reading parts of the manuscript. I would especially like to thank Ian Birchall, who read the manuscript through. Early drafts of different chapters were read at the Alternative Futures and Popular Protests Conference organized by Colin Barker in Manchester, and at the London Socialist Historians' Group seminar at the Institute of Historical Research. Parts of the section on Tottenham have appeared in a local history pamphlet published by Haringey Trades Council to celebrate the twenty-fifth anniversary of the Battle of Wood Green, and an early version of a planned chapter on anti-fascism in Manchester, Liverpool and the North West appeared instead in a special issue of *Northwest Labour History*.[7] I would also like to thank Chris Bessant of New Clarion Press, for all his assistance in the publication of this book. The greatest debt I owe – as always – to Anne Alexander. But to all who have helped me, many thanks!

Acknowledgements

The author and publishers are grateful to the following for permission to reproduce photographs used in the book:

Peter Alexander, pp. 117, 164
Geoff Brown, pp. 43, 86, 116
Kathy Gaffney, p. 83
Searchlight, pp. 20, 30, 62

Chronology

1967		National Front formed; leaders include John Tyndall, Andrew Fountaine and A. K. Chesterton.
1968		Arrival of Kenyan Asian refugees.
	April	Enoch Powell's 'River of Blood' speech. Dockers march in support of his anti-immigrant message.
1970		General election: Conservative government formed. Ten National Front candidates obtain a total of 11,449 votes, at an average of 1,145 where they stand.
1972		Arrival of Ugandan Asians. Unofficial strikes by dockers and printers bring an end to Edward Heath's Industrial Relations Act.
	December	NF candidate wins 2,920 votes at a by-election in Uxbridge.
1973	*May*	NF candidate wins 4,789 votes at a by-election in West Bromwich.
	September	Salvador Allende's government overthrown in Chile.
	October	Twenty-four building workers from North Wales tried in Shrewsbury for offences under the Industrial Relations Act.
1974	*February*	General election: results in hung parliament. Fifty-four National Front candidates obtain a total of 76,865 votes, at an average of 1,423 where they stand.
	April	Portuguese revolution.
	October	General election: Labour government formed. Meanwhile, 90 National Front candidates obtain a total of 113,844 votes, at an average of 1,265.
1975		American forces withdraw from Vietnam.
1976	*January*	Unemployment stands at 1.2 million. Disputes within the National Front. John Kingsley Read attempts (and fails) to expel John Tyndall.
	February	James White bill attempts to remove abortion rights.
	March	Right to Work demonstration. Harold Wilson resigns as prime minister, replaced by James Callaghan.
	April	Strikes on Liverpool docks, among engineers in Kirkby and Warrington.

May	Arrival of Malawi Asians. They experience hostile coverage in the *Sun* and *Daily Mirror*. Fiftieth anniversary of General Strike. Local elections: eight National Party candidates in Blackburn receive on average 40 per cent of the vote. National Front secures nearly 15,000 votes in Leicester.
June	Gurdip Singh Chaggar murdered in Southall. Sixty London dockers sign an open letter welcoming Malawi Asians to Britain. Soweto uprising.
July	National Front candidate wins 3,255 votes at a by-election at Thurrock.
August	Start of Grunwick strike. Eric Clapton speech. Eighteen people arrested at Notting Hill Carnival.
September	*Sounds*, *NME* and *Melody Maker* publish the letter that leads to the formation of Rock Against Racism.
October	Strikes at Trico succeed in winning equal pay.
November	Eighty thousand march in London against public sector cuts. Twenty-five thousand march against racism.
December	Sex Pistols' 'obscene' interview with Bill Grundy.
1977 *January*	Twenty-five thousand strike in Sheffield against job losses.
March	Unemployment reaches two million. National Front candidate wins 2,955 votes at a by-election at Birmingham Stechford.
April	Conservative-run Gravesend Council bans Sikh festival. Three thousand confront National Front in Haringey.
May	Local and Greater London Council elections: National Front receives 5.7 per cent of the vote where it stands, pushing Liberals into fourth place in nearly one-quarter of constituencies. NF announces plans to stand in more than 300 seats in next general election.
June	Queen's Silver Jubilee. Sex Pistols at no. 1. Police anti-mugging arrests in Lewisham. Fighting between police and pickets at Grunwicks.
July	Tom Jackson of the post workers' union calls an end to solidarity action in support of strikers at Grunwicks. Mass pickets continue. NF members attack 'Lewisham 21' protest, many injured. Unemployment reaches 1.6 million.
August	White-collar APEX union calls off Grunwicks pickets, threatening to stop the workers' strike pay. Anti-fascist success at Battle of Lewisham.
November	Anti-Nazi League formed with Paul Holborow, Peter Hain and Ernie Roberts as three leading members. Local groups set up in most cities in Britain. Bournemouth East by-election: National Front candidate fifth with 725 votes.

1978	*January*	Margaret Thatcher's interview for *World in Action*: 'People are rather afraid that their country might be rather swamped by people with a different culture.'
	March	National Front candidate wins 2,126 votes at a by-election at Ilford North.
	April	First Anti-Nazi League/Rock Against Racism Carnival. Communist Party of Great Britain agrees to back the Anti-Nazi League.
	July	Anti-Nazi League conference. Manchester ANL Carnival; also events in Cardiff and London. Demonstrations to remove NF from Brick Lane.
	September	Second London Carnival.
1979	*January*	Iranian revolution, Shah toppled. 'Winter of discontent': strikes by bakers, journalists, social workers and lorry drivers.
	February	Idi Amin driven out of Uganda.
	April	General election: Tory government elected. During campaign, Blair Peach killed at Southall; 303 National Front candidates obtain a total of 191,719 votes, at an average of 633 in each seat. All NF candidates lose their deposit. NF begins to split into rival factions and is now clearly in decline.
1980		Rise of British Movement as violent home for ultra-Nazi former members of National Front. Large number of racist attacks. Anti-Nazi League re-launched specifically to confront BM. St Paul's riots in Bristol.
1981		Combined far-right vote in 1981 Greater London Council elections is just 2.1 per cent. But continuing racist attacks, and 13 die in a blaze in New Cross. Anti-Nazi League members participate in Campaign Against Racist Laws. Youth and international conferences, anti-fascist marches in Oxford, Leeds, Coventry and elsewhere. Riots in Toxteth. Anti-Nazi League slowly wound down from autumn.
1992–4		Growth of fascist parties in France, Germany and Austria. Anti-Nazi League re-launched and confronts the British National Party in East London.
2002		Three British National Party candidates elected to Burnley council. Other BNP councillors follow in subsequent by-elections. Love Music Hate Racism launched.
2003		New anti-racist coalition Unite Against Fascism launched.

1

In 1977, I Hope I Go to Heaven

In 1970s Britain, fascism was on a high. The National Front (NF) won a total of 44,000 votes in local elections in Leicester in 1976, and combined with another far-right group, the National Party, the total fascist vote reached 38 per cent in local elections in Blackburn. In March 1977, the NF beat the Liberal Party in a by-election at Stechford in Birmingham, and pundits warned that it could displace the Liberals as Britain's third main political party. The NF received 119,000 votes in the May 1977 Greater London Council (GLC) elections, and almost a quarter of a million votes in local elections, across the country. During this period, the National Front claimed to have up to 20,000 members, while it had the money and the resources to distribute 5 million leaflets each year. The Front stood 413 candidates in local elections in 1977, and promised to stand 318 candidates in the 1979 general election.[1]

In response to the success of the NF, a number of groups attempted to combat its threat, including the Socialist Workers Party (SWP), the magazine *Searchlight*, the Communist Party of Great Britain (CP/CPGB) as well as the Campaign Against Racism and Fascism (CARF), the Jewish Board of Deputies and many others besides. The most important anti-fascist organizations were Rock Against Racism (RAR) and the Anti-Nazi League (ANL). This book is a history of the Anti-Nazi League and of the campaign as a whole.

At the start of this history, it is right to place anti-fascism in the context of its time. The action took place in Britain, overwhelmingly in England, and in one distinct period, between 1977 and 1981. Within England itself, the centres of the conflict included London, the West Midlands, Yorkshire and the North West. The past is always a foreign country, even a past through which you lived. But what was England like then? At the most superficial level, 1977 was a year of youth fads, including Pot Noodles, skate-boarding and *Star Wars*. Tourists were held up in Heathrow following strikes by air traffic controllers. The books of the year included Tolkien's *Silmarillion* and Alex Haley's *Roots*. A predominantly Asian workforce struck at Grunwick. Red Rum won the Grand National and Geoff Boycott scored his hundredth first-class century at Headingley. Scotland fans tore down the Wembley goalposts, and Liverpool won the European Cup. It was also Silver Jubilee year. In June, Elizabeth II celebrated 25 years as queen, the Tories organized tea parties, and the Sex Pistols' 'God Save the Queen' ('She made you a moron / Potential H-bomb') was banned by the self-censorship of the music business from taking its no. 1 place in the pop charts.

Beneath the surface, three key processes shaped the history of racism and anti-racism in late 1970s Britain. One was the decline of British empire, which had provided many British people with a sense that 'their' country played a leading role in world affairs. A second factor was the decline of the British economy, which had been until recently the second largest manufacturing and trading economy in the world. Finally, the National Front and its enemies existed within a political world shaped by the strengths and weakness of the Labour movement. The Labour Party was in power, but moving to the right. The gap between the Labour leadership and Labour supporters created the political space both for the NF to recruit disillusioned urban voters, and for anti-racists to organize a radical campaign against it. There was a crisis in late 1970s British society, and there was no certainty as to how that crisis would end.

No colonies

The National Front was a fascist party. Like all such organizations, it thrived at times when large numbers of people felt that their world was in crisis. The Front spoke of national decline and rebirth, couching both in racist terms. The secret to revival could be found in the removal of black influence from British life. The NF was able to win an audience because Britain in the 1970s was a society ill at ease with itself. At the end of the 1940s, Britain had ruled directly over whole chunks of the globe. Thirty years later, the lion's share of empire was gone, and the sense of national decline hung like a cloud over British public life. Many people were nostalgic for a British empire whose passing was a matter of recent memory.

One key justification for the fact of the British empire had long been racism. All evidence suggests that the modern doctrine of racism, the idea that racial categories are fixed, was *invented* to serve the purpose of empire.[2] It emerged in the seventeenth and eighteenth centuries at a time when the values of the Enlightenment were coming to the fore. There was an obvious contradiction between the popularity of ideas of liberty, equality and fraternity, and the practice of empire. It is hard to occupy another people's land, without claiming in justification that the subject people are not fully human. But racism did more than this: it told the colonisers that the black and Asian subjects of empire could never be human, and would always need to feel the civilising hand of foreign, British rule.

The generally accepted view of the subjects of colonial rule was that they were sub-human. Such values did not limit themselves to the white people living in the colonies, but were felt in Britain as well. As black sailors came to live in Britain, racism was imported back to the mainland.

In 1731, the Corporation of London banned companies from employing black people. By the 1780s, the British government began to enforce the repatriation of former slaves to Africa. The *Encyclopaedia Britannica* described Africans in the following terms:

> Vices the most notorious seem to be the portion of this unhappy race. Idleness, treachery, revenge, cruelty, impudence, stealing, lying, profanity, debauchery, nastiness and intemperance are said to have extinguished the principles of natural law and to have silenced the reproofs of conscience. They are strangers to every sentiment of compassion and are an awful example of the corruption of man left to himself.[3]

It would be wrong to suggest that everyone who lived in eighteenth-century Britain was racist. Instead, slavery was undermined by a series of popular movements. One was the revolt of the slaves themselves. C. L. R. James's book *The Black Jacobins* tells the story of Toussaint l'Ouverture, the leader of the great Haitian slave revolt, which did more than anything to encourage the British and French governments to ban the slave trade.[4] But parallel to the resistance of the slaves was a British-based movement of workers. In the eighteenth century, the London Corresponding Committee organized tens of thousands of white workers in the campaign against this unjust system.

In the eighteenth and nineteenth centuries, racism was strongest amongst the propertied classes. It was not restricted to the authors of encyclopaedias, but was further extended by the most articulate scientists of the day. The notion of eugenics was developed, to argue that blacks and Irish should be bred out of British life. Social Darwinism often combined this doctrine of progress through the elimination of unfit nations, with further support for the elimination of unfit individuals. Sections of British society came to use the language of euthanasia, or to associate immigrants with 'the unfit'. At the start of the twentieth century, the British Brothers League organized a campaign against Jewish immigration, in alliance with the Parliamentary Alien Immigration Committee, the London League, and the Immigration Reform Association.

These days, many historians talk about the British empire in a remarkably value-free way. The empire existed in the past, they say, and it would be wrong to impose our values on a different time. But the reason for mentioning racism here is not to criticize the values of previous generations, but instead to make a point about Britain in the 1970s. By this time, the values of empire were associated in people's heads with race. To be British meant to have an empire; to be white meant to be the rulers of empire. To be nostalgic about the British empire in a country that was in decline meant that you would almost certainly also blame the decline of Britain on the former subject peoples, including Asians, blacks and their allies on the political left.

So where did it all go wrong for the British empire? Both of the two world wars had reduced the economic security of the British state. The second, in particular, left Britain dependent on American loans. In this new situation, the state was increasingly unwilling to bear the cost of a huge standing army. India demanded its independence, which was granted in 1948. Meanwhile, the people of the Third World also grew in confidence. They were no longer willing to remain a subject people. The decisive moment came in 1956, when Colonel Gamal Abdel Nasser nationalized the Suez Canal. The Israeli army occupied the Sinai, while France and Britain landed troops at Port Said. Determined not to see its own prospects for regional hegemony challenged, America refused to back the invasion. Meanwhile, in Britain there was considerable opposition to the war. Dockers, fire fighters and electricians threatened strike action, and in smaller incidents, engineers and building workers did actually walk out.[5]

Under American pressure, Britain, France and Israel were compelled to withdraw. British imperial power had been humbled, and the struggle for the liberation of countries across Africa drew sustenance from this victory. Over the next twenty years, Britain was forced to cede almost all of its remaining possessions. It withdrew its troops in favour of client regimes where they existed, and out of fear of the dangers posed by national revolts. Meanwhile, those powers that attempted to remain in Africa fared even worse. France and Portugal were defeated in full-scale colonial wars.

Those who had believed in empire now experienced the trauma of defeat. The Tory politician Enoch Powell addressed his speeches to those nostalgic for the past. 'Our generation', he said, 'is one which comes home again from years of distant wandering. We discover affinities with earlier generations of English, generations before the "expansion of England", who felt no country but this to be their own.'[6]

All the racist anxieties were magnified, after 1950, by the presence of black migrants in London, Birmingham, Manchester and elsewhere. Between 1953 and 1961, the number of Commonwealth migrants travelling to work in Britain increased from 2,000 a year to over 100,000. Michael Billig's work on the mind-set of National Front voters shows that many believed that black people had actually and measurably lower intelligence than whites. They thought that Africans and Asians were ungrateful for the gift of empire and incapable of developing their own culture now. They maintained that black people were 'taking over' Britain. One subject told Billig:

> It is frightening to think that these strange people should be massing all around you all the time, and doing things contrary to your culture … and not conforming or anything, and not trying to live in peace with us in any way and just sticking in their separate cliques. And that to me is very frightening.[7]

It was in this context that the Queen's Silver Jubilee in 1977 took on such symbolic importance. Tens of thousands of street parties were put on. Rural England drowned in flags and bunting. Outside the inner cities, attendance was near compulsory. But all over Britain, the young wanted out. In families up and down the country, a war of manoeuvre began – a conflict of values of suburbia against the city, the past against the future, the generation of the Blitz against Tucker, Benny and the *Grange Hill* kids. What was at stake was the British memory of empire, and all that went with it. The demise of Britain was bound up with the defeat of empire, and black people were blamed. There was space in society for a right-wing movement more radical than any Tories could be.

No cash

When people attempt to make sense of economic change, they often cast around for non-economic explanations – they might name sunspots, tides, the mysterious factor 'confidence' or whatever. By the late 1970s, many people chose to explain the decline of the British economy in terms of the general decline of the British military machine. The direction of this explanation was almost certainly wrong. The British economy did not decline because of the weakness of the empire. Instead, the British state lost possession of its empire precisely because it no longer had the economic resources to subdue people who were the unwilling victims of imperial rule.

The irony of British decline was that it took place in conditions of relative affluence and full employment: the problem was that moderate growth occurred just as other countries witnessed unparalleled boom. Between 1950 and 1973, the world economy grew at a faster rate than ever before. Real growth rates increased at a rough average of 4 per cent a year, four times faster than they had between 1913 and 1950, and three times faster than they had in 1870–1913.[8] Even in Britain, the 1950s saw full employment and growing state spending on welfare. Ralph Darlington and Dave Lyddon describe the mood in the workplaces:

> Until the mid-1960s unemployment levels were typically two per cent or less. Workers becoming unemployed could often find work within two or three weeks – and that was only for those who bothered to sign on at the labour exchange because they could not immediately walk into another job.[9]

These historians are describing Britain, but in every country people's living standards rose, as did their confidence that that a new era of stability had been achieved. Indeed, most economies grew much faster than Britain's. So although living standards rose, the British economy was actually in relative decline. While many workers genuinely felt that life was on the up in the 1950s and 1960s, British business came to the exact opposite conclusion. Full employment meant more work, and a greater share of the national wealth going to labour. But while, in 1900, gross domestic product per head had been higher in Britain than anywhere else in the world, by 1979 the UK had fallen behind its competitors in America, Australia, Canada, Denmark, France, Germany, the Netherlands, Sweden and Switzerland.[10] Production was only one indicator, and a more rational system might not assume that national economies should only be judged competitively. But the sense of decline seemed real to managers, politicians and bosses at the time.

Even the boom was incomplete. While workers were able to secure increases in wages, and better working conditions, there was no comparable improvement in the housing stock – or not until later. Thus one of the most powerful complaints against new immigrants was not that they were taking British jobs, but even more that 'they' were stealing 'our' houses. Fears about housing were a factor behind two early race riots: Notting Hill and Nottingham, both in 1958.

For the people charged with supervising the British economy, the fact that Britain was falling behind was a matter of urgent concern. The Labour Party argued that incomes were growing too fast relative to the increase in factory output. Its solution was voluntary wage restraint. Labour called on the trade union leaders to police their members. As early as July 1966, Harold Wilson's government was discussing the value of higher unemployment, as a means to reduce inflation and increase productivity.[11] The problem for Labour Chancellor and then Prime Minister James Callaghan was that higher unemployment never came. Wages continued to rise, and inflation with them.

In contrast, the leaders of the Conservative Party thought that the explanation of Britain's economic failure was the corporate economy, in which trade unions and big business confronted each other as relative equals. Edward Heath's Tories tried to smash the unions by passing an Industrial Relations Act. Unofficial strikes were to be banned and unions would have to ballot before taking action, or their funds would be sequestered. In the early 1970s, this strategy fell apart in the most spectacular way. Strikes by miners, rail workers, engineers, dockers and building workers destroyed the Industrial Relations Act. In 1974, the Conservatives called a general election asking 'who runs the country?' Should it be the government or the unions? The government lost the vote.

While the economy was expanding, the contradiction between high economic growth and relative economic underperformance could just about be tolerated. But the oil crisis of 1973 marked the end of the long global boom. Suddenly, inflation soared and real growth rates tumbled. It is difficult now to appreciate the extent of the blow. We live on the other side of this first postwar slump; boom and bust are part of our lives. But for those people who had lived through 25 years of low unemployment and high growth, the crash of the mid-1970s marked the beginnings of a new and profoundly shocking time. For two whole years, almost continuously, the stock markets fell. Even when that financial crash had ended, people still had to endure a world of higher unemployment and declining services. There was no obvious way by which stability could be restored.

Two statements may be taken as truisms. First, in all societies, whether the total economy is rich or poor, the wealthiest people remain on top. Short of a social revolution, the dominant people in any society are going to be the existing ruling class. Second, the general conditions of economic life shape the general habits of society, not in any direct way, but as a pressing influence. In other words, the crisis of the mid-1970s did not lead immediately to a transfer of social power between one group and any other. But the crisis did have an impact. Those who were poor already became poorer. Those who had most wealth or power became more anxious to defend them from any threats.

The British ruling class and their supporters entered the mid-1970s in a condition of absolute panic. One writer, Chris Harman, describes the fear that followed union victories in the early 1970s:

> *The Times* spoke of the need for its readers 'to impose a policy of sound money at the point of a bayonet'. John Davies, Heath's former industry minister, told his children that this might be the last Christmas they would be able to enjoy. Heath himself 'relied heavily for advice' on his top civil servant, Sir William Armstrong; by the end of January 1974 Armstrong was talking wildly of coups and coalitions. The head of the CBI tells how, 'We listened to a lecture on how Communists were infiltrating everything. They might even be infiltrating the room he was in.'[12]

The paranoia was pervasive. *Time Out* journalist Tony Bunyan documented the wild schemes that sections of the ruling class were willing to contemplate. One representative figure was Peter Hamilton, security consultant to Chubb, and some-time adviser to Heath's Conservative Party. Hamilton believed that society was under assault by espionage and subversion, 'moral if not always legal crimes . . . concerned with gain and redistribution of wealth'. He was especially concerned with the success of the left in industry. Hamilton argued that the state should jail militant shop stewards, in much the same way that the police should apprehend a common thief.[13]

In 1976, Tory MPs in the House of Commons, acting on MI6 information, accused the trade unionists Jack Jones, Ernie Roberts and Hugh Scanlon of being 'prime targets for Soviet Bloc intelligence'. In 1977, George Kennedy Young (formerly of MI6) told David Yorck of the American CIA that Wilson's government had contained 'five ministers of the Crown whose membership of the Communist Party of Great Britain is not known to have been renounced and overlapping with them, other ministers whose ultimate allegiance is outside Britain'. If there was a conspiracy however, it was not in Wilson's cabinet, whose left credentials can only be exaggerated, but in the repeated attempts to destabilize an elected government, made by fractions of an embittered ruling class. The social historian Edward Thompson complained in the *New Statesman* of 'pre-packaged juries, tapped phones, a compliant press, a managed television [and] the gross suppression of public truth'.

Thompson portrayed the Labour as complacent in face of the Neanderthal Tory right.[14]

In a context of economic stagnation, fragments of the ruling class were beginning to question the extent of their own support for liberal democracy. But in this process, the militants of the Tory right faced various obstacles. One was the still-limited extent of the economic crisis, which was not yet enough to encourage full-scale panic. Another was the preference of most businessmen for mainstream Conservatism. As strategies go, it was the safer option. But in the paranoid world of the far right, these two problems were not insurmountable. Surely the crisis would intensify, and then more people would come to accept their views? A third, potentially decisive, obstacle was that these people inhabited a world of big business, country houses and military uniforms. If they seriously hoped to build an anti-socialist coalition of big business, small business and groups of patriotic workers, they would have to find a cause around which a more popular right could converge. The issue was anti-immigration. The audience was the product of Labour's decline.

No fun

All these processes tended to make life easier either for fascists, or at least for a much-radicalized Conservatism. The crises of empire and industry converged to create a moment that was pregnant with possibilities for the far right. But before coming on to examine how the National Front sought to situate itself within the crisis, it is important also to examine a third process, the weakening of the link between the British working class and Labourism. The decline of Labour identification opened up spaces to its left and right alike.

As late as the mid-1950s, most workers had still looked to the Labour Party to bring change. Even the Communist Party of Great Britain, the largest party to the left of Labour, insisted that socialism could only begin with a radicalized Labour government. In the words of the Communist Party's programme, *The British Road to Socialism*, 'British Communists declare that the people of Britain can transform capitalist democracy into a real people's democracy, transforming Parliament, the product of Britain's historic struggle for democracy, into the democratic instrument of the will of the vast majority of her people.'[15] One prominent champion of the New Left, Peter Sedgwick, has described the political feel of the 1950s. The politics of the Labour Party were still an expression of values deeply held in the Labour movement. Even Labour's constitution reflected the relationship between the two.

> The organisational mythology of the committed Left amounted to the construction of a vast shadow panoply of trade-union structures, manned by conscious militants at branch and district level, and by progressive or

reactionary, Left-wing or Right-wing, responsible or autocratic General Secretaries and Executives in their national offices. Like the constitutional map of Soviet Russia projected by Sidney and Beatrice Webb in the 1930s, the initiatives of the rank-and-file were supposed to send countless pressures upwards, channelled and summed in the block votes of six or seven digits that were cast at the annual Trade Union Congress or the Labour Party Conference. As the neurologist's recording equipment marks the gross electrical rhythms of the brain, each stroke on the graph representing the aggregate of millions of tiny voltages from the individual neurons, so the Conference or Congress vote aggregated the voices of invisible throngs: or rather would do so, provided that the recording machinery itself were not spiked by treacherous leaders.

By 1971, when Sedgwick's article was written, everything had changed. Demonstrations and strikes still happened, but were no longer acknowledged by Labour's leaders. The movement had been forced into a much more antagonistic relationship with the British state. 'The Labour MPs are more prosperous since then, and more remote.' Recalling the miners protests of the early 1950s, Sedgwick wrote, 'nowadays you would not get a militant lobby like that, simply because very few workers would have enough faith in Parliament to take a day off and come down to London to waste their time and breath.'[16]

From the mid-1960s, socialists and trade unionists began to question their unflinching loyalty to Labour. The 1966 seamen's strike marked the onset of a period of disputes. Prime Minister Harold Wilson denounced the strikers as a 'tight knit group of politically motivated men', accusing Communists of having orchestrated the protest. Ironically, their party had limited influence within the seamen's union with the leading role being taken by young militants from the Labour Party. The full-time official with responsibility for the strike was John Prescott, now the Deputy Prime Minister under Tony Blair.

From the mid-1960s onwards, young socialists increasingly diverged from Labour. The radicalization of the 1960s was expressed in anti-Vietnam protests, 'ban the bomb' marches, student struggles and a growing willingness of younger workers to take strike action. This trend towards militancy was most visibly demonstrated in the May 1968 events in France, where student revolt sparked off a general strike. This process of radicalization was to throw up many New Left political formations, and give a significant boost to the fortunes of even small groups of revolutionaries. Tiny organizations mushroomed into sizeable if often unstable and ultimately short-lived parties. In Britain, the Labour and Communist Parties faced for the first time significant forces to the left that were able to tap into and exploit the mood of popular radicalization.[17]

The Labour Party won the two general elections of 1974 on the back of a leftward-moving popular mood. Its manifesto was popular, promising as it did the abolition of the House of Lords and public schools, and increased taxes for the rich to pay for better public services. Tony Benn and

Michael Foot joined the cabinet, while TUC left-wingers, including Jack Jones and Hugh Scanlon, were brought into close contact with the government. Bitter struggles continued through the five years of Labour rule, but the overall result was to reduce the levels of militancy within society. The number of strikes fell rapidly, while the government held the line on its incomes policy. Unemployment rose from 600,000 in 1974 to over 1 million five years later. 'Career opportunities', the Clash sang, 'the ones that never knock.' The government reduced spending on public services, demoralising its most ardent supporters. Inequality rose, faster the longer that Labour was in office. The period of the Wilson–Callaghan government was a time of sharp popular disillusionment, which paved the way for the Conservatives' election victory in 1979.

Within the trade unions the established lefts were confused by Labour's lurch to the right. Supporters of the Labour left and the Communist Party of Great Britain were forced to choose whether they were for or against the party that they had helped to elect. Ultimately, this generation's loyalty to Labour proved to be not tactical but strategic. The union full-timers and leading shop stewards, and the prominent activists in social campaigns, did not believe that any alternative force could emerge to displace Labour. Consequently, many leftists found that they had no choice but to explain away or excuse the cuts in working-class living standards.

These debates within the workers' movement were frequently played out in full public view. One prominent factory was the British Leyland works in Longbridge, where the key union figure was the convenor, Derek Robinson. Leading Communist activists such as Robinson saw their role as winning the loyalty of the rank and file for a restructuring plan that entailed job losses and speed-ups on the production line. Inevitably, the gap between the workers and their convenors grew. In February 1977, skilled tool-room workers at Leyland came out on strike. Their union leader, Hugh Scanlon, declared the strike unofficial and denounced the strikers. Derek Robinson encouraged other Leyland workers to cross their picket lines. When he was later sacked, the same workers would not fight to defend him. In 1978, firefighters went on strike against pay restraint. First supported by the TUC General Council, they were then abandoned by their leaders. Traditions of solidarity, patiently built up during the long boom of the 1960s and early 1970s, were falling apart. In the winter of 1978–9, public sectors workers went on strike, but their actions lacked the élan, the generous spirit, of the disputes of the early 1970s. In their hearts, millions of workers were leaving Labour, some moving rightwards fast.

Perhaps the most important single factor in explaining the mood of working-class frustration with Labour was the rise in unemployment. In January 1975, there were 678,000 people jobless. By the end of the year, this number had risen to 1,129,000. In December 1976, the number of people out of work was up again to 1,273,000. In September 1977, it stood at 1,609,000. Unemployment was twice as high among blacks as among whites. Such high levels of unemployment had not been seen in Britain since the 1930s. They help to explain the militant, aggressive edge to politics at this time. Young workers were alienated from the system, and looked to more radical politics for a solution. The National Front gained from the failure of the Labour government. First set up in 1967, the NF grew in prominence through 1968. That year, Enoch Powell gave his infamous and racist 'Rivers of Blood' speech, calling for the repatriation of black workers. London dockers and Smithfield meat porters struck in support of his racism.[18] Two active supporters of the British fascist Oswald Mosley, Pat Duhig and Danny Harmstone, led the marches. Although outmanoeuvred in 1968 by Enoch Powell himself, the National Front did receive valuable publicity.[19] It was able to stand in ten constituencies in the 1970 election, reaching an average of 3.6 per cent of the vote. The NF grew under Heath's government, and claimed 17,500 members in 1973, but only really took off under Labour. It suffered a split in 1976, with a more Conservative wing breaking off to form the National Party, but the party grew. In 1976, the NF received 15,340 votes in Leicester. The following year, it achieved 19 per cent of the vote in Hackney South and Bethnal Green, and 200,000 votes nationally.

The real strength of the National Front was on the streets. According to Ken Leech, then working as a priest in London's East End, 'Between 1976–8 there was a marked increase in racist graffiti, particularly NF symbols, all over Tower Hamlets, and in the presence both of NF "heavies" and clusters of alienated young people at key fascist locations, especially in Bethnal Green.' By 1976 and 1977, the NF had more activist members than ever before. It was also more visible, putting up graffiti and leaflets. The National Front's cadres waged a violent race war, committing dozens of racist attacks. Between 1976 and 1981, 31 black people were killed in suspected racist murders.[20]

But Labour's declining hold over its core voters also enabled the emergence of a radical left, which would not restrict itself to parliamentary opposition to fascism. In July 1976, the poet (and former International Socialist) James Fenton wrote a piece for the *New Statesman*, describing an NF meeting addressed by Robert Relf in Tilbury, Essex. Fenton asked, 'Who speaks against the National Front?' In his article, you can sense the frustration of a generation of young anti-racists who were fed up of waiting for Labour to take a lead:

> 'Parliamentary language' barely conceals the assumptions which the Tilbury meeting shared. Indeed it is in a way refreshing to go from Westminster to such a gathering and hear people say what they really mean. As for Labour, the issue is fought in the worst possible terms – arguments about numbers, and whether the pool of immigrants will ever dry up. And all the while there is an air of congratulation – all the participants in the debate, or nearly all of them, are being so responsible. Thank God we can sit down together and discuss the matter in a civilised way.

'If the Front have grown', Fenton continued, 'to the point where they are no longer treated as a joke, it is not because the Left have sometimes opposed them on the streets; it is because Parliament has been embarrassed to meet them head on.'[21] Such views were rapidly becoming common sense, not just among the people attached to organized far-left groups, but in colleges and workplaces, and in the heads of young Labour activists. Further conflict lay ahead.

2

Race and Racism

So far, this book has said little about race or racism. But the history of resistance to fascism would make no sense without saying something of the generation of black British people who fought back. There have been black people living in Britain for several hundred years. As Peter Fryer points out, 'There were Africans in Britain before the English came.'[1] Because of the multi-national nature of the Roman armies, there were Arabs and black Africans living in England over 2,000 years ago. They included skilled workers, such as the Mesopotamian builders who finished the fort at the eastern end of Hadrian's Wall. The Anglo-Saxons only appeared 500 years later. By the eighteenth century, the black population of Britain included sailors, slaves and freed men and women, as well as the children of rich Africans sent to Liverpool or London to receive their education. By 1800 there were settled black populations in each of these cities, and Bristol and Cardiff also.

One reason why black or Asian people have come to Britain is the British Empire. Imperialism encouraged economic links, which have always worked in both directions. As Tony Bogues pointed out in 1979, 'Trade with Africa meant ships with African sailors.'[2] The whole direction of imperialism was towards the impoverishment of black people. Between 1876 and 1897, catastrophic harvests affected every tropical country in the world. Famines were worst in countries such as India where the British were in charge. The sacred doctrine of free trade insisted that it was better to starve people to death than feed them. In total, somewhere between 30 and 60 million died.[3]

In the twentieth century, the British Empire required black and Asian men and women to serve in its army, notably during the two world wars. In the period after 1945, a series of British politicians toured the countries of the Empire (and later the Commonwealth), inviting black people to migrate to Britain, to do the work that white British people were no longer willing to do. One future opponent of immigration, the Conservative politician Enoch Powell, spent the 1950s campaigning to bring nurses from the West Indies to Britain.[4] Given the often impoverished conditions at home, it is no surprise that people came.

There were already some 20,000 black people in Britain by 1945, but the great symbol of postwar migration to Britain was the arrival of the

13

Empire Windrush in June 1948, with 400 Caribbean workers on board. Over the following ten years some 125,000 West Indians and 55,000 Indians and Pakistanis came to Britain.[5] The arrivals were British citizens, and many had been educated to believe the myths that the British state had put out in its own defence. England was supposedly a free society, the very cradle of parliamentary democracy. Despite these pleasing myths, black and Asian people in Britain were received most often with contempt. Customs officials treated every black face as a potential criminal. Police, headteachers, every authority seemed to regard these foreigners as little more than savages. Homes, hotels and pubs were barred. Following the victory of an anti-immigration Conservative candidate, Peter Griffiths, at Smethwick in the 1964 general election, both major parties came to the conclusion that the British public would vote for immigration controls.[6] Since then, every government has passed legislation making it harder for black people to migrate here.

A tacit arrangement has been at work, and most evidently in periods of Labour government. In return for taking further steps to limit the numbers of new black migrants, the British government has also promised to act against the worst excesses of white racism. Harold Wilson introduced the Race Relations Act and the Community Relations Commission. Yet far from acting decisively to stop racism, the focus of such models has been just as much on taming black 'extremism', either by incorporating black radicals into the lowest levels of the state machinery, or by prosecuting those who overstepped the bounds. One of the first people to be charged under the Race Relations Act was Michael Defreytas, prosecuted in 1970.

In face of a hostile society, one solution was self-organization. As Paul Gilroy points out, 'blacks have been actively organising in defence of their lives and communities ever since they first set foot in Britain'. There is a history of black and Asian opposition to racism that goes back at least to the eighteenth-century London Corresponding Society's campaign against slavery. One black radical, William Davidson, took part in the famous Cato Street Conspiracy of 1820. Motivated by anger at the government's killing of two dozen unarmed workers at St Peter's Field in Manchester in 1819, Davidson and his allies planned to blow up the British cabinet. They were trapped by informers, caught and executed. Twenty years later, William Cuffay, the son of an African slave, became one of the leaders of the Chartists. Black sailors played a part in the 1866 strikes on the Tyne.[7] In 1945, the fifth Pan-African Congress took place in Manchester, involving a generation of future African leaders, Kwame Nkrumah, Jomo Kenyatta, George Padmore and Ras Makonnen. Early anti-racist organizations in Britain included the West Indian Standing Conference, the Campaign Against Racial Discrimination and the Joint Council for the Welfare of Immigrants.

Through the 1970s, the younger generation (both black and white) became ever less tolerant of racism. The radicalism of US campaigners such as Martin Luther King and Malcolm X left a mark in Britain. Racist policing was no longer ignored. *The Times* reported one 1971 march against immigration controls: 'Indian, Pakistani and West Indian organizations from all over Britain marched through London . . . A dozen organizations including the Supreme Council of Sikhs, the Indian Workers Association and the West Indian Standing Conference took part.'[8]

In Manchester there was a Black People's Political Alliance, while the (Jamaican) People's National Party organized branches across Britain. The IS had a black newspaper, *Flame*, evolving in the direction of a separate black section, while the most important groups for Asian workers included the Indian Workers' Associations (IWAs) and the Asian Youth Movements.[9] By 1976, there were three main IWAs: one in Southall, led by Vishnu Sharma; a second, around Prem Singh, linked to the Communist Party of India (Marxist); and a third, led by Avtar Jouhl, with politics closer to Maoism, which was strong among foundry workers in the West Midlands.[10]

Trade unions were often criticized for their perceived failure to protect black and Asian workers from discrimination in the factory, or from racist laws. In the 1950s, some branches in engineering factories and bus depots did indeed maintain closed shops in an attempt to exclude black workers from employment. By the late 1960s, however, such practices were rare. Slowly, the unions became an ally of black labour. The few moments when racists did attempt to use trade unions to exclude black workers – as at Imperial Typewriters in 1974 – were met with outrage and resistance within the wider movement.

By the late 1970s, younger blacks and Asians, the second generation, did not share their parents' naïve sympathy with British justice. Tariq Mehmood's novel, *Hand on the Sun*, describes a cycle of official racism through the 1970s, in which every authority worked together to keep young blacks and Asians down. One result was a generational conflict among the Bradford immigrants themselves. In *Hand on the Sun*, this struggle is represented by the arguments between Jalib and his father. Racist thugs attack Jalib at school and at home. He finds it almost impossible to hold down steady work. He has no understanding of the conditions back home which forced his father to leave Pakistan; the debts, the poverty of rural life. Jalib's father can no more understand why his son is so determined to pick fights, or to get into trouble with the police. The incomprehension is mutual.[11]

One symbol of what was wrong with Britain was the response of the authorities to the Notting Hill Carnival. Having first been established in 1965, the carnival became the largest celebration of black culture to be found anywhere in Britain. Two hundred and fifty thousand people attended the 1975 event. Middle-class whites in North Kensington disliked the carnival, and in March 1976 were able to find 500 people to sign an anti-carnival petition, which received police backing. By 1976, the scene was set for clashes. Aggressive policing encouraged youngsters to fight back. Three hundred and twenty-five police were wounded; 60 people arrested and charged.[12] Having suffered their wounds, the police then arrested 18 young men in Islington. These people were first accused of 'suspicious behaviour' and then questioned in custody. There, according to the police, the young men spontaneously volunteered the information that they had gone to the carnival in order to steal and attack the police. The status of these 'confessions' was crucial to the case. Seventeen of the men provided evidence that they had been assaulted in police cells. In court, the judge demanded convictions. Eventually, the jury came up with 43 not-guilty verdicts, eight of guilty and 28 undecided.[13]

The second generation of black British people came of age. Darcus Howe expressed their anger at the time:

> After an account of his humiliation in his first job in Britain, as a postal sorter in Mount Pleasant, a Bunyanesque railway-station quarter of London, he asserted that the present black community 'is no longer willing to live in the room, traipse after the police, do the employer's bidding so that they can create their wealth. We are no longer that defeated, demoralised working-class. And *that* is why the authorities are compelled to attack.'[14]

By the late 1970s, a popular movement had grown up against state racism. Jamaican writer Rodney James lived in Leeds and then London. He remembers well the arguments. One influence on him was Jamaican religion. Another was the image of Black Power in the USA:

> Most of my generation of Afro-Caribbeans in Britain was in one way or another profoundly affected by the Rastafarian movement that swept across the Atlantic to Britain in the early 1970s. Besieged as we and our parents were by British racism, we welcomed its attack upon white supremacy and its attempts to decolonize our minds. From the United States, Black Power also came to Britain and we became familiar with the writings and struggles of George Jackson, Huey Newton, Bobby Seale, Angela Davies and Stokeley Carmichael.

James came into contact with activists from the Caribbean and from Africa. Reading and political discussion made him a revolutionary:

> At university in particular, I met people from every part of the British Caribbean community . . . My closest friends at the University of Leeds, where I did my first degree, were from Grenada, Guyana and South Africa. I also had a close friendship with a comrade from Chile who had been driven into exile by Pinochet and I knew a number of Palestinians on campus. I also developed friendship with Asian comrades from the Indian subcontinent and East Africa, many of whom had been radicalised by the insurgent and murderous fascism of the far-right National Front in the 1970s.[15]

One sign of the rise of this new generation was the emergence of a more politicized black music. Black British acts Burning Spear, Aswad and Steel Pulse were then at their height. George Csapo, front-man for the two-tone band Bethnal, opened his gigs with anti-National Front slogans, while his songs reflected his anger against racism: 'It's a long time since we've been here / We're the second generation / You can talk on the phone / And you wouldn't even know / Who dat you talk to.' This is how Csapo articulated the band's political strategy: 'They're hitting at us so we've got to hit back. We're not going to go out with guns and try and stop 'em, but we can do it in our music.'[16] Soon acts like Bethnal would find their counterparts in the white music scene as well.

Racism was the enemy, including both the concealed, institutional racism of the police, and the public racism of the National Front. In both its forms, it was a poison that black people were increasingly unwilling to accept. The point has already been made that the NF was encouraged by a mood of cynicism as the Labour government turned right. Beyond this, at least three other social forces also played a part, namely the press, the police and immigration controls. Before coming on to the NF, we should say something about each of these in turn.

State racism

The success of the National Front was made easier by the hostile report-ing of immigration in the press. Throughout the 1970s, the media coverage of migration was overwhelmingly racist. Such press headlines as 'Asian Influx will swamp us', or made-up stories of refugees enjoying the good life, undoubtedly encouraged people to believe the NF's claims. The local and the national press were both to blame. In 1978, the Labour Party dedicated a party political broadcast to anti-NF politics. In response *The Yorkshire Post* criticized 'cheapjack politicians' for 'raiding' the film archives.[17] Isaaq Ahmed of the Campaign Against Racism in the Media remarked on the link between press scares and racist attacks:

> On May 2, 1976, the *News of the World* had a headline which read 'One slips in on every boat'. Three days later, Asian parents in Redbridge made an appeal for safety, after they were constantly attacked on the school playground. On May 6 the *Sun* headline read 'Another 20,000 Asians on the way' and 'Storm over two-wife immigrant', that night an Asian shop in West Essex was repeatedly attacked.[18]

Nor was the national press only to blame for its cowardly attacks on refu-gees. The papers also consistently ignored anti-racist events. So the huge marches against racism following the murder of Altab Ali in May 1976 did not receive any coverage in the *Daily Mail*, the *Daily Telegraph* or the *Express*. *The Times* gave the protests 35 words on page four, the *Finan-cial Times* just 31 words. When the Anti-Nazi League organized a 35,000-strong anti-racist carnival in Manchester, the biggest political protest that Manchester had witnessed all century, the local *Manchester*

Evening News failed to notice or report the event.[19] The national media showed no greater interest.

The police force was a second source of racism in society. There were dozens of incidents in which officers failed to prosecute white racists following attacks. Two examples will suffice. In the summer of 1976, Mustafa Siddiqui was badly stabbed by a white man in a Brick Lane butcher's shop. The police arrived and the assailant was released without charge. When Mustafa's family protested, the police insisted that the case should be dropped for the sake of 'good community relations'. Again, in April 1977, the four Virk brothers, Balvinder, Mohinder, Sukhvinder and Joginder, were attacked and badly hurt by a white gang. Sukhvinder Virk went to call the police. On their arrival, the brothers were arrested and their attackers released. In court, the police brought charges of common assault and occasioning actual bodily harm against the Virks, and their attackers became the chief prosecution witnesses. 'Justice in this country is even-handed,' said Judge Michael Argyle. *New Statesman* journalist Francis Wheen quoted one friend of the Virks: 'If I am attacked in the street I have the choice of either allowing them to beat me up, so that I end up in hospital, or defending myself, in which case I shall be metaphorically beaten up in the courts and sent to prison . . . why should I have to make such a choice at all?'[20]

Such action on the part of police and judiciary became routine in the 1970s. Perhaps more important in terms of encouraging popular racism was the role of senior officers, who repeatedly claimed that all black youth were to blame for crime. The Institute of Race Relations documented the racist attitudes of the police in its evidence to a Royal Commission on Criminal Procedure, which was later published under the title, *Police Against Black People*. The force did not reflect public values, but helped to create racism, 'through stereotyping the black section of society as muggers and criminals and illegal migrants.'[21]

This mention of migration raises a third driver of racism, immigration controls. The 1968 and 1971 Immigration Acts were both justified using a language of liberal anti-racism; limitations were necessary if black people were to be integrated within British society. Whenever race returned to the political agenda, after Lewisham, Southall or the 1981 riots, the press and liberal commentators called each time for further restrictions on migration, to take the heat out of anti-immigrant racism. So each time black people were attacked, the solution offered was to keep black people out of Britain. This polite racist approach was summed up in Margaret Thatcher's infamous 1978 television interview, which explicitly defended 'hostile' white responses to immigration: 'People are really rather afraid that this country might be swamped by people of different cultures. The British character has done so much for democracy, for law . . . that if there is any fear that it might be swamped, then people are going to be rather hostile to those coming in.'[22] Britain's tough immigration laws legitimized racist arguments. They made racism respectable.

A bitter history of coups and expulsions

What about the NF? The National Front was originally an alliance of different racist parties. The first chairman was A. K. Chesterton, a firm supporter of Oswald Mosley in the 1930s, then an ally of William Joyce (Lord Haw-Haw), and later the leader of the League of Empire Loyalists, an imperialist rump that attacked the Conservative Party for allowing the decline of Britain's Empire. Chesterton was able to raise funds for the NF, partly through his links to apartheid South Africa. He resigned in 1970, as the NF drifted even further right.[23]

Other leading members of the National Front had been active in the neo-Nazi milieu of the 1950s: Andrew Fountaine in the National Labour Party, Colin Jordan in the National Socialist Movement, John Tyndall and Martin Webster in the Greater Britain Movement, and so on. These organizations were all small and extremely violent. The Anti-Nazi League was never short of pictures of leading members of the NF in full neo-Nazi uniform. Through the 1970s, the NF was divided by ongoing turf wars. Some factions wanted to transform it into an openly Nazi party; others into a more standard formation, which would find it easier to recruit disgruntled Conservatives. One split led to the formation of a rival National Party, which attempted to organize along those more conventional lines. One common route into this milieu was via the Conservative Monday Club. Members of the National Front were found to have successfully infiltrated one of the Monday Club's offshoots, the 'Halt Immigration Now Campaign'.[24]

Paul Holborow recalls the tactics of the National Front:

> The Nazi strategy was conceived in the 1960s and early 1970s and they stuck to it until 1979. They wanted to establish themselves as part of the mainstream of British politics. They exploited the arrival of the Malawi and then the Ugandan Asians. They ran a serious number of candidates in the 1979 elections. They did well at West Bromwich. They did well in 1974: Tyndall polled well in Bromley by Bow. It culminated in spring 1977, when the Front won 119,000 votes in London.

The key to the success of these tactics lay, he argues, with the NF's leaders: 'Martin Webster was a very unpleasant man, but he had a real flair for organization and theatre. You could see it in the NF marches, with drums, flags and poles with emblems on top. Webster was quite consciously emulating the Nazis in the 1930s. He would hold press conferences. He was often on TV.'

Martin Harrop's study of the National Front, based on interviews conducted in 1977 and 1978, estimated that 6 per cent of the population could be considered 'potential' NF voters. Most NF supporters, he suggested, were young men, manual workers from urban areas. More came from London and the West Midlands than elsewhere. The outlines of this picture fit with the image of the National Front presented in its own literature.

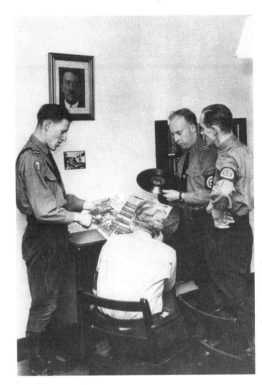

John Tyndall (with record), later to become National Front leader, pictured inside the National Socialist Movement headquarters in west London, 1962

In contrast to Harrop, Colin Sparks, an anti-racist activist writing at the time, suggested that the NF was more middle class and found most of its cadres among small employers. Part of the argument was not about who joined the National Front, but who led it, especially at a local level. Sparks' view that the NF was ultimately a middle-class party is supported by studies of its parliamentary candidates, most of whom were men in their thirties, educated to age 18, self-employed, professionals or managers.[25]

Anti-racist campaigners saw the National Front as fascist or even Nazi. The two terms were used interchangeably, individuals terming themselves 'anti-fascist' or 'anti-Nazi'. Some activists preferred to call the NF 'Nazis', rightly understanding that this phrase would connect it in people's minds to the horrors of the Nazi Holocaust. The archives of the anti-fascist magazine *Searchlight* produced many photographs of NF leaders wearing the paramilitary garb of their earlier, pre-electoral days. Fascism and Nazism were seen as like.

More recently, the historians of fascism have tended to criticize this approach. Richard Thurlow published a set of articles in the journal *Patterns of Prejudice*, arguing that fascism and Nazism were distinct traditions.[26] Drawing closely on the work of postwar fascist ideologues including the American writer A. James Gregor, Thurlow suggested that fascism unlike Nazism had not been biologically determinist:

Fascism was rationalised in terms of an idealist political philosophy which emphasised the striving of the human will to create higher spiritual forms, and the transformation of political society within the confines of the nation state and its dependent territories. Nazism, on the other hand, saw the function of will power as being subordinate to a materialist base. The function of the will was not to enhance aesthetic and moral values within human society, but instead merely to implement the deterministic laws of nature by a process of Darwinian natural selection.[27]

It followed that the National Front in Britain (despite its Nazi leadership) was only a fascist party, and that the 'Nazi' tag was ill judged.[28]

I have argued elsewhere that such formulations are mistaken: the National Front looked and behaved like the German NSDAP, and its leaders consciously copied Hitler's movement as their model.[29] But perhaps this debate is too academic. For the activists who opposed the right when they marched, it was enough to know that the NF saw itself as presenting a revolutionary challenge to the status quo, and that this movement behaved like the armed fascist parties of the interwar years. The leaders of the NF had their own approach to the question, judging by an interview that appeared in the *Sunday Telegraph* in 1977. '"When we are knocking at the gates of power in Britain", said Richard Verrall, "there will be a new generation, the 14- and 15-year-olds will see us for the force we are, a new force, a virile force." He smiled, "And when that happens", he said, "they won't give a damn who was a fascist, and who was a Nazi."'[30]

In contrast to previous fascist parties active in Britain in the 1930s and 1940s, the National Front was more working class and much more violent. Irrespective of the highs and lows of the party's membership, it always had a much more obvious presence on the streets, on the terraces and on some council estates. Compared to this public work, electoralism was always a secondary activity. According to *Searchlight*'s Gerry Gable, 'The hard Nazi core always believed in Dr Goebbels' maxim: who controls the streets will win the final victory.'

The organization had some success in recruiting workers, and set up a National Front Trade Union Association as early as 1972.[31] Two years later, an NF intervention among white workers helped to undermine a strike by Asian workers for equal conditions at Imperial Typewriters in Leicester.[32] Also in 1974, the NF benefited from the defection of Bill Roberts, a former executive member of Bolton Labour Party and convenor for the Amalgamated Union of Engineering Workers at Edbro Bros. Roberts stood as a candidate in a council by-election and received 14.6 per cent of the votes.[33] By 1978, the NF was believed to be collecting £100 a week at the Upper Street Sorting Office in Islington. There was even a small NF group in the mines. Such developments were clearly threatening.

The left-libertarian paper *Big Flame* interviewed one anti-fascist who had grown up in Wolverhampton in the 1950s, and had then supported Enoch Powell. 'Just like lots of lads and girls, racism was attractive to me, in that it meant you could rebel against the system with the implicit support of your family . . . But the real clincher for why I became a firm Powellite was the reaction of the middle-class, whose abstract, liberal tolerance was totally irrelevant, ill-informed and patronising.' The correspondent could remember vividly 'a TV discussion following on a documentary about racism in Wolverhampton in which a middle-class do-gooder from Hampstead said, "To be terribly frank, one finds the speech of the white people in Wolverhampton quite as alien as that of the ethnic minority."' Any effective anti-racism had to break through the link that could sometimes bind racism with elements of class feeling. 'I still get creeps', the *Big Flame* journalist wrote, 'when I hear that "One race, the human race" line, because it allows the NF to manipulate the germ of class-consciousness in a racist direction. That's why they try to nail the revolutionary left as "nigger lovers", students and "do-gooders".'[34]

The National Front's support varied over time, but was consistently linked to the development of white racism in the cities. Ricky Tomlinson briefly joined in Liverpool in 1968. 'I was politically naive and poorly educated,' he remembers. 'I had a mixture of left- and right-wing views, having been a shop steward and at the same time coming from a very patriotic family.' The NF presented itself as a single-issue anti-immigration campaign. 'I just wanted to draw the line under how many we could take because there didn't seem to be enough to go round.'[35]

'Members and supporters are attracted predominantly by the National Front's stand on immigration', wrote Zig Layton Henry, 'and for this reason this is the issue which dominates NF campaigns and publicity.' Harrop suggested that as many as three-quarters of all new recruits to the NF joined out of racism. Indeed, the NF itself was happy to claim the mantle of white racism. One BBC *File at Four* programme, broadcast on 9 November 1977, featured the following interview with Martin Webster, a leading NF spokesman:

> *Martin Webster:* I sometimes think it doesn't get across. The reason why we publish a poster saying 'The National Front is a Racialist Front'[36] is because we *are* a racialist front. You must understand what that means. It means that we support the concept of the nation as the means whereby our society is to be organised and we believe the only rational basis for having nations is some kind of a degree of ethnic homogeneity.
> *Interviewer:* And if you're outside that degree of ethnic homogeneity your rights will be limited?
> *Webster:* Well you won't have any rights at all, because you won't be a citizen of the nation, because you won't be part of the community.[37]

The first sign of National Front success came in 1968, following Powell's campaign against immigration by Kenyan Asians. This pattern was repeated. *Searchlight* estimated that the NF's membership doubled between October 1972 and July 1973 following the arrival of refugees from Uganda. A similar impetus was provided in 1976 by the arrival of the Malawi Asians. The press ran dozens of racist stories, with the *Sun* claiming that refugees were being put up in four-star hotels. In an atmosphere of racism, the NF recruited around 3,000 new members.[38] Another *Searchlight* estimate holds that the party recruited a total of 64,000 people between 1967 and 1979, the gap between this figure and the NF's peak membership of 17,500 being caused by the rapid turnover of support, with few new members remaining in the NF long.

As well as Powellism, other events generated widespread press coverage (not always positive) for the National Front. In June 1974, clashes between fascists and anti-fascists around London's Red Lion Square culminated in a mounted police charge against anti-racist demonstrators. One of them, Kevin Gateley, was killed. Lord Scarman headed the public inquiry.[39]

By 1976 or 1977, the National Front was riding the crest of a wave. Membership was on the rise and the organization was receiving wide publicity in the British press. For example, in July 1976, a parliamentary by-election in Deptford (which includes the area of Lewisham) saw the two far-right parties, the National Front and the National Party, win a combined vote of 44 per cent, more in fact than the victorious Labour candidate, who won with 43 per cent of the vote.[40]

The leadership of the National Front used this very moment to tack right. Articles began to appear in the NF's magazine *Spearhead*, reminding its readers of John Tyndall's past in the Greater British Movement. The August 1977 issue included articles claiming that the Jews were responsible for the Second World War, and another repeating claims that the Holocaust had never happened. In April 1978, *Spearhead* went even further, dismissing the murders as 'a fantastic tale':

> Six million Jews, after being relieved of their dentures, wooden legs and gold teeth, were secretly exterminated at a synthetic rubber factory in 2,000-capacity death chambers disguised as shower-baths with an insecticide gas that was lighter than air but dropped from the ceiling, after which the millions of corpses were disposed of in slow-burning, four-at-a-time cremation ovens.[41]

Such language was intended, of course, to offend anyone concerned with the memories of the dead. In talking up the racist and anti-Semitic content of their ideology, the leaders of British fascism also desired to firm up the fascist politics of the NF's new recruits.

The left and anti-fascism

For those anti-racists who could remember the heady days of the 1960s, a wretched change had occurred. The leading members of the Anti-Nazi League were recruited from a generation of socialists who had lived through the events of 1968. They had seen Vietnamese forces score extraordinary victories against the greater military power of the USA, they had watched the Soviet invasion of Czechoslovakia in August, and the student protests and general strike that broke out in France in May 1968. In Britain, these exciting events had an impact at first in terms of people's ideas, convincing thousands that socialism was a real possibility. Only later, and especially after 1972, did the revolutionary ideas generated by 1968 begin to manifest themselves in terms of mass action. The campaign of the Pentonville dockers against the Industrial Relations Act, and the two miners' strikes of 1972 and 1974, broke the back of the Heath government. There were great opportunities of the left. One party, for example, the International Socialists, grew from just over 400 members at the start of 1968, to around 2,000, six years later.[42]

Set against the background of the more optimistic 1960s and early 1970s, Roger Huddle saw the late 1970s as a 'frightening period':

> It came up like a time bomb. You'd just come out of 1972–4 when the workers had brought down a Tory government. And the Labour Party was in power. And you were waiting for the honeymoon to be over and the upturn of workers' struggles to start again. And suddenly there were people strutting the streets of Walthamstow with swastikas.[43]

Socialist-feminist writer Sheila Rowbotham noticed the downturn for the first time around 1976. Somehow, the movements of the late 1960s and early 1970s had begun to lose their confidence. For the first time, it no longer seemed certain that the new political movements would actually win. 'We were very active', she recalls, 'but there was some peculiar notion of a pause.' For Rowbotham, the gap between upturn and downturn was marked by the rise of separatist feminism:

> It only became evident later. I was working around the Essex Road Women's Centre. There were local groups in Hackney and Islington; we would try to get them to report what was going on. There was lots of activity around hospitals and community politics. Also trade union struggles, like equal pay. Then we started to have meetings on women and literature, women and film. Then I was pregnant. It seemed to be something happening to me.
>
> In 1976, the government started to make cuts. We had to defend things. It no longer seemed that workers' control was going to happen. By 1977 we started to have revolutionary feminism. The idea that all men were evil seemed obnoxious, but we didn't know what to do. I had a baby boy; I couldn't go along with them. But for the first time, there were people saying to us that they were more feminist than thou!

In autumn 1976, another anti-racist, Lorraine, wrote to her friend Di in Oxford. Friends were cowed by unemployment, she reported, afraid to complain at work, 'Any job must be grasped, fed and kept . . . I too have those intimations that England is tilting, tilting, and from below evil is rising.' She wrote of how 'manifestly politically dispirited many comrades are – the crisis resonating into our own lives: bone-cold fears.'

Left-wing activists were shocked by the resurgence of the right. Ian, a member of the International Socialists since the early 1960s, describes a common feeling of anxiety on the left: 'You felt the threat, in terms of graffiti, in terms of the numbers [the NF] could put on demonstrations, in terms of the results they were getting in elections. They clearly were a significant presence, and they were trying to implant themselves in the localities.' John was a young lecturer living in south London. He had first been politicized by a student strike in 1968. Ten years later, he suggests, things felt very different:

> We were in a hopeless situation. People would go on about 'the Pakis'. Generally, it wouldn't go anywhere . . . We used to sell *Socialist Worker* in Woolwich. When we turned up the NF would be standing opposite us, selling. They seemed to be the ones that had the resonance . . . A lot of lefties, ex-students, gave up. They said that the working class was racist.

Dave Widgery describes the NF graffiti seen around the area of London's Brick Lane. 'By 1978 it had become impossible for anyone living or working in the E1 area not to have witnessed the provocations; doorstep and bus-stop abuse, the daubing of menacing graffiti, the window-breaking and air-gun pot shots, the stone- and bottle-hurling sorties on Sundays, and the threatening atmosphere around certain estates and tube stations which produced a de facto curfew.'[44]

Keith was then a student activist, dividing his time between Essex and Middlesbrough. He recalls a climate in which the right was able to intimidate the left: 'We had already spent years fighting the NF and not just because we hated Nazis in general, but also because the NF meant for us physical attacks and fights on paper sales.' Christine used to sell *Socialist Worker* on Lewisham High Street: 'the National Front would come along and try to beat us up'. By 1977, some activists were already volunteering to defend more than one sale. The danger was that individuals could be 'beaten up more than once in a day'.[45]

Through 1976 and 1977, the National Front was able to organize a number of attacks on left-wing stalls, paper sales and other events. Mike was living in west London:

> I remember a number of events on the Old Oak Common Road. The National Front was clearly building. It was bad enough in 1976 and 1977. Our sales were being attacked many weeks. We had to have someone at the back of the stall, this big guy, he worked as a heating engineer, we needed him just to make us feel safe. There was a real build-up of fear. Then, sometimes we would go to East London, and there were rumours about no-go zones.

Left-wing bookshops were also a target. In autumn 1977, ten bookshops held a joint protest against attacks by fascists. They held the event in the Unity Bookshop, which had been firebombed by Nazi sympathizers. In addition to Unity, Bogle-L'Ouverture had been attacked three times and

New Beacon books twice, Centreprise had been firebombed, Soma books had received threatening phone calls, and Headstart books had had its windows smashed. At no stage had the police made any arrests.

But while the physical attacks on the left were important, we should not exaggerate their extent. The National Front did not recruit primarily as an anti-socialist organization. It won new members rather by giving them a political excuse to go out and attack blacks. In spring 1977, *Race Today* described a climate of spiralling racist attacks in the East End:

> Already, the beatings, the knifings, the kickings are on the increase. A few days ago, a young Asian, on his way home from work in London's East End, almost had his ear severed from his head by a gang of knife-wielding white thugs. The life of another Asian hangs in the balance after he was bludgeoned by racists who broke into his flat.[46]

At the end of the National Front's ideas were racist murders. This was a truth recognized – and even celebrated – by members of the NF and other far-right groups. The National Party's elected councillor John Kingsley Read responded to the news of the racist murder of the Sikh Gurdip Chaggar by saying, 'One down, one million to go.'[47]

Why was anti-fascism so important to the activists of the labour movement? Of course, the campaign was important in itself. If you believe in an equal society, you cannot accept a situation in which racist values are becoming mainstream, and black people are being beaten on the streets. But other factors accentuated the emotional importance of anti-fascism for the left. One was the memory of interwar Spain, when thousands of anti-fascist volunteers had left the mines and factories of Europe and America to fight in the anti-fascist International Brigades. Even as late as 1977, it was still true that some leading activists within the Communist Party, and in the trade union movement more generally, had fought in Spain. Others had been part of the generation that welcomed them home afterwards.

White socialists feared that the National Front might gain a position within the white urban working class. As early as May 1974, Christopher Hitchens (then a member of the International Socialists) observed that many local NF activists, even parliamentary candidates, had begun as socialists within the Labour Party. He mentioned Michael Lobb, a former Marxist, who had campaigned for the NF in Silvertown, using the issue of redundancies at Tate and Lyle. In Bolton, the NF candidate was Bill Roberts of Edbro Engineering: 'Although he goes on about frightened old ladies, falling property values and the other stand-bys he is certainly no fascist and he estimates that half his local branch are ex-Labour voters.'[48] Hitchens' article raised the ultimate nightmare for the left – the possibility that the NF could undermine its core support by appealing to groups of angry, disillusioned white workers. It followed that if the left ever wanted to get anywhere, then it needed to put its own house – the labour movement – in order.

Although some socialists saw the rise of the NF and became demoralized, others remained optimistic. Many were influenced by the legacy of the anti-racist tradition. By the late 1970s, important black self-defence organizations included the Hackney Black People's Defence Association, Blacks Against State Harassment, Brixton Black Women's Group, Peoples Unite, Southall Black Sisters, and the United Black Youth League. Indeed, it has not only been blacks who have taken part in anti-racist campaigns. In the 1930s, the growth of Oswald Mosley's British Union of Fascists was stopped by a large anti-fascist movement, led by the Communist Party of Great Britain and including Jewish and ex-servicemen's organizations. After the war, the revival of fascism led to the formation of the 43 Group, another network of militant anti-fascist Jews. By the 1960s, the 43 Group had transformed itself into the 62 Group, and several of its former activists also helped to set up the anti-fascist publication *Searchlight* in 1965.[49] Other anti-racist organizations included the Campaign Against Racial Discrimination, established following Martin Luther King's visit to England in 1965, and the Council of Liberation, which called the demonstration at Red Lion Square.

Many of those who took part in anti-racist work in 1976 and after had been involved in campaigns against the National Front since the early 1970s. They were part of an existing organized anti-racist milieu, which was very strongly linked to the political left. The various political parties, however, responded to the fascist threat in very different ways. To its credit, the Labour Party organized a nationwide anti-racist campaign, which culminated in a march of 30,000 people on 8 July 1976. However, the Labour Party's response to the NF was generally uneven. It was, after all, a Labour government that was tightening immigration controls and putting across the message that immigrants were not welcome. Constituency Labour Parties were often deeply ambivalent towards anti-racist protests. According to Peter Hain, one of the founders of the ANL, who spent much of the late 1970s touring Labour Party branches trying to persuade them to affiliate to the League, 'the main political parties had attempted to depoliticise race, with Labour in particular arguing that the racists could not be taken head on.'[50]

A party political broadcast transmitted on 14 September 1976 summed up the contradictions of Labour's response. Michael Foot spoke, along with Tom Jackson of the Union of Post Office Workers and Mrs Millie Miller MP. Tom Jackson argued against the National Front from a class position, saying that 'the trade union movement was founded on solidarity, unity and international brotherhood. We must not allow anything to divide us, not race, not colour, not creed.' Michael Foot, by contrast, reminded his audience that Labour was already tough on refugees: 'Some people don't seem to realise just how strictly immigration to Britain is controlled already under the existing law.'[51] Whatever the strengths of Tom Jackson's message, Foot's speech made concessions to the argument that there should be more immigration controls, more rules to exclude black people from settling in Britain. Such an approach was different from arguing that it was *wrong* to be racist.

By 1976 and as late as early 1977, the largest single umbrella group was the All-London Campaign Against Racism and Fascism, backed by the Communist Party of Great Britain. Although this party was still by far the largest and best-rooted force to the left of Labour, it was split over the regimes in the Eastern bloc. In many areas, it divided into two hostile factions: 'Euro-Communists' were younger, more middle class, keener to stress their party's independence from the Soviet bloc; 'tankies' often older, better represented in the unions and more loyal to the USSR. The Communist Party's membership declined in the late 1970s, to under 20,000 at the end of the decade. What is more, the party was in retreat politically. Its 'Popular Front' strategy of making alliances with liberals, bishops and other respectable figures, was cutting it off from new generations of radicalized young workers. The leadership of the Communist Party rejected the strategy of the younger parties to its left, which called for physical confrontation to stop the National Front. The party opposed the anti-fascist confrontation at Lewisham, and although it did eventually sign up to the Anti-Nazi League, the Communist Party seems to have been very much tailing events, not leading them.[52]

With the mainstays of the traditional left unable to take a decisive lead in the anti-racist campaigns, the initiative often fell to local networks of rank-and-file trade union activists. Trades councils became more important, as did black organizations and members of the younger far-left parties, including the International Socialists and the International Marxist Group. From August 1976, the workers at the Grunwick film-processing labs were on strike. This protest, which initially involved around 200 workers, mostly Asian women, quickly became the focus of a national campaign. Workers at Cricklewood sorting office refused to handle any mail coming into the plant. Trade unionists and socialists called for mass pickets. According to Mrs Desai, one of the best-known leaders of the Grunwick strike,

> Our experience is that there is a difference between the ordinary union members and the higher level. The ordinary unionists who come on our picket line, they support us because I think they understood how we suffer. Some may have racialist attitudes, but there is a genuine sympathy. At the higher levels, I am not so sure, because they are not *doing* anything.[53]

Although the Grunwick strikers eventually lost, the strike of Asian women was part of the mass movement of black people against racism that made the Anti-Nazi League and other campaigns possible.[54]

Christine was then working full-time as the staff-side representative at Lewisham Council. An active socialist, she remembers a series of political campaigns in which socialists and trade unionists sought to challenge racism. In the council, there were three reps, one for white-collar workers, one for direct labour and one for blue-collar workers. The last, she felt, was an 'out-and-out racist' who tried to prevent black people from working in his section. This rep was later exposed. Trade unionists in Lewisham also gave their support to the Grunwick strike and later mobilized for the huge black protests in 1981. Life itself was a giddy whirl of political events: 'Every Saturday we used to go to Hyde Park . . . It was a different world.'

In these campaigns, it was often members of the smaller parties, especially the International Socialists, who came to the fore. A young Spurs fan, Richard, recalls leafleting against fascist candidates in London in 1974, and also joined demonstrations in 1976 against Robert Relf, the racist homeowner in Leamington Spa, who offered his house for sale to whites only. John from south London remembers that for a member of the IS, active in 1972–4, 'There was a lot of racism about. Our main activity was countering the Front in by-elections. It was the central thing we did.' The IS took part in a large anti-fascist demonstration in Blackburn in October 1972, and helped to call two large anti-Front mobilizations, in Leicester and central London in August and September 1974. In March 1975, the organization supported to an anti-Front rally in Islington, and that September the IS confronted an NF 'anti-mugging' march through Hackney.

By 1976, the mobilizations were almost too many to list. In February, 1,500 anti-racists opposed a National Front march in Coventry. In March, the International Socialists called a picket of the BBC, for allowing racists on its *Open Door* programme. In April, two large marches confronted an NF demonstration through Manningham in Bradford, while in May there were large anti-racist marches in Birmingham, Portsmouth and Southall. In June, there were more protests in east London, Southall, Brixton and central London. In Rotherham, members of the IS divided themselves into two contingents. One hundred and fifty took part in an Engineers' Union demonstration for 'racial harmony', while around the same number again acted as a mobile picket, heckling the NF march and defending Eastwood, the Asian area of the town.[55] BBC studios were occupied in Newcastle and Leeds, as a protest against interviews with the right.

One of the National Front's best-known personalities was the landlord Robert Relf. He placed a sign outside his house in Leamington, 'For Sale to an English family'. Relf was prosecuted under the Race Relations Act, and convicted. Despite previous membership of such parties as the National Socialist Movement and the Ku Klux Klan, Relf was given an easy ride in the press, and presented as some kind of martyr. In July 1976, the NF attempted to organize a march through London to demand Relf's release, where the place of honour was to be taken by Relf's original sign. Members of the International Socialists managed to thwart these plans. They captured the sign, and took it instead to Southall, where a joint demonstration called by the International Socialists, the Southall Youth Movement and the Indian Workers' Association took great delight in burning the offensive sign.[56] Steve Jeffreys was one of the organizers. 'We completely filled Southall,' he recalls. 'It was so important. For me, that was what socialism was all about – internationalism – or it didn't mean anything.'

Paul Holborow was another activist in his late twenties. He had been active politically from 1969, mainly around Vietnam. 'I joined the International Socialists in autumn 1969 at Queen's College, Dundee. I went to London, to SOAS, and then later to Wolverhampton Technical College for a qualification to teach in further education. They were two hectic years, with the miners' strikes, Heath . . .'. From winter 1971, he was working full-time for the International Socialists:

> I was in London, by autumn 1974 or spring 1975, then an organizer in east London until summer 1977. It was a busy time. We had 30 to 40 members in a party branch at Ford's. I can also remember growing opposition to the Nazis. East London was one of their main targets. They were constantly holding paper sales. They held public meetings in Haggerston School. They wanted to establish their presence at the top of Brick Lane. Socialists were constantly focused on opposing them. It was an arduous campaign that lasted for two or three years. There were physical confrontations. Tyndall and Webster had backgrounds in Nazi groups. They believed in both the boot and the ballot box. They said they had a right to march and reclaim black areas for white Britons. It was symbolic to them. They also understood the importance of a paper. They used it to shove down the throat of immigrants, and also to recruit new members.

The protests continued right through the year. In central London, 15,000 supported marches called by the two Indian Workers'

The National Front at Brick Lane, east London

Associations against racism in July. Four thousand people protested against the National Front and the National Party in Blackburn in September, and 1,000 demonstrated against a large NF by-election march. In October, 250 people picketed the National Front's annual general meeting, while a weekly confrontation began between NF paper-sellers, and members of the International Socialists in Brick Lane. In November 25,000 joined a TUC march against racism, and another thousand demonstrated in support of Asian immigrants fleeing to Britain from Malawi.

In all these protests members of the International Socialists played a prominent role, helping to organize and publicize the marches. But the IS were not the only organization to take part. Besides the Communist Party, whose members provided the leadership of many local campaigns, other groups included the International Marxist Group (IMG), whose contingent at Red Lion Square included the murdered student Kevin Gateley.[57] For most contemporaries, the IS were distinguished mainly by the enthusiasm with which they took part in the campaigns, yet signs of a distinctive approach towards anti-fascism were beginning to emerge. In the words of one IS activist, Pete Alexander, 'We were against calling for bans; we were willing to engage in confrontation; we looked for opportunities to unite with people to the right of us (and joined "official" marches as well as counter-demonstrations); and we had an orientation towards winning trade union support.' In autumn 1976, members and supporters of the IS would play a crucial role in founding a new political organization, Rock Against Racism, which through its skilful blending of music and politics enabled the anti-fascist movement to reach a vast new audience, and in turn acted as an inspiration for the Anti-Nazi League.

3

Reggae, Soul, Rock and Roll

In August 1976, rock guitarist Eric Clapton played a gig in the West Midlands. Clapton had recently enjoyed a hit with a cover of Bob Marley's reggae classic 'I Shot the Sheriff'. He interrupted the concert to begin a speech. Members of his audience heard Clapton mutter, 'Vote for Enoch Powell . . . stop Britain becoming a black colony . . . get the foreigners out . . . I used to be into dope . . . then a foreigner pinched my missus' bum . . . now I'm into racism . . . It's much heavier . . . man.' When one teenager, the later writer Caryl Phillips, tried to talk about the affair to his white friends afterwards, they just kept quiet.[1] Clapton wasn't the first musician to make such comments: in 1975, Bowie had declared Adolf Hitler to be the world's first rock star. Following Eric Clapton's outburst, the photographer Red Saunders wrote a reply, which was published in the *New Musical Express*, *Melody Maker*, *Sounds* and *Socialist Worker*. The letter set the tone for a new movement.

> When I read about Eric Clapton's Birmingham concert when he urged support for Enoch Powell, we nearly puked.
>
> What's going on Eric? You've got a touch of brain damage. So are you going to stand for MP and you think we are being colonised by black people. Come on . . . you've been taking too much of that *Daily Express* stuff. You know you can't handle it.
>
> Own up. Half your music is black. You're rock music's biggest colonist. You're a good musician but where would you be without the blues and R&B?
>
> You've got to fight the racist poison, otherwise you degenerate into the sewer with the rats and all the money men who ripped off rock culture with their cheque books and plastic crap.
>
> Rock was and still can be a progressive culture not a package mail order stick-on nightmare of mediocre garbage.
>
> Keep the faith, black and white unite and fight.
>
> We want to organise a rank and file movement against the racist poison music. We urge support for Rock Against Racism.
>
> P. S. Who shot the Sheriff Eric? It sure as hell wasn't you![2]

Saunders and friends then followed the letter by organizing a series of anti-NF concerts. Rock Against Racism (RAR) published 14 issues of a magazine, *Temporary Hoarding*, and artists, musicians and writers participated in the creation of a musical style that drew its influence from French surrealism, Marxist politics and the best of punk. The message was angry, exciting and compelling. This editorial in the first issue of *Temporary Hoarding* was RAR's manifesto: 'We want Rebel music, street music. Music that breaks down people's fear of one another. Crisis music. Now music. Music that knows who the real enemy is. Rock against racism. Love Music Hate Racism.' Widgery's description of RAR gives a sense of the goals that the young movement set itself: 'Wilhelm Reich, the avant-garde German psychiatrist who diagnosed as a fatal weakness in the German left's opposition to Hitler its refusal to take seriously the cultural and sexual dimensions of fascism's appeal, would have loved it.'[3]

An issue of Temporary Hoarding

Jazz, funk and punk . . .

'Red Saunders had been planning something for months,' Roger Huddle recalls. 'He'd been planning a Rock Against Racism gig first, as a way of protesting against David Bowie.' Saunders was a member of a theatre group, the Kartoon Klowns. They were rehearsing a play, *Yes, but: Socialism or Barbarism*. 'All sorts of people signed the letter,' Saunders recalls, 'even if they weren't that political.' Pete Bruno, the Klowns' drummer, signed and 'Mike Stadler, my agent, an American anti-racist but liberal, he was more outraged about Clapton than anything.' Originally, the group was strictly informal, a coalition of friends. But after initial coverage in the music press, the *Socialist Worker* agreed to print a full-page ad, inviting people to write in to a 'Rock Against Racism ad hoc committee', and messages of interest or support started to arrive in large numbers. Red and his allies sought to convert enthusiasm into organization:

> There was Roger Huddle, Syd Shelton, Ruth Gregory. They were the first lot. After the letter appeared, people came back and contacted us. A lot of the well-known people, the second lot, Laurie Flynn, David Widgery, didn't get involved till later. Wayne Minto, John Dennis, and a whole lot from Tom Robinson's entourage, young, students, concerned, Chris from Misty, then Misty, Aswad, Mutumbi. Our attitude was always, if you'd like to get involved, do it. One guy called up from Aberystwyth. I said, 'Right, you're the RAR Aberystwyth committee'. He said, 'Can't you help?' I said, 'No, I've only got two rolls of Sellotape and that's it.'

Following the publication of the first Rock Against Racism letter, some 600 people wrote in to express their support.[4] A collective emerged and began to meet. Members of the emerging RAR collective hoped to put on just about any sort of gig with the first headlining act they could find. Roger Huddle explains that 'Rock Against Racism started off as a kind of retrospective – soul, funk, pub rock – 'cause that's what we thought we could do. That was the prevailing independent music, away from the big pop stars.'[5]

The first Rock Against Racism gig took place on 10 December 1976, with Carol Grimes at top of the bill. Grimes was a surprising choice. A working-class woman and a single mother, she was best known for her blues band Delivery, which had folded some four years previously. Her style was soul or blues, after the fashion of Janis Joplin. Her music was interesting rather than cutting-edge. The innovation would come later. To advertise the concert, members of RAR spray-painted an image onto a massive plain white sheet, photographed it, and then reduced the image to normal size. In their enthusiasm, they originally forgot to put on the time of the gig. The concert itself seemed 'very studenty'. It was after the second concert, with members of the reggae bands Aswad and Steel Pulse in the audience, that members of RAR began to see the real potential of the new movement. By spring 1977, plans were afoot for an RAR fanzine, which began publication in the autumn. There was also talk of putting on much larger events.

People from outside the inner core of Rock Against Racism began to take notice. Jerry Fitzpatrick had been the central London organizer of the Socialist Workers Party since 1975. By winter 1976–7 he was a 27-year-old veteran of rank-and-file groups in the actors' and musicians' unions.

> You saw with RAR a coming together of fairly diverse individuals, even if several of them had a shared history in the same party. They would

meet in Red Saunders' studio. Some of the discussion was uncoordinated but even by spring 1977 the core themes were beginning to blossom. I remember the Carole Grimes gig in December 1976, and even then you could really see the potential.

The first issue of RAR's magazine *Temporary Hoarding* gives a sense of the group's perspectives. Printed on two sides of A2, folded twice to A4 size, the fanzine included on its front the words of the launching statement, 'We want rebel music, street music.' The insides folded out to reveal a large A3 poster of the Clash, and beside them the words of their song, 'White Riot': 'All the power is in the hands of the people rich enough to buy it'. A second, smaller poster showed a family watching a National Front march on television: 'Don't sit back and watch it . . . SMASH RACISM!' The text was found almost entirely on the back cover and consisted of detailed advice on setting up gigs in each local area. 'Is there a bar? If so what happens to the takings? . . . It's going to cost probably a minimum of £180 to break even. Think of that when deciding how much to charge for tickets.' From the local concerts something bigger would emerge, but slowly and as part of a wider movement.

Our music

By spring 1978, a number of bands had played on Rock Against Racism platforms. They included Aswad, the Cimarons, Carole Grimes and the London Boogie Band, Belt and Braces, the Derelicts, the Diamond Jack Band, Bamboo, Plummett Airline, Mutumbi, Nice One, Black Slate, Red Rinse, The Adverts, the Fall, Limousine, Foxy Lady, Life Mask, Steel and Skin. What made Rock Against Racism *work*? Red Saunders identifies four processes:

> First, there were people whose radical experience went back to the sixties. They knew how to make movements work, because they'd been through ten or twenty which hadn't. They were pot heads, they'd gone through the Beatles, Pink Floyd, and now they were on the same side as the punks. Second, the SWP gave absolutely unequivocal support. They gave us an address, Cotton Gardens, and everything we asked for. Third, there was always an immense do-it-yourself ethic about punk. Finally, there were the Carnivals. They put RAR somewhere else.

Rock Against Racism was the first political movement to root itself in popular music, or as John Hoyland and Mike Flood Page put it, the first to understand pop music 'from the inside'. These were the years of punk, when the old millionaire stadium bands of the 1970s lost touch with their audience and a new music sprang up, based on simple cord sequences, music that anyone could play. The strength of punk was not expressed primarily in terms of chart success, but as a youth counter-culture that had a huge impact on how people dressed and looked. The musical was libertarian, in the best sense of the word. As Caroline Coon wrote in *Melody Maker*, in August 1976, 'The musicians and their audience reflect each other's street cheap ripped-apart, pinned-together style of dress . . . The kids are arrogant, aggressive, rebellious . . . Punk rock sounds simple and callow. It's meant to. The equipment is minimal, usually cheap. It's played faster than the speed of light . . . No indulgent improvisations . . . Participation is the operative word.'[6] Sex Pistols manager Malcolm McLaren emphasized the anger of the new punk style: 'If it was the music, the bottom would have dropped out of this business ages ago. It's the attitude that counts.'[7]

By spring or summer 1977, however, the early radicalism of punk had begun to fade. Punk was increasingly taken over by people who had the spare money to buy into its new style. Along the way, punk antagonized many of its earliest followers, who felt cheated. George Marshall describes the increasing bitterness that street punks began to feel towards bands like the Sex Pistols:

> When it became High Street fashion with High Street price tags, it also became the preserve of those who could afford it rather than those who could feel it. Buying a pair of ready-made bondage trousers for thirty quid down the King's Road could hardly be chalked up as one in the eye for the system. And neither could paying a fiver for a ripped bin liner.

As early as 1978, the graffiti went up, 'Punk is Dead', a view echoed by two music journalists, Julie Burchill and Tony Parsons in their book, *The Boy Looked At Johnny*, and confirmed when the fanzine *Sniffin' Glue* printed its last issue.[8]

One influence that helped Rock Against Racism to grow was the experience of the Sex Pistols. It would be hard to imagine a more confused legacy. On the one hand, the Pistols were arrogant, destructive and utterly mercenary. While many other punk icons have retained some vestige of their youthful anger, the Pistols rapidly became a parody of their earlier days. Once Sid Vicious had died and Johnny Rotten split, remaining band members would release turgid, formulaic dross. But in Jubilee year (1977), the Pistols briefly spoke in an authentic language of rebellion. The charts had never contained angrier songs than 'God Save the Queen' or 'Anarchy in the UK'. Pistols manager Malcolm McLaren still dines out on his memories, his collaboration with Situationist artist Jamie Reid and his days as a young radical protesting against the Vietnam War.[9]

The quick demise of bands like the Sex Pistols created a space that was partly filled by a revived skinhead subculture, with which the National Front attempted to connect. Here it was helped by the traces of ambiguity that punk displayed towards fascism. The style was anarchistic, but reckless in its allegiances. According to Jake Burns of punk act Stiff Little Fingers,

Youthful energy can often be mistaken for violence and I think this was the case in a lot of these instances. Also, I don't think a lot of the bands' lyricists were the brightest people on the planet and wrote basically 'boy's comic' type lyrics. If you are setting out to outrage the older generation, very little works as potently as summoning the ghosts of the Nazis. Sadly, the National Front saw this as a licence to annex the songs.

Members of the Sex Pistols wore swastikas, not to support fascism, but simply from a desire to shock. Yet such nihilism could spill over into a rejection of ordinary people. One of the Pistols' last songs pronounced 'Belsen was a Gas', in bad humour, as well as bad taste.

The sound of punk, with its jagged three-chord repetitions, was the antithesis of reggae or dub. In Jon Savage's phrase, 'the style had bled Rock dry of all black influences'. The Clash song 'White Riot' told dispossessed youth to go out and emulate the Notting Hill rioters. Fascists found it easy to misrepresent its message as a call for race hate. At other times, they tried a different message, threatening to ban everything they didn't like. The National Front's Martin Webster promised to stop black music, claiming that reggae was for 'degenerates and monkeys'.[10]

One historian of Rock Against Racism, Ian Goodyer, insists that punk showed evidence of both left- and right-wing potential. He describes interviewing a former member of the Young National Front, who told him that 'the Sex Pistols legitimised the swastika'. NF members took encouragement from any lyrical reference to the far right. 'In this context, the Clash's "White Riot" presents an obvious example, but even the phrase "too many right-wing meetings" in the Jam's song "Down in the Tube Station at Midnight" could provoke such a response.'[11]

The people who organized Rock Against Racism deliberately endorsed the rougher music of bands like the UK Subs or Jimmy Pursey's Sham 69. Sham in particular stressed their street origins. Songs like 'I Don't Wanna' and 'The Cockney Kids are Innocent' were written for an audience of unemployed young workers, the people whom the National Front and RAR both sought. Sham had a reputation for being a band with a violent following. Rumours maintained that Sham counted NF members in their road crew.[12] In 1977 and 1978 their gigs at Kingston, the London School of Economics and Middlesex Polytechnic and their set at the Reading Festival all ended in mass brawls. The Middlesex Poly gig had been organized by RAR, but soon broke out of the organizers' control. NF supporters were much in evidence. They fought with organizers and security and briefly took the stage. Photos from the event show large numbers of people giving the Nazi salute. Eventually the NF supporters were repulsed, and the gig ended with Jimmy Pursey back on stage and singing alongside the Rasta group Misty. The night ended on a note of hope, as one RAR activist Syd Shelton recalls: 'There was an affinity, a wonderful moment of black and white unity'.[13]

Sham 69 gave anti-racists a route into the minds of young skinheads. In adopting this street music, Rock Against Racism grabbed it out of the hands of the white racists. George Marshall pays testament to the power of the band:

> Lyrics to songs like 'Borstal Breakout' and 'If the Kids are United' might look simple and naïve on paper, but they weren't being entered into a sixth form poetry competition anyway. And it's only when played live that they genuinely come into their own and sound as sharp as any Stanley blade. The pride and passion with which Jimmy belted out his three minute masterpieces, and the way every word was unanimously echoed by the crowd, is what it's all about. And going to Sham 69 was about being part of something, a part of probably the best band ever to tell it as it was on the streets.[14]

The Rock Against Racism carnivals of summer 1978 are described fully in Chapter 7. The first took place in May 1978. Some 70,000–100,000 people gathered in Trafalgar Square and marched along Fleet Street, all through the City, and out to the East End of London for a massive concert in Victoria Park. Sham 69 did not play the first RAR carnival, but Jimmy Pursey did join the Clash live on stage to sing 'White Riot'. Writing afterwards, John Hoyland and Mike Flood Page praised Sham's support. Pursey's hard-core following consisted of skinheads whose allegiance had been to the National Front:

> They import the aggressive solidarity of the football terraces to Sham's gigs, and their NF chants formed a disturbing counterpoint when Sham 69 played the Central London Poly for Rock Against Racism a couple of months back. Pursey has hitherto refused to take a stand on his followers' politics . . . [yet] the presence of Pursey and his erstwhile Front following on the march and at the gig could be a sign of something changing.[15]

Although Sham 69 was important, it was the support of the Clash that gave Rock Against Racism real credibility among the majority of young punk fans. The band had a political edge that the other punk acts lacked. Their music was angrier, sharper and more dynamic. Their total sound gave a purpose to the DIY mentality of punk. The comedian Mark Steel, then a bored young punk living in the suburban south, describes listening to his first Clash album in 1978:

> While the lyrics were indecipherable, the meaning boomed out of the chipboard speakers and echoed around the Swanley walls. It was all right to be angry. You be angry, mate. There's a whole generation of us, expected to be grateful, well about how this for gratitude – 'Career opportunities, not one will ever knock / The only job they offer you's to keep you out the dock'. So it wasn't just me.[16]

Julian Cope, a more cynical member of the Liverpool punk scene, recalls seeing the band for the first time at Eric's, during the Clash's 1977 'White Riot' tour: 'They were totally brilliant. It was just as cartoony as the

Ramones, but blazing with colour. And they all moved in rigid formation
. . . The club burned on free energy for the rest of the night. All the
right-on guys loved Strummer. All the women wanted to fuck Simonon.
All the secret rock stars wanted to be Mick Jones.'[17]

The great Rock Against Racism carnivals brought together white punk
rockers and black reggae bands, Jimmy Pursey alongside Misty, Tom
Robinson with Steel Pulse. Writing after the first RAR carnival, John
Rose told the readers of *Socialist Review*:

> 'White Riot', by the way, was made after the riots at Notting Hill. For a
> while some skinheads who support the National Front and the other more
> overtly Nazi British Movement believed that this was their song. They
> have been disappointed. Clash belongs to the same movement as Rock
> Against Racism – RAR. 'White Riot' says that white kids riot in solidar-
> ity with black kids – not against them.

Chris and Clarence from Misty were active members of the London RAR
Committee. They travelled up from Southall to Hackney for the weekly
committee meetings and gigged for Rock Against Racism, playing Carnival 2, the RAR tour, at Southall Park, with Jimmy Pursey, the Ruts and
the Mekons, 'more times than we can remember'.[18]

Reggae, soul

While the stadium sound was giving way to punk rock among white musicians, black music was also changing. Since the late 1950s, the black
British sound had been imported via sound-system dances organized in
Jamaica. For the next two decades, the music remained home-based. Moments of chart success in Britain came and went. By the mid-1970s, two
things had changed. First, the success of Bob Marley had given reggae an
international audience. Second, a number of British acts had also started,
without the traditional links to the Caribbean. Jamaican society was stag-
nating under the sway of corrupt politicians and violent gangs, even as its
music was conquering the world. Lloyd Bradley, reggae's biographer,
describes its hold over Jamaican life:

> Never was this power more graphically illustrated than on 22 April 1978,
> at the National Stadium in Kingston and the One Love Peace Concert. A
> 30,000 capacity show, headlined by Bob Marley and the Wailers, sup-
> ported by, among others, Pete Tosh, Dennis Brown, Leroy Smart, Inner
> Circle, Trinity and the Mighty Diamonds, brought together both Peo-
> ple's National Party and Jamaican Labour Party politicians and gunmen
> to endorse the ghetto gang treaty that had been signed on 5 January that
> year. The gunman truce had already been marked in music by tunes like
> Jacob Miller's 'Peace Treaty Special', Dillinger's 'The War is Over' and
> Culture's 'Natty Dread Taking Over' – all best sellers during that year –
> but the concert was to bring it to the attention of the entire Jamaican
> people, regardless of class or colour.[19]

While reggae acts were experiencing unheard-of chart success, the patronizing notion that there was just one black music was giving way under the pressure of different black sounds – soul, disco, the first hints of rap, all of these from the USA. Isaac Julien was then a teenage follower of the latest club sound. He remembers the pronounced division between supporters of reggae and soul, and Julien sided with the latter:

> Reggae was more tied up with black nationalism and certain rigidities of sex and race – tough masculine left politics. Soul, on the other hand, allowed for inter-racial relationships and challenged some of the structures of black masculinity. It opened up a less fixed and more fluid space and, of course, conventional left politics condemned this as anti-political, but that's where most of the energy for *Soul II Soul* or Kiss FM came from.[20]

One problem for black bands was to break down the apartheid that still separated black and white audiences. Musicians mixed, but audiences did not. By 1978 or 1979, the walls had begun to fall. Steel Pulse toured with the Police.[21] Their album *Handsworth Revolution* sold over a quarter of a million copies. Aswad's 'Warrior Charge' is one of the great monuments to this period, a horn-loaded crossover between reggae and dub; it captures the confidence of the time. The song later became the title-track for British film *Babylon*, described by Lloyd Bradley as 'the most enjoyable documentation of British reggae culture'.[22] Venues opened up to reggae acts in a way they never had before.

Two Tone

As Rock Against Racism developed, so did the sound of the main acts. There had been bands before that had tried to fuse 'black' and 'white' sounds. What was different now was the extent of the fusion. In late 1970s London there was no real white audience for black music. RAR bands deliberately set out to break through this barrier. Nicky Tesco of the Members remembers playing alongside Misty at RAR gigs, sharing their instruments, learning from their sound. According to Jake Burns, 'what was particularly significant about RAR shows was the active cross collateralization of music. Invariably we would be on the bill with Aswad or some other reggae band . . . RAR's raising of cultural awareness meant more and more people started experimenting with the type of bill to put on.'

Other acts learned in the same way. The Clash recorded 'Police and Thieves', based on Junior Murvin's original song, said to have blared out over the anti-National Front riot in Lewisham. They also hired a black producer, Lee Perry, and wrote perhaps their greatest song, 'White Man in Hammersmith Palais'. The narrator is the only white man at a reggae night. Looking for an evening of authentic political music, he senses that everyone else is there for entertainment. The words of the song move to unease, even despair, while the music of the song takes up the pauses and missed-beats of reggae, subverting the message of the lyrics and offering an alternative sense of hope.

The race was on to find a sound that could unite black and white. After the Clash, the Specials were the next to try. Rather than marrying punk with reggae, the Specials turned instead to an earlier Jamaican sound, ska. They promoted an entire new look, based on porkpie hats, wraparound shades, mohair suits and black loafers. The name of their label – Two Tone – summed up the appeal of their music. Other two-tone acts included Bad Manners, the Selecter and Madness.[23]

The Ruts also tried to fuse reggae and punk styles, while Sham 69 mixed together the 'workers united' slogan of the Portuguese revolution with football terrace chants to produce 'If the Kids Are United'. Siouxsie and the Banshees, having worn swastikas in 1976 and 1977, now wrote 'Metal Postcard', based on the collages of the German anti-fascist Johnny Heartfield. Elvis Costello's 'Less than Zero' warned of a 'Mister Oswald', named presumably after the British fascist Oswald Mosley, who commits crimes, including murder, but 'has an understanding with the law'. The Slits sang about the blandness and boredom of ordinary women's lives.

The Gang of Four also turned towards a funk–punk fusion. Originally a bunch of anarchists from Leeds University, the band actually met on an anti-fascist demonstration.[24] Their guitarist, Andy Gill, describes their sound as the product of the crisis of its time: 'There was terrible violence, pitched battles between students and British Movement members on the University campus. We could see the struggle between the SWP and the BM capturing the stray youth. We were sympathetic to the SWP, we had done some benefits, but we didn't make our own approach in those broad political terms.'[25]

The Tom Robinson Band was one of the most consistent of the Rock Against Racism performers and a member of the RAR steering committee right from the start. Today, he speaks proudly of his role in the campaign, 'To see National Front leaflets frightened and annoyed me. They were posing as a serious political party. All these international rock superstars, Eric Clapton, David Bowie giving the fascist salute, even Rod Stewart declared "Enoch's our man", all these people had made their living out of black music. I made up my mind to get involved and do everything I could to help.'

Robinson was 27 at the time of the first carnival. According to Pete Alexander, 'The style was more melodic than punk, and the words were more significant. I think his appeal was more to the activists than the new youth audiences. He was also good at relating to both the punk and the black musicians.' Tom Robinson also worked closely with the original RAR performer Carol Grimes. A member of the Campaign for Homosexual Equality, Tom Robinson was best known for his anthem, 'Glad to Be Gay', but his anti-fascism was also felt in other songs, including 'Up Against the Wall': 'Consternation in Mayfair', he sang, 'Rioting in

Notting Hill Gate / Fascists marching on the high street / Cutting back the welfare state / Operator get me on the hotline / Father can you hear me at all? / Telephone kiosk out of order / Spraycan writing on the wall.' The music of Rock Against Racism was urban, edgy. There had never before been a chart music that combined the energy of times with the radical politics of songs like this.

The relationship between the music of punk and the politics of Rock Against Racism was at its most productive in the first six months of 1978. RAR filled a musical gap created mostly by the big political crisis of the decaying Labour government, and partly also by the events of punk's decline. The Pistols were breaking up, and the bands of the moment, the Clash and Sham 69, were at the forefront of RAR. According to John Savage, 'Early 1978 was the time of RAR, not only because some public show of solidarity seemed necessary to disassociate punk and its culture from any taint of racism, but also because its amphetamined politics filled the black hole left by the Sex Pistols' demise.' New bands including the Mekons, the Ruts and the Gang of Four started out at RAR benefits. Music and politics came together, as *New Musical Express* journalist Steven Wells describes:

> Punk wouldn't have had so much impact outside London without the anti-fascist movement, but then the anti-fascist movement would not have had so much impact without punk. In Leeds, where the Young National Front were really strong, some of the early punks had formed fascist groups like the Dentists and the Vents. Punk was apolitical in that context; many people saw it as fascistic even though Martin Webster came out against it. RAR caused punk to make real contact there – the time when most people see punk as being diluted was the time when it was gaining substance.

Keith briefly organized RAR gigs as a young activist living in Middlesbrough. He compares Rock Against Racism in its heyday to the Chartist practice of exclusive dealing. 'If a band or a musician did not support Rock Against Racism then they were in serious trouble. They were deeply untrendy and people would not get their records.'[26]

The music magazines and fanzines were friendly to Rock Against Racism. *New Musical Express* interviewed most of the major bands and ran plugs for the first RAR carnival, quoting Tom Robinson: 'It's important to realise that you're not helpless. If people join together they become strong.' The *NME* covered Sham 69's central London gig, and a cartoon summed up the paper's hostility to the far right. Beneath a drawing of a typical NF march came the speaker's words, 'Friends, we've got to make England safe again – for psychopaths, morons, inadequates, sadists and power-mad bastards like ourselves.'[27] RAR's success may have helped build up the structures of the alternative music scene. The *NME* and *Sounds* built up their sales in this politicized milieu. Meanwhile, RAR helped to establish venues for punk bands. The Squat in Manchester was

Rock Against Racism, Manchester

then in the hands of university students, running a sit-in. The first RAR gig in the city was held there, and the venue remained in use at least until 1980, when New Order played a semi-secret gig at the same location.[28]

For Roger Huddle, writing at the time, Rock Against Racism converted a music that was already revolutionary into an organization that could match its potential: 'RAR's fight is amongst the youth whose life style is rebellious . . . Punk is not just the music. It was visual, it revolutionised graphics, it's anti-authority, anarchistic and loud. It has a lot to give Rock Against Racism and RAR has a lot to give it.'[29] People like Huddle had a dual notion of the relationship between music and more conventional, historical processes. First of all, the character of musical innovation was said to be conditioned by the character of the society in which it emerged. Its edge was determined by the feelings and activity of its audience. Second, once music existed, there was an obligation on its audience – in this case, revolutionary socialists – to engage with it. Theory needs to be raised to the level of practice. The quality of music places demands on the people who intervene in it.

It was new to see the far left taking pop music seriously. Before the 1970s, the dominant approach on the left had been to look for socialist politics in the folk songs of earlier times.[30] In Britain and the USA, left-wing artists modelled themselves on the nineteenth-century singing tramps. The socialist politics of artists like Woody Guthrie, Pete Seegers and Ewan MacColl was used to support the belief that the only properly left-wing music was folk music.

The idea that traditional music was more radical was famously expressed at Bob Dylan's May 1966 gig at the Manchester Free Trade Hall.

As Dylan went electric, people heckled, and the shouts of 'Judas' were recorded in countless bootleg albums. Even a decade later, a generation of radical folk musicians still maintained that their music was innately more radical than the guitar bands could ever be. Dave Haslam, the historian of the Manchester music scene, observes that Ewan MacColl despised rock music as an American import. 'You'd think MacColl would have lightened up in his later years, but he always maintained his belief that rock & roll was (in his words) "politically suspect" right up to his death.'[31]

Such conservatism was not limited only to older groups, like the Communist Party of Great Britain, and their fellow travellers such as Ewan MacColl.[32] In July 1977, the Italian Trotskyist paper *Quotidiano dei Lavoratori* ran a long article arguing that punk was a proto-fascist art form. The author, Nemesio Ala, linked punk to 'the acceptance of social repression' and insisted that 'it is a good thing that punk rock has so far taken only a limited hold in Italy'.[33] This disdain was the very opposite of the RAR approach.

According to Simon Frith and John Street, Rock Against Racism was also partly defining itself against Music for Socialism (MFS),

> a group of progressive rock musicians and writers who had come together the previous year in a kind of last throw of 1960s idealism. MFS (which was particularly influenced by Italian examples) was more interested in the politics of music making and the music-industry and its initial response to punk (as voiced by the Maoist composer, Cornelius Cardew) was overtly hostile: punk was denounced as "fascist".

Rock Against Racism's artistic-political activism came from a different, Brechtian tradition, 'and punk's shock value use of the swastika (the key evidence in the Cardew line) would be challenged directly, on the streets'.[34]

Precisely because of its musical radicalism, Rock Against Racism was adopted by young punks, including many who did not consider themselves 'political'. According to Lucy Toothpaste, 'Many people who came along didn't have political persuasion, but they responded to the statements made by musicians, that it was necessary to challenge people who were putting forward racist ideas.' Caroline was then aged 19 and living in a squat in London. She heard about the first RAR gig and was attracted by the music and its anti-establishment feel, although she described herself as either 'unpolitical' or 'an anarchist' and never identified with the full politics of Rock Against Racism.

> It was part of our culture, living in London as punks. We were getting harassed by the police. We naturally identified with other people getting harassed by the police . . . It didn't matter if you had green hair or were black, you would be stopped by the police, for any reason . . . We felt like victims of an authoritarian state.

Caroline's memory is of taking part in a politicized movement, but what did she contribute? Her most specific memory is of passing leaflets overhead, from the stage backwards into the crowd.[35] Her memory is something vaguer than the organizers' ideal, of 'a liberated space within which the fecundity of free cultural exchange could be demonstrated and experienced'.[36]

Always writing sideways

Several of the founding members of Rock Against Racism came from backgrounds in the International Socialists, including Dave Widgery, Roger Huddle, Syd Shelton and Ruth Gregory. What was the relationship between RAR and this party? Academic historians have variously accused the IS (which in January 1977 became the Socialist Workers Party) of taking a parasitic attitude towards social movements, supporting them for purely selfish reasons, joining them from the outside, and then dropping them at the first opportunity. Such is Richard Thurlow's account of relationships between the SWP and the Anti-Nazi League: 'the decline of the NF was partially due to the successful undermining of it by the Anti-Nazi League. When the latter itself was blatantly taken over by the Socialist Workers Party the organization folded as the bulk of the membership refused to tolerate being controlled by a notorious factional hard-line Trotskyist group.'[37] The relationship between the ANL and the SWP is discussed more fully in Chapter 6, but given that RAR was to act as a sort of parent to the later movement, is there any sense in which the equivalent relationships provided a pattern for the future?

Rock Against Racism was decentralized from the start. According to Syd Shelton, 'It was an organization of activists. If you got your feet dirty and your hands dirty and rolled up your sleeves and got involved, that was it, that's all you did. There was no leader.'[38] If a local group had the idea for a gig or an action, the group in London happily let them do it. There were arguments among RAR activists, including over the question of sexism, as we shall see. There is no evidence, though, of any consistent 'line' being argued by members of the SWP.

Although such socialists threw themselves into Rock Against Racism, they did not regard it as their possession. The greatest complaint of surviving RAR activists is not that the International Socialists or Socialist Workers Party crushed their campaign by sending too many people into it, or 'taking it over'; rather they complain that the party often failed to do enough: by failing to keep up sustained levels of involvement, or by not taking the campaign sufficiently seriously. Syd Shelton and Ruth Gregory of RAR remember negotiating with leading members of the IS and later the SWP within the Anti-Nazi League, and compare the experience to 'arguing with your parents'. Members of the parent organization would perhaps respond that the activists within the movements were failing to challenge oppression in its totality. It was all very well talking about music, but fascism had to be defeated by well-organized campaigns. Like Shelton, Red Saunders recalls occasional tensions, but his tone is more patient:

> We sometimes used to have arguments about where the ANL or the RAR banners should be. 'Uncle ANL', I used to say, 'has just come and messed up our vegetable patch.' But the ANL was a link through the SWP to the unions and the Labour Party. People always think I'm a bit mad, because I've been into culture all these years. But even I could see that there were limits to what RAR could do on its own – that the working class is essential to socialist politics.

Those members of the International Socialists who provided some of the leadership of Rock Against Racism in 1976 were drawn from a particular layer. They were relatively young. Several worked at the IS print shop. They were active members of the party, loyal, but not always the most orthodox of Leninists. They did not try to bring the whole party behind them, rather they tried to involve just as many activists – IS members or not – as were needed to make the campaign work. Peter Alexander recalls:

> Rock Against Racism was an initiative from outside the leadership. Although there were occasional tensions, it was always backed by the [SWP] Central Committee, and branches, to varying degrees, mobilized for RAR events and sometimes organized RAR gigs. The 'tensions' and the 'varying degrees' were inevitable and proper – there were, after all, other priorities as well, and these varied from one locality to another.

In winter 1976, it was not obvious that Rock Against Racism would take off. Nor was it the only lively campaign at the time; it had to compete with the rival attractions of student or industrial campaigns, the Right to Work marches, the Southern Africa Solidarity Campaign. The relationship between Rock Against Racism and the party would later change with the formation of the Anti-Nazi League, and as anti-racism and anti-fascism came to dominate the day-to-day practice of the Socialist Workers Party, but this process is described more fully in subsequent chapters. In 1976 and 1977, most members of the International Socialists and the SWP regarded Rock Against Racism as just one possible campaign among many. They supported it, but they took part in many other movements as well.

Members of the Socialist Workers Party also disagreed among themselves in analysing the new movement. Because it was aimed at punks, and not at existing socialists, many party members regarded Rock Against Racism with some suspicion. John from south London was one of this minority: 'I was thirty, and conscious of my age . . . The general problem was that there wasn't enough politics talked to the audience. We tended to surf a wave, rather than building a permanent organization.'

Tensions between Rock Against Racism and the Socialist Workers Party were a reflection of a wider debate within the latter. Several leaders of the SWP, including Chris Harman, felt in 1977 or 1978 that their paper, *Socialist Worker*, was too preoccupied with the concerns of young music fans. According to one of Harman's comrades, Pete Alexander, 'I think the issue was more about how the paper related to the new audience. Should it reflect its immediate level and interests, or should it be used to draw people towards Marxism?' The activists from RAR replied that the SWP leadership underestimated the punks. Whoever was right, one thing should be clear: the SWP in this period was rethinking its attitude on a whole range of problems — like whether or not still to support Labour in elections — and attitudes towards Rock Against Racism were pulled in.

Rather than seeing the relationship between RAR or the ANL and the SWP as one in which the latter dominated the former, it would be far more accurate to see the two in a reciprocal relationship. The politics of the International Socialists and the Socialist Workers Party did shape Rock Against Racism, but it is also true that the populist, youth politics of the RAR had their impact on the parent organization. Richard was then working for the party and remembers selling *Temporary Hoarding* outside his local dole office. 'It was a really brilliant atmosphere, and we went really overboard. Lots of comrades became punks. I remember one Jewish comrade who had both a skullcap and a Mohican. We did get a fantastic number of people involved, but we overemphasized how politicized they were.'

Despite occasional tensions, Rock Against Racism operated as a successful example of anti-fascist unity. Such was the opinion of even sceptical independents. This, for example, is how Nicky Tesco of punk band the Members recalls late 1970s: 'Punk was renowned for its nihilism, which was pretty anathema to a lot of hard-core Socialist Workers people. But that side of it never really impinged. You never had a commissar show up at the dressing room and try to convert you, or anything like that.' Music journalist Gavin Weightman, writing after the first RAR carnival, described the relationship between the socialists and the movement at its height. He saw thousands of people marching because they wanted to march. He saw their so-called leaders not at the front, but struggling to catch up with them. He saw a movement that abounded in colour and creativity. 'If there is a conspiracy, with the carnival the chief manifestation of it so far, the only possible culprit would be the Badge and Banner Manufacturers Association (if there is one).'[39]

Music our prayers[40]

Perhaps the best-known member of the Rock Against Racism generation was Dave Widgery. In previous years Widgery had been among the first members of the party to grasp the significance of women's liberation, the campaign to defend access to abortion and the gay rights struggles of the 1970s. He was a talented writer (who compiled two dazzling left-wing anthologies), a doctor in Limehouse, a former editor of the magazine *Oz*, and an incurable activist. Born in 1947, Widgery was a victim of the 1956 polio epidemic and spent five years in reconstructive operations, graduating as he described, 'from wheelchair and callipers to my first pair of shop-bought shoes'. It was a horrific experience for a child to go through, trapped in a hospital ward without his parents, 'crying, as I so clearly remember, ourselves to sleep at night with our nurses in tears at their inability to comfort us'.[41]

Widgery joined CND and took part in the Aldermaston march, and also wrote for the national school students' *U Magazine*. At the age of fifteen, he read Jack Kerouac's great novel *On the Road* and discovered in it 'a coded message of discontent'. Later he would claim that Neal Cassady, the hero of the novel, was the 'Leon Trotsky of his time'. Dave Widgery bunked off from school to listen to jazz bands at the Rikki-Tik club in Windsor. He was expelled from his grammar school for publishing an unauthorized magazine, *Rupture*. In 1965, he interviewed Allen Ginsberg for *Sixth Form Opinion*, and was seduced by him, before escaping on his Lambretta. Later that year, Widgery spent four months travelling across the United States. He arrived just as Watts, the black district of Los Angeles, exploded in riots. Widgery then journeyed to Cuba and later to the West Coast, taking part in anti-Vietnam protests called by members of Students for a Democratic Society.[42] Paul Foot describes his friend:

> David was a restless man. He was always driving his body further than it could go in feverish pursuit of something unattainable. He was quite unlike the popular image of a revolutionary. He was the opposite of Dave Spart or Citizen Smith. He was not one for party exclusivity. Most of his friends were outside the party. If he disagreed with the party, he said so. Indeed, so terrified was he of the image of the party hack that he would often say he disagreed when he didn't.

Widgery brought to Rock Against Racism a love of blues and jazz. An ardent champion of Billie Holliday and Bessie Smith's blues, a man who boasted of having seen Jimmy Hendrix play live, he was the linchpin around which Rock Against Racism grew.[43]

Dave Widgery had the ability to bind around himself a group of friends who shared his general outlook towards questions of politics and culture. He learned from them and they learned from him. One friend, Roger Huddle, worked as a designer in the SWP studio. Another ally, Red Saunders, recalls the Rock Against Racism group:

> I was just a working photographer and then the art got to me, typography, Rodchenko's posters, Mayakovsky's poetry. I was educated by the theatre group CAST [the Cartoon Archetype Slogan Theatre], it was the rock on which everything was based . . . So that we would be reading Preobrazhensky this week, right, then we're off to see the Prague Theatre of the Black and then it's *The Crimes of M. Lange* at the Kilburn Grange.

It trained you for cultural fanaticism. We'd go back to the flat, eat sardines on toast, get herbed up and analyse it all night.[44]

Widgery was an activist in the movement, and later its first historian. His book *Beating Time* gives a back-stage view of RAR, rightly celebrating the movement he helped to build. 'It took to the end of 1976', Widgery recalled, 'for the little RAR group to hammer out its ideas and consolidate a core of visual artists, musicians and writers who could drive the project ahead. But for that group the feeling of fear and passivity against the Front's advance was over, at least in our heads; we were going to strike back kung-fu, rub-a-dub, surrealist style.'[45]

The Rock Against Racism paper *Temporary Hoarding* relayed left ideas in a radical format. The magazine was based around large A3 sheets, which could be folded out in poster style. The look relied on collage, images and irony. Not everyone liked it. Colin was an 18-year-old member of the RAR committee in London. Although his parents were radicals, Colin was less overtly political. He thought the magazine was too political for its own good, and not enough a fanzine. 'I was a music press and fanzine reader and I wanted to read interviews with bands . . . I wasn't going to read an article about internment, whatever that meant.' But between these two extremes, there were thousands of people who loved the magazine.

Creative Marxists like Widgery, Red Saunders and Widgery's friends Ruth Gregory and Syd Shelton hoped to use Rock Against Racism to generate a new political language, less verbal and more visual, more populist than the socialism that they had inherited. 'The graphics of Rodchenko', Ian Godyer writes, 'and El Lissitsky, the poetry of Mayakovsky and the polemical imagery of Grosz and Heartfield, all inspired RAR's attempts to creative an imaginative fusion of politics and art.'[46] Such cultural politics were expressed in Rock Against Racism's decisions to record a compilation album (ironically with the future multinational, Virgin Records), a video and slide shows; even the choice of a logo — a five-pointed star, based on old symbols of labour. Much of their enthusiasm was undoubtedly musical in origin. Writing afterwards, Widgery went so far as to claim that reggae *drove* his own life and the lives of his friends, their sex lives and their waking time. It gave his group their rhythm and purpose:

> Black music was our catechism, not just something we listened to in our spare time. It was the culture which woke us up, had shaped us and kept us up all night, blocked in the Wardour Street mod clubs, fanatical on the Thames Valley R&B circuit, queuing all down Gerrard Street to see Roland Kirk in Ronnie Scott's old basement. It was how we worked out our geography, learnt our sexuality, and taught ourselves history. There was no question of slumming or inverted snobbery, we went for black music because it was so strong rhythmically, there was a passion in it, it was about life and had some point to it. And if white musicians were as

good and as exciting (as George Fame, Alexis Kormer and the early Stones certainly were) we worshipped them too.[47]

The politics of Rock Against Racism can also be seen in a one-off magazine, *Rentamob*, published in 1977 as the 'Agitprop bulletin of the SWP and supporters'. Beneath the title, 'Down with Slogans', *Rentamob* set out a vision of how RAR and similar initiatives could transform the left. 'Go to the average left-wing meeting – a dull pub room, a speaker who may be good, but followed by a generally lifeless question-and-answer session and a list of exhortations from the chair. Yet the struggle for socialism is the struggle to tap the immense creative, imaginative ability of working people, the enthusiasm that is crushed by class society.' Posters, street theatre, bands and graffiti, all were promoted, with the longest article dedicated to the success of the 'Stuff the Jubilee' badge.[48]

One passage from an article he wrote for the magazine *New Socialist* in 1981 expresses Dave Widgery's belief that propaganda had to be relevant, or it had no value at all: 'If socialism is transmitted in a deliberately doleful, pre-electronic idiom, if its emotional appeal is to working class sacrifice and middle class guilt, and if its dominant medium is the printed word and the public procession, it will simply bounce off people who have grown up this side of the 1960s watershed. And barely leave a dent behind.'[49] Writing about the death of Steve Biko, in *Temporary Hoarding*, Widgery began with the events of the Soweto uprising and proceeded to describe in detail the repression of the South African state. Only then did he turn his readers' gaze to the role played by their own leaders.

> The British government voted in the United Nations, yet again, against business sanctions contra South Africa . . . Almost a quarter of South Africa's exports go to Britain and 4 per cent of British exports are destined for South Africa . . . The state that killed Steve Biko is, despite the diplomatic talk, deeply connected to Britain. To help black Africa to freedom, we will have to free ourselves.[50]

The force of this writing depended on its passion. It was the expression on paper of the musical politics that made Widgery. But cultural styles, alone, build no movements. That requires people. Even once a style had been developed which would make possible a fusion of radical music and politics, there was still a need to win the support that Rock Against Racism and others could then shape.

4

Lewisham

From spring 1977, the pace of the protests quickened. On 23 April, a 1,200-strong National Front march through Wood Green was opposed by some 3,000 anti-racists, members of Haringey Labour Party, the Indian Workers' Association, local West Indians, trade unionists, and members of Rock Against Racism and the Socialist Workers Party. While Communists and churchmen addressed a rally at one end of Duckett's Common, a contingent of anti-fascists organized by the SWP broke away and subjected the NF column to a barrage of smoke bombs, eggs and rotten fruit. Some 81 people were arrested, including 74 anti-fascists. Still, anti-fascists held that the Wood Green mobilization had been a victory: reducing the NF to 'an ill-organized and bedraggled queue'.

According to Ian, 'We pursued the Nazis – large amounts of things were hurled at them. We didn't stop them, but they got a very vigorous response.' Balwinder remembers 'coming out of the Tube station and finding a whole gang of NF giving out their racist filth. Fortunately there were also many anti-racists present who directed us toward the common. Then as the National Front march came around the corner of the common suddenly they came under an attack of flour, eggs, tomatoes and worse.'

The police had relatively few officers on duty and the left had a relatively free hand to frustrate their opponents.[1] Richard recalls an angry, confident counter-demonstration: 'Someone had the wit to set off a smoke bomb. There were Turkish, Greek and black kids fighting against the Nazis.' Anna from Islington also found herself at Wood Green, and recalls watching the young people throw anything they could against the National Front: 'All the shops lost one shoe in every pair.' Another anti-Nazi veteran, Andy, remembers protests getting hotter and hotter: 'We had a crack at the Front at Wood Green, and I felt that we got very close.'

Jerry Fitzpatrick was then working full time for the Socialist Workers Party in central London. He was sent to Wood Green and played a prominent part in organizing the protests at Duckett's Common: 'I'd come from an Irish background. I had been at Derry in 1969. I had seen the resistance on the Bogside – that was a factor. We wanted to organize in the same way. We had a keen eye on confronting the NF.' The smoke bombs that Richard recalls were in fact marine flares. 'I bought them from a boatyard. I thought they would make an effective public spectacle. We sought a non-violent context. But we were willing to sharpen the demonstration, to give a sense of colour and cover as people confronted the Nazis.'

The left has had long had a presence in Haringey, and 25 years on from the protests, many local people are willing to describe their memories. Dave Morris, later a defendant in the famous 'McLibel' trial, attended as part of an anarchist group. He saw the anti-fascists charge the National Front march, but remembers that the NF were eventually able to regroup and continue along their way. Morris then recalls the police removing the public and protesters from the pavements at the side of the NF march:

> Somehow I got through, seemingly the only one who did at that time. For half an hour I walked alone alongside the fascist demonstration as it completely dominated the streets, protected by police who cleared away most of the public in general. It was eerie . . . After getting increasingly funny looks from cops and marchers despite my innocent whistling and humming and pretending to admire the cracks in the paving stones, I sloped off.

Another anti-fascist protester, David B, was even closer to the centre of the fighting. His diary provides a vivid record:

> We walked to Turnpike Lane where the counter-demonstration was assembling in the presence of vast numbers of police . . . We met up with Steve and watched the Front march form up a hundred yards away, with plenty of verbal exchange between the two sides. It seemed incredible to me that the police could allow such an obviously explosive confrontation to occur . . . A little way along Wood Green High Road the march was attacked. Red smoke bombs filled the air and a battle was soon under way. Everything that could be thrown was thrown at the fascists in an attempt to stop the march. Police horses appeared on the pavement, and if shoppers got in their way that was hard luck.

David and his friends eventually found themselves standing outside the school in which the National Front was holding its post-march rally.

> I suggested that we try and go inside. At this point Steve said we were crazy and left. There was some dispute at the door about whether to admit us but finally we got in and I heard a couple of minutes of the meeting. 'If they're black, send them back'. The atmosphere was one of rabid anti-intellectualism, clearly thought was a sign of weakness. Then somebody said 'they're commies', and we were recognized as anti-fascists, which I thought was obvious anyway. The mood was ugly so we made to leave but they weren't able to restrain themselves, we were jostled and pushed out. Robin, a yard behind me, received a number of blows and kicks until blood was running from his nose. Some of this happened outside, but the police stood around nearby, ignoring it.

This was the rally at which NF leader John Tyndall declared, 'I think World War Three has just started out there.'

Still more fighting took place later, on the trains heading back to London. According to Gerry Gable,

> the British Movement sent in its Leader Guard. They were not just good street fighters but had received paramilitary training from former Special Forces officers. At first they did a lot of damage, but as the train journey away from Wood Green continued they were cut down and down until finally a handful of them remained battered and bleeding and they made their escape.

The experience of seeing the National Front at close hand convinced David B. that anti-fascism was an urgent necessity. 'It had been quite a day. I'd never been through a demonstration like it and left determined that the National Front must be opposed with absolute ruthlessness wherever it dares to appear. Any illusions I may have had about non-violent means of opposing them were destroyed in that school.'[2] Ted Parker travelled up from south-east London to be at Wood Green. 'What I really remember from Haringey is how close we came. The National Front were brought in by the police, with a lot of protection, a lot of secrecy. We didn't really think we could stop them. But one day, we would.' Jerry Fitzpatrick was also thinking towards the future: 'I drew two lessons. First, we needed logistics, more supporters in the set area, more street planning, a better sense of what the police tactics would be. Second, there had to be an intense effort towards organising among the local community.'

Two weeks after Wood Green, the National Front attempted to hold an election meeting at Shoreditch School in Hoxton. Five hundred people turned out to prevent them.[3] The mood was hardening. The magazine *Race Today* called for black defence patrols in the Brick Lane area of the East End. But the attention of activists was moving quickly from east to south London, and to Lewisham in particular.

The real muggers

The roots of the protest in Lewisham go back to a police campaign against young blacks. In May 1977, 21 people were arrested and charged with conspiracy to steal purses. This action was perceived locally as a crude attempt to create some kind of anti-mugging backlash. The journalist Paul Foot described the character of the arrests:

> 5.30 Monday Morning. Six policemen break down the door of 21 Childeric Road in Deptford, South East London, with an axe. Another six smash down the back door. They pour inside, overturning furniture, ripping open drawers, and turning people out of their beds. Christopher Foster, aged 16, is frog-marched into the road in his underclothes. Insults and questions are shouted at him. He and four other young people in the house are rushed to Penge police station. These include Cathy Cullis, a young white girl. She is stripped to her underwear in a cell. Two

policemen come and joke about the 'disease' she has caught living with black people.[4]

The action was recorded within the Lewisham force as 'Operation PNH'. The acronym was said by local activists to stand for 'Police Nigger Hunt'. Over 60 black youngsters were detained, and 18 of them charged. Campaigns were then launched in their defence.

Rumours came out about the treatment of the Lewisham defendants. They were only accused of being petty criminals, but the police had assaulted them, smashing down people's doors before arresting them. It had been an apartheid-style raid. Tony Bogues of Flame and Kim Gordon of the Socialist Workers Party met up with David Foster, the father of Christopher Foster. They set up a defence committee. Later Gordon spoke to Prince Charles outside a black youth club that the prince was visiting. The prince suggested a meeting between the police and the defence committee.[5] Police Commander Douglas Randall then agreed to a meeting where he would speak to the families of the defendants. Slowly, more of the defendants agreed to take part, until a majority of them were involved. The police were pushed on to the defensive. They then responded by arresting members of the defence committee, adding another three names to the original Lewisham 18.[6] Tony Bogues has clear memories of David Foster:

> David was an ordinary, nice fellow who had believed in the early stages of his life the myths about British justice, but on arriving in Britain he was immediately aware of the question of race. How could he deal with race, raise his kids and still be respectable? David did it with a certain dignity. We sat down and talked with him for days. His house became the community house. There were large meetings, quiet meetings. The question of self-defence from the fascists and the police came up in discussion with the youth. We spent a lot of time, a lot of time, persuading people to work with us.

Gerry Gable was then a journalist working for London Weekend Television.

> The *Evening Standard* was running horror stories about young black muggers. They showed an elderly lady battered and bloody and said that blacks had mugged her. We found the battered lady and she had not even seen her attacker as she was pushed down from behind. We met mixed-race gangs where a white kid would be used as the stop as no person in their right mind would stop if a couple of black kids asked them the time. Many of the victims of purse stealing on the local bus queues were black women. When the police approached the victims and asked them to give evidence there was a universal refusal as they hated the police more than those who stole off them.

Summer 1977 also saw the climax to the picketing at Grunwick in north-west London, and many of those who took part in events at

Lewisham were graduates of the Grunwick picket lines. The first mass pickets in support of the striking film-processing workers took place in the spring of 1977, when Right to Work marchers who had walked to London from Manchester joined the strikers to express their support for them. From 23 May, a number of left-wing newspapers including *Socialist Worker* began to call for mass pickets. Slowly the number of large protests grew. By June 1977, these were taking place weekly, and then daily. On Friday 17 June, 1,500 people turned out to support the 100 or so Grunwick strikers. The following week, members of the police Special Patrol Group were used to send non-union, 'scab', workers across the picket lines. The violence escalated and was soon being shown nightly on national television. This was one of the first all-out strikes where the workforce was composed almost entirely of immigrant labour. Many identifiable leaders emerged, not least Mrs Jayaben Desai, chair of the strike committee.

On 9 July, the owner of Grunwick, George Ward, was able to defy the picket lines by bringing in support mobilized by the National Association for Freedom. NAFF turned out 250 volunteers and 150 vehicles. Two days later, on 11 July, the National Union of Miners called for a day of action in support of the Grunwick strikers. Some 20,000 people turned out, outnumbering the police three to one. Twenty-four pickets were arrested. A second national mobilization was called for 8 August (the week of the Lewisham marches), but called off at the instigation of the strikers' union, APEX. Together with the police and the courts, and shielded by the equivocal support given to the strikers by their own union, Ward was just about able to keep his plant open.[7]

At the same time as Grunwick, there was a strike at Desoutters in north London. Mike was a member of the support group, and later took people from that dispute to Lewisham. 'One of the most active stewards was ironically a member of the Front. He held together one of the gates during the strike. He received a phone call from Tyndall putting pressure on him to break with the strike. In the end, he left the Front.'

In south-east London, meanwhile, the mood was rising. Ted Parker was the Socialist Workers Party district secretary. He describes how 'there were different groups in the party'. One was the black socialist group Flame; 'they leafleted the whole area for weeks'. One of its leading figures was Tony Bogues, a socialist from Jamaica who 'looked more like a poet than an activist'. Some support came from Thames Poly. The SWP also backed workers at Reinforced Steel, who occupied their plant against the threat of closure.

'Lewisham was the climax', recalls Tony Bogues, 'of a series of activities in the black underground.' Bogues himself had only been in London for a year, having arrived from Jamaica.

I came from there, the Manley regime, the destabilization attempts being run by the CIA. We said that Jamaica should not become the next Chile

. . . My politics was all about self-organization. There was a way in which you talked with working-class people. You started from what they thought. It was a different style from the British left. We didn't leaflet people. We asked what they thought . . . I made initial contacts, with the people in Flame, and also with family, friends, the sorts of people you drink with in the bar. After a year, I knew a lot of people, some friends, some political. There were the people in the SWP. Kim Gordon was militant, quick-witted. The International Marxist Group had a guy called Fitzroy, from Nigeria. There was the Black Marxist Collective in Croydon. It was a different kind of politics, based on the immigrant cultures.

Parker himself had been brought up in Folkestone, in a very patriotic family. He joined the Royal Air Force at 16, on a three-year apprenticeship. They had education classes at the base, which set him thinking. Together with a friend, Mike, he joined the Campaign for Nuclear Disarmament. They were court-martialled and given eight-month sentences. A campaign was launched on their behalf. Parker later ended up at the London School of Economics during the heady years of 1966–9. In 1967, he toured South Africa, delivering clandestine leaflets for the banned African National Congress. By the mid-1970s, he had been a union activist in the print union SOGAT and the lecturers' union ATTI. Through 1977, Parker recalls,

> we had been selling *Socialist Worker* in Lewisham Town centre. The Front would storm in and break us up. We had to rally as many people as we could to protect us. People used to come down from east London to help us out. There was one estate in Catford, where most of the Front lived. It became notorious for racist attacks. They also attacked a Sikh temple in Woolwich.

On 18 June, the central committee of the Socialist Workers Party wrote to their counterparts in the political committee of the Communist Party suggesting that their parties should agree to work together around two very specific areas: the defence of trade union rights to strike and 'joint meetings of the committees of our two parties responsible for anti-racialist activities, with a view to launching a joint campaign within the Labour movement to drive the fascists off the streets'.[8] Events on the picket lines at Grunwick may have influenced the first suggested area of joint activity; events in Lewisham certainly shaped the second.

On 2 July, members of the National Front attacked a demonstration in support of the Lewisham detainees. One teacher was kicked unconscious by the fascists. Although this time it was the left that was under attack, the police still managed to arrest 23 anti-fascists alongside 27 fascists.[9] Dave Peers of the Socialist Workers Party warned his comrades to expect further attacks:

> The attacks on the demonstration by the Nazis – and in turn by the police – are the culmination of a month of growing fascist and police

harassment in the area. We have received well-founded reports that this represents a change of tactics by the Nazis . . .

We have been informed that their South London branches have been given a free hand to attack left-wing demonstrations. This is a danger that no anti-fascist – SWP member or not – can ignore. The local SWP will be contacting trade unions, Labour Parties and all anti-fascists in the area to defend the right to demonstrate and to meet in public free from fascist harassment.[10]

Although the Socialist Workers Party appeal to the Communist Party for joint action proved unsuccessful, it did focus attention on the next set of demonstrations due to be held in the area. The National Front called an anti-mugging march for 13 August, to assemble near New Cross station. An All-Lewisham Campaign Against Racism and Fascism counter-protest was organized. The police planned to route it far away from the NF march. The SWP and the Lewisham 21 defence committee promised to challenge the NF. According to that week's *Socialist Worker*,

Panic is breaking out in high places as the Nazis of the National Front prepare to march through Lewisham's black community this Saturday. Newspapers like *The Sun* and the *Daily Express* have called for the march to be banned. So have a number of Labour MPs and the Labour-controlled council. Their concern is not so much with the threat to black people as with the pledges being made by the left to stop the Nazis marching, regardless of what the police do.[11]

The sky darkened

On 13 August, around 6,000 anti-fascists, including large numbers of local black youths, prevented around 800 supporters of the National Front from marching through Lewisham. The original NF demonstration was publicized as an anti-mugging march, to tap into the furore cause by the arrest of the Lewisham 21. Activists were determined to halt the NF and prevent them from gaining control of the streets. The police, armed with long batons and perspex shields, were equally determined to keep the march going. Although many groups were represented at Lewisham, it was members of the Socialist Workers Party who took the lead in organizing the confrontation with the fascists.

By mid-June, Jerry Fitzpatrick had received word of the planned National Front march.

A group of us set up headquarters in a building on Clifton Rise. We occupied a house and used it as an organizing centre. Norma, a local activist, was central to this organization, and Ted Parker. We created an atmosphere among black youth. People came in to collect leaflets and posters. You got a sense of people organizing things themselves. There was one incident – it was a small, trivial thing, really. About three weeks before the demonstration, the police were chasing a black youth, and he ran into our building. They grabbed him, and me too, accusing me of providing him with a false alibi. In court, we provided him with a solicitor. He didn't get off, but it was a light sentence. In the days after, I had a really strong sense that the barriers had come down. The word went round that we would help people against the aggressive police.

The organizers called for backing from different Lewisham groups. According to Fitzpatrick,

There were lots of Irish people who provided us with logistics and support. They were hardier than some others. And there were other ways in which the Irish community contributed. There was an Irish hall next to our centre. We were allowed into there, and into the Irish pubs and dances, to raise money, to speak about the NF as the latest incarnation of British imperialism, and to appeal for support.

Steve Jeffreys was a member of the Socialist Workers Party's central committee:

We had so many plans for Lewisham. I've never been on a demonstration that was so well organized. We knew that coaches were coming from all over the country. We knew from Lewisham that there would be a kind of local uprising. We discussed hiring a lorry, and using that to block the road, but we thought that would put the organizational details in front of the politics. We knew we had the numbers; we didn't need to militarize the struggle. We planned groups – for when the NF attacked, the police, we had everything planned in advance. There are lots of times that I've heard people talk about demonstrating, maybe even confronting the police, but never with the sort of confidence that we had then.

Ted Parker attended the High Court hearings that discussed whether the National Front march should be banned. He was interviewed in the Lewisham *Mercury*. 'I tried to draw parallels with the Battle of Cable Street in the 1930s. Mosley had been anti-Semitic and violent. In Germany, the fascists were allowed to march. But in Britain, at Cable Street, they had been stopped.' What about the police? he was asked. 'I said I had a friend in the police who hated the Front as much as I did. But if the Front march, and the police protect them, we're ready to fight if that's what it takes.'

Parker's other jobs included purchasing the rotten fruit to throw at the National Front. 'We bought marine flares to signal where people were needed – we'd learned that from Wood Green. I went to the market and brought absolutely barrel-loads of rotten fruit. We gave that to people in carrier bags.' By the week of the demonstration, Parker's greatest fear was that the NF would somehow get to the demonstrators, by attacking them the night before. He was not the only one to consider that possibility. According to Jerry Fitzpatrick, 'The day before the march, the police raided the centre. They were looking for megaphones, banners, the things

we would need for the demonstration. But they found just two
walkie-talkies. We were expecting raids and had already cleared out.'
Parker spent Friday evening in Brockley.

> We looked at the terrain. We were absolutely sure we could win. The
> plan was simple; we would try to get as many people as possible to
> Clifton Rise, New Cross Station. We knew the police would try to keep
> the groups separated, on each side of the railway lines. We'd make some
> effort there, at the beginning, but it was a feint really. If we couldn't stop
> the Front at Clifton Rise, we would let the Front go North along New
> Cross Road. Smaller groups would ambush them. We'd leave a few
> people in New Cross to protect the families of the Lewisham 21. But our
> largest number would turn round and march quickly along Lewisham
> Way. That's where we were going to make a real effort. The police
> would try to stop us getting across the bridges. We'd have to storm any
> barriers. But we'd then hold Lewisham High Street. There was no way
> the Front could get through.

Some of the group later returned from Brockley to Lewisham, in an attempt to drum up last-minute support for the mobilization. Andy was
there:

> There were four of us from the leadership, and a group of young black
> comrades who'd joined the SWP recently. We spent the evening touring
> round Lewisham. We met people on the estates, black kids, gangs and
> their leaders. We talked to people. We explained that tomorrow we'd be
> organizing the biggest march that any of them had seen, that we'd take on
> the NF, and also the police. Some people didn't know what to make of us
> – they were calling us this and that. But we talked to a lot of people. And
> the day after, you got a real sense. There was a large group of black
> people. Hundreds, thousands even. They were waiting and watching.
> And when things really kicked off, they got stuck in.

Tony Bogues of Flame has similar memories: 'The night before the demonstration, we drove around the entirety of Lewisham. We knew that the
violence was going to happen. We said to the fascists – if you come into
our community, we'll stop you. We knew what would happen.'

The Socialist Workers Party was not the only local group to call an
anti-National Front protest. The day began at 11 a.m. with a march called
by the Communist Party, Catholic organizations, councillors and members of the All-Lewisham Campaign Against Racism and Fascism
(ALCARAF). Mayor Godsif of Lewisham and Mervyn Stockwood, the
bishop of Southwark, led the march. Each of the three main parties was
represented. The 4,000 people who took part expressed their opposition
to the NF, and then many of them left the scene. According to the *Sunday
Times*, 'The [marchers] wanted to demonstrate peacefully against the National Front by marching from Ladywell Fields along Lewisham High
Street and Lewisham Way to Railway Grove. Although this was peril-
ously close to where the National Front was due to assemble, ALCARAF

argued that its march would be over at least 90 minutes before the Front assembled.'[12] Dave Widgery was less kind towards these moderates, 'The official protest march, including the Catholics, the councillors and the Communists, made indignant speeches against fascism in Lewisham and carefully avoided going within two miles of the fascists who were assembling behind the British Rail station at New Cross where the atmosphere was less forgiving.'[13]

Having taken part in the first demonstration, members of the Socialist Workers Party then handed out a leaflet calling upon the demonstrators to join a second protest, which would assemble at the National Front's planned assembly point. In Jerry Fitzpatrick's words,

> In the negotiations leading up to the demonstration, we tried hard to persuade the other groups, the Communists and the church people, not to call a counter demonstration at the same time at a different venue, but to organize theirs in such a way that if people then wanted to march with us, they could. In the event we succeeded because their demo finished in time for the bulk of them to join us at Clifton Rise. There needed to be a broadening of our appeal. If we were seen simply as boot-boys then we would fail. We had to convince the Communist Party, the Labour Party, the trade unions to join with us and broaden our support.

Some refused the call. A Communist Party leaflet expressed that organization's hostility: 'We totally oppose the harassment and the provocative march planned by the SWP.' The leaflet attacked 'those who insist on the ritual enactment of vanguardist violence'.[14] Yet hundreds did join the second march. According to Ted Parker,

> We knew one pivotal thing was to get as many people as possible from the first march up to Clifton Rise. We had lorries on the first march, telling people what the plan was, urging them to join us. The fascinating thing was that people wanted to march to Clifton Rise, but they just wouldn't line up behind an Socialist Workers Party banner. You could see it. We had the numbers. Eventually, we found some members of some other group like the IMG with a banner for some united campaign against racism and fascism. People agree to group behind that. It taught me a lesson for later – many people would support a united campaign, they didn't all want just to line up behind the SWP.

Red Saunders was part of the crowd who joined both the first and second demonstrations:

> What I really remember is that there were all these Christians and Communists, telling us to go home. Most people stayed. But we were all just milling about, when this old black lady, too old to march, came out on her balcony. She put out her speakers, as loud as they could, playing 'Get up, stand up'. That did it for me.

Pete Alexander recalls attending the Communist-led demonstration and successfully encouraging many people to march with him and join the second protest at Clifton Rise.

> I was part of the SWP contingent sent on to this march. Not only was this part of our general approach of backing all mobilizations against the fascists (we were very non-sectarian); it was also so that we could pull people to the counter-demonstration at New Cross. Until Lewisham there were still many people – students especially – who were confused about the best way of fighting fascism. We were actually pretty successful. I and the people I pulled arrived at New Cross just as the fun began.

Angus MacKinnon, a journalist on the *New Musical Express*, actually missed the first protest, arriving directly at Clifton Rise, 'On the day', he wrote,

> I arrived at New Cross and couldn't get any further. It was about eleven o'clock and there were already a lot of people there – most were trade unionists. It said in the press the next day that there were three thousand, but it must have been twice that number. They said it was the standard rent-a-mob. It wasn't. Many had come from all over the country, for the same reason as myself – enough was enough.

Similar feelings were expressed by Bev, a graduate student who came to the demo with socialists and trade unionists from Nottingham. 'I had no idea what to expect, but there was such a strong feeling that the National Front shouldn't be allowed to hold their march unchallenged.'[15]

The fighting began near Clifton Rise at 1.30. According to John Rose,

> The whole of New Cross High Road and the top of the Nazis' intended assembly point, Clifton Rise, was occupied by anti-fascists. It was then that the police made their first, unprovoked attack. Foot police tried unsuccessfully to clear a path for the Nazi march, and then mounted police moved in. They too, were soon forced to retreat – but not before the police had taken revenge by grabbing people at random. Unable to clear the top of Clifton Rise, the police finally made the Nazis move up onto the main road through a side road 200 yards along. The Nazis were allowed through police cordons to join the march by showing their Nazi membership cards. Suddenly, hundreds of police and a score of police horses began to charge down the road clearing a path for the head of the Nazi column. The crowd of anti-fascists exploded. Sticks, smoke bombs, rocks, bottles, were thrown over the police heads at the Nazis.[16]

'As the Nazi honour guard swung on to Lewisham High Street,' Paul Holborow continues, 'you had the marvellous sight of the master race scuttling away. I remember one on his knees, hiding behind a policeman, himself desperately trying to hide from the bombardment.'

Another activist, Einde, has described the battle that followed. He was a member of the Socialist Workers Party, from Derry, then studying sociology at City University in north London. Einde recalls joining big crowds at the junction in New Cross, which was located strategically

Anti-fascists and the local community fight with the National Front and police at Lewisham: Clifton Rise

between the two nearby metropolitan stations. It was also the top of a hill, a natural vantage point:

> There was a huge police cordon between us and the NF's meeting place. As the Front march set off, it had to come out on to the main road at the bottom of the hill. We had linked arms by this stage and were facing the police cordon that stood between us and the NF march. I was with the comrades from the university in about the seventh or eighth line. To be quite honest I didn't want to be in the first row as I knew what was supposed to happen.

The plan was simple. The fascist march was located downhill from the anti-fascist contingent. As the National Front neared, their opponents would see the march side on. On hearing a signal, anti-fascists would charge down the hill at the NF group.

The sign to attack was delivered by Jerry Fitzpatrick. 'Jerry had glasses and busy fair hair', Einde remembers; he was 'a wheeler-dealer, a magnificent organiser'. Fitzpatrick and other stewards had decided not to confront the main National Front honour guard, composed of the hardened street fighters, marching at the front of their contingent. Instead, the comrades from the SWP would pile into the middle of the fascist procession. Einde remembers Fitzpatrick standing on a box, by the traffic lights, waiting for the NF as they crossed the road at the bottom of the hill.

> We charged down the hill against the police cordon. The rows of demonstrators in front of me broke under the strain of the pushing, but by the

time our line came to the front, the police cordon had weakened sufficiently and we broke through into the middle of the march. I can
remember that we grabbed an NF banner and in a tug of war we managed
to get it off them, all the while maintaining linked arms – how we did it I
don't know. Eventually the police managed to push us back, but I remember that there was a hail of bricks from some convenient building
sites alongside the route of the march and assorted other stuff, including
at least one dustbin.

The anti-fascists' charge had a dramatic effect. Pete Alexander recalls, 'I
still remember seeing National Front marchers with green faces. They
were so scared. I'd never seen people go green before.'

These memories are confirmed in Dave Widgery's account:

> In New Cross Road, just down from Goldsmiths' College, a crowd of
> 5000 anti-NFers had assembled by midday. People gently milled; here
> surging forward under banners that sprang and swooped like kites, there
> breaking out into feminist war whoops, elsewhere shouting recognition
> in noisy South London patois . . . At the front, a ram-packed contingent
> of South London Afro-Caribbeans cordially but expertly blocked off the
> police's first attempts – uphill and on foot – to open a way for the NF . . .
> An officer with a megaphone read an order to disperse. No one did;
> seconds later the police cavalry cantered into sight and sheered through
> the front row of protesters.

So, continues Widgery, it might have ended,

> except that people refused to melt away from the police horses and jeer
> ineffectually from the sidelines. A horse went over, then another, and the
> Front were led forward so fast that they were quickly struggling. Then
> suddenly the sky darkened (as they say in Latin poetry), only this time
> with clods, rocks, lumps of wood, planks and bricks . . . The Front found
> it most difficult to dodge this cannonade while upholding the dignity ap-
> propriate to a master race inspecting soon-to-be-deported underlings.
> The NF march was broken in two, their banners seized and burnt.

According to the report that appeared in the *Sunday Times*,

> Hundreds of demonstrators attempted to force the police cordon but rein-
> forcements appeared and moved steadily through the stamping crowd in
> single file. A woman in a green mac was crushed on a [wall] outside a
> house. In New Cross Road, National Front supporters numbering about
> 1,000 were met with a hail of bottles, bricks, wood blocks, beer cans,
> smashed paving stones and smoke bombs. Mounted police charged up,
> clearing a way for the marchers. Police snatch squads darted into the
> yelling crowds, seizing missile-hurling youths.

'After about 20 minutes of confusion', the paper continued,

> the police regained control of the whole of Clifton Rise and the top of
> New Cross Road. Their tactics then were to hide the National Front in

Achilles Street and then send the marches up Pagnell Street into New Cross Road and on their way to Lewisham. The plan almost worked. The left-wingers were milling around at the top of the Front column emerging from Pagnell Street [But with the police outnumbered on New Cross Road, left-wingers were able to charge through and catch the middle of the National Front demonstration] . . . When they reached the march, a wedge of police tried to hold the two sides apart. But demonstrators simply hurled the ammunition they had collected along the way at the Front and the police protecting them became sitting targets.[17]

To summarize the events so far: the National Front arrived at New Cross Road at about 1.30 p.m. They tried to assemble at Clifton Rise. There they were attacked, and when they did set off, their march was broken up by the group including Einde and Jerry Fitzpatrick. But the police charged back at the anti-fascist demonstrators, who then broke away. The NF were just about able to reassemble, and then they marched east along New Cross Road in the direction of central Lewisham. Crowds threw fruit at the retreating members of the NF. Smaller groups attacked them from the side streets.

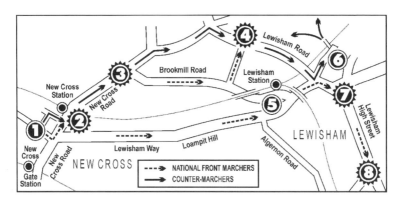

Lewisham: route of the demonstration and counter-demonstrations

One group of anti-fascists was caught and held by the police at Clifton Rise. Morgan was a young Irish steelworker and a member of the Socialist Workers Party. His workplace, Reinforced Steel, was a small factory owned by British Steel. Having come out on strike in support of a group of nurses at the local hospital, Morgan's fellow-workers were then threatened with the sack, and responded by occupying the plant. In the weeks running up to Lewisham, Morgan found himself attacked and threatened by members of the National Front. One work colleague, a former NF supporter, even came to warn Morgan that he was being followed. 'They attacked us on the High Street, they also attacked Labour. That was regular.' Two of his work colleagues joined Morgan on the anti-NF protests. But they got no further than Clifton Rise. Arriving there after 2 p.m.,

Morgan and his friends found themselves penned in by the police, and unable to march. His group was held like that for several hours.

Much larger numbers, however, were able to follow the anti-fascists' original plan, and march east along Lewisham Way. Ted Parker led on a megaphone, shouting 'Defend the clock tower!' Why the clock tower? 'It's right in the middle of Lewisham. If we went anywhere else, I was worried the police might pen us in, and lead the NF through by one of the side streets.' Marching east, anti-fascists were actually walking along a similar route to the National Front – but along a shorter and more direct way – and without the fighting that slowed down the NF march. By 2.30, this large contingent had arrived at central Lewisham, about the mid-way point in the NF's planned route. In this way, they were able occupy the ground before the NF arrived.

David L came from a Jewish background in north London. These protests were part of a life's struggle against racism. He recalls the diversity of this anti-racist march, the presence of women's contingents, alongside a few members of the Trotskyist group Militant:

> There was a large contingent from Women against Racism and Fascism. Next to them was a Militant contingent. At one point, the main women's steward said, 'Right, women this way.' Someone from Militant then chipped up, 'Oh, can I have one?' It was all the stewards could do to persuade the women, 'Massacre them next week, it's the Nazis we're after today.'[18]

Charli from the International Marxist Group takes up the story:

> When my contingent reached the police, we couldn't turn round because at that point the demo came to a complete halt . . . We were the first banner, and marching with no police 'escort' at all, but by the time we'd done half a mile there was a group of black youth, generally in the 14 to 20 age range, demoing ahead of us, and this group grew until it was maybe 400-strong as we went along. Big contrast between the all-black youth ahead of us and the 95 per cent plus white contingents from the original demo. There were people hanging out of windows and waving and cheering as we went along. Totally amazing. Made you feel good.

Jerry Fitzpatrick agrees. 'There was a buzz on the day, a networking. It wasn't communicated by posters or leaflets, but by people talking. This was West Indian youth making a stand.' Where had all the numbers come from? Charli continues:

> There was a difference between April and August, in that Turnpike Lane was predominantly white at the north . . . It is these areas, white ghettoes where there is racist fear but very little experience of actually living among black or Asian people, where the fascists have gained most support and tactically the NF were marching hoping to win support. Lewisham, on the other hand, was a predominantly black area and an NF march there could only be seen as an insult to the locals.

By 2.30 p.m., the bruised remnants of the National Front march had reached Lewisham train station. The marchers could then look south, where the whole of Lewisham was occupied by the largest group of anti-NF protesters, outnumbering the police and the NF several times over. Not daring to continue along their planned route, the NF headed north towards Blackheath, where they stopped in a deserted car park and NF leader John Tyndall gave a short, concluding speech. Tyndall called for the police to be armed with guns. His followers slunk away.[19]

By 3 p.m., the National Front had been dispersed. Yet the euphoria that greeted this news was diminished as people realized that the police were still determined to clear all anti-fascists from the streets. Ted Parker was now at Lewisham clock tower. 'There was a tide of people blocking the road. There were no signs of the police at all. Marchers were even redirecting the traffic. Then the police began to appear.' The *Sunday Times* blamed the subsequent fighting on the left: 'The most violent scenes came when some 3,000 demonstrators realized that a secret arrangement between the police and National Front had allowed the NF marchers to slip away. Enraged left-wingers rioted along Lewisham High Street, smashing windows, wrecking police vehicles.'[20] It would be more accurate to say that people were defending themselves from the police.

At 3 p.m., Einde was standing near the clock tower:

> This was where the Nazi march was supposed to come on to the High Street. The police attempted to clear this area several times, but without success. Then they brought out the horses. This was the first time I'd ever encountered police horses. It's quite a frightening experience, but together with some other comrades we got the people to link arms facing the police lines and retreated slowly and without panic. Shortly after we heard that the National Front had had to break off their march and hold their rally in an isolated car park. At that time the pavements along Lewisham High Street were being newly paved with conveniently sized bricks. These were used to pelt the police. It was quite terrifying at first. We were occupying the street facing a line of police. Behind us were large numbers of young blacks who were lobbing half-bricks over our heads into the middle of the police – miraculously none of us seemed to be hit. The police would charge us, our line would part and the young blacks would simply melt away into the side streets. Then the whole thing was repeated facing in the other direction. At some stage the police brought out the riot shields, the first time they had been used on the 'mainland'.

Pete Alexander takes up the story.

> The black youth were especially interested in attacking the cops – after Operation PNH and much else this was understandable, and this is partly why the riot became blacker as the day went on. A lot of SWP members also enjoyed having a go at the police. We were fed up with them defending the Nazis and many of us had been unfairly arrested and intimidated

by them, and there was probably a matter of solidarity with the black kids. It wasn't just the fascists who were beaten; it was also the cops. Heavy drink cans and bricks were used to knock them off their horses and they had to resort to trying to clear the streets using cars at high speed.

Now that the fascists had left, the conflict that remained was a battle between anti-fascists and the police. Charli was there:

I saw the riot shields in use outside the Odeon cinema, and later further south towards Ladywell there was a police motorbike abandoned, covered with green paint and on fire. Lots of dented and scratched police transits with big holes in their windows were zooming round, but there was no other traffic whatsoever. There were bricks and stones all over the street, but I saw just one smashed shop window. I heard later that there had been a lot of confrontations between local youth and police in Lewisham that day, obviously related to the huge police presence due to the demo but not directly concerned with it. Just the usual provocations writ large.

A third of the entire Metropolitan Police force was on duty that day. It was the first time that riot shields had been used on the mainland, and even on their own terms, the police hardly knew how to use them. BBC footage shows the police in gangs, three or four officers at a time, running behind their great over-sized screens. The officers charged, in broken lines, arresting more than 200 demonstrators. People were clubbed, as they stood, grabbed and taken. Police and protesters could reach out and touch. There were no lines, just a mêlée.

John, a teacher from south London, was caught up in the fighting. He was arrested, charged and accused of having planned the events:

I had been spotted by snatch squads operating at the end of the day as the demonstration was dispersing. I was clubbed, kicked and punched by police armed with riot gear and shields. I ran but was run down by a police motorcycle, and bundled into a Special Patrol Group carrier. As the van raced through the streets, they amused themselves by trying to jump from the seats on to my head. It proved more difficult than they had imagined. They could only break the bones in my hand. I was charged with police assault; the assault of an unknown member of the Metropolitan Police force, who was never produced or named.

Maeve was a young black teacher, of South African origin. She worked at the same school in south London as John. In the run-up to the events at Lewisham, she recalls sticking up posters for the demonstration. A prominent activist, she was sure that she was going to be arrested. 'I washed my child's teddy bear. I took him to my mother's. I didn't want her to say anything, if she had to look after him for several days.' Maeve recalls being at Lewisham Way, as the police lines scattered. 'I was cut off, round the back from the clock tower. The police were really abusive. One said to me, "If I wasn't in this uniform, I'd show you, Nigger."' Maeve was separated from her brother, who was also marching, and from other activists. By now, the crowd was much younger and blacker. 'I remember one of the organizers was on the megaphone shouting to us to all link arms, but when I turned to the people next to me, they just laughed.' The crowd was more divided than it had been earlier. Parts were also angrier. According to Parker,

> The cry went up from the marchers, 'Let's go to Ladywell station', but we meant to go to the train station, to go home. The black youth took it up, 'To Ladywell, Ladywell police station'. That was the nearest police station. I heard later from people who'd been arrested earlier in the day that just as we were getting ready to depart, suddenly all the cops stopped doing any paperwork. They began preparing the building for what they saw as an inevitable attack. And the black youth did go there. They stoned the station.

After several hours of fighting, one thing was clear: the National Front had failed to pass. According to Dave Widgery's *Beating Time*,

> We were frightened and we were brave and proud and ashamed at the same time. As the day became more brutal and frightening, and the police, furious at their failure, turned to take revenge on the counter demonstrators, there was one big flash of recognition on the faces in the groups: between dread and socialist, between lesbian separatist and black parent, between *NME* speadfreak and ASTMS branch secretary. We were together . . . the mood was absolutely euphoric. Not only because of the sense of achievement – they didn't pass, not with any dignity anyway . . . but also because, at last, we were all in it together.[21]

Maeve's strongest memory is similar, of an overwhelming feeling of elation that sustained her for weeks afterwards.

The last word belongs to Ted Parker.

> I was on Lewisham High Street, with a megaphone, when I was hit on the head by the police. After that, I was completely groggy, my mind went, my memory. I think I must have bumped into a couple of comrades. They wanted to take me to Lewisham hospital, but I insisted they take me to one in Westminster, so I wouldn't get arrested. Next thing, I wake up in hospital. I don't even know what day it is. I was even thinking – maybe it was the Friday, we'd been attacked, and the whole thing never happened. I ask the nurse, the patients. It was OK, it was the Sunday. Was there a riot? There had been. I couldn't remember a thing. I phoned my wife, and said, 'I'm in hospital, I've lost my memory.' She said, 'That's the tenth time you've rung me with the same cock and bull story.' Then I was feeling shaky again. I phoned Jerry Fitzpatrick from the hospital, and I asked him, 'How was it? Did I do all right?' He said, 'Ted, you were bloody marvellous.'

Who will defend the communities?

After Lewisham, the media took the side of the police. Daily and weekly newspapers ran with the hundreds arrested and the 50 policemen injured, ignoring the causes of the protest and portraying the conflict as a senseless battle between two parallel sets of extremists. The front page of the *Sunday Times* reported David McNee, the Metropolitan Police Commissioner, condemning the 'determined extreme element' of the left for preventing a 'lawful march' from taking place.[22] The *Sunday People* featured the headline, 'Bobbies pay the price of freedom'. A leader in *The Times* blamed the Socialist Workers Party, 'whose members and adherents, some of them armed with vicious weapons, came prepared to fight. That their belligerent intent so soon transferred itself from their avowed enemy, the Front, to the police is an appalling indictment of their true philosophy.' The *Daily Mail* used a front-page picture of a policeman holding a studded club and a knife, weapons supposedly found at Lewisham, and beside him was the headline, 'After the Battle of Lewisham, a question of vital importance, now who will defend him?' The *Daily Express* went further: 'We have no time or sympathy for the Front . . . All the same, the Front does not go in for violent attacks on the police or on authority.' Journalist Hugo Young, then working for the *Sunday Times*, solemnly announced that the SWP was 'a forerunner of the forces of darkness'. Tory leader Margaret Thatcher informed the press that 'Your Communism is the left foot of Socialism and your Fascism the right foot of it.'[23]

Linsday Mackie of the *Guardian* was no more sympathetic to the demonstrators, only more detached, asking in a strangely dispassionate manner whether the police could claim any sort of victory.

> Mr David McNee, Metropolitan Commissioner of Police . . . advised the Home Secretary, Mr Merlyn Rees, that his force could control events in Lewisham; and the many calls to ban the march were therefore not successful. With 56 of his men injured – 11 of them seriously enough to be detained in hospital – Mr McNee on Saturday night said that the violence in Lewisham was the result of an 'orchestrated and violent attempt' by extremists to prevent the National Front march taking place. He said that the police function was to deal 'effectively and impartially with breaches of the law' and he said that this was done on Saturday.[24]

Several Labour Party voices claimed that Socialist Workers Party demonstrators amounted to 'Red fascism', an equally despicable counterpart to the National Front. The *Daily Mirror* claimed that the SWP was 'as bad as the National Front', while Michael Foot, a left-winger since the 1930s, insisted that 'you don't stop the Nazis by throwing bottles or bashing the police. The most ineffective way of fighting the fascists is to behave like them.' The Liberal Party called for a ban on marches by 'extreme left-wing organizations'. Sid Bidwell, the Ealing Labour MP and a one-time revolutionary socialist, announced that he had time neither for the NF nor 'for those crackpot adventurers who have yet to take their part in responsibility in the real Labour movement. We cannot counter them by a strategy of trying to out-thug the thugs of the National Front, because we have the strength to do otherwise.'[25] As well as the press backlash, the SWP had to deal with attacks from members of the NF. They threatened known socialists, broke the windows of several SWP members' homes, then attacked and set fire to the party headquarters in September 1977.[26]

After the deluge

Despite the consensus in the national press, a few voices did attempt to stem the flood of the anti-anti-fascist backlash. The *New Musical Express* devoted an entire page to a free-wheeling subjective account of the march, written by Julie Burchill and Tony Parsons: 'the unforgettable faces of marching Nazis were the stuff of nightmares; they looked twisted, sick, bigoted, and ultimately pathetic'. Tom Picton of *Camerawork* observed that the Fleet Street papers blamed anti-racists for the violence at the Lewisham. 'None of [the papers] will accept that it is a violent act to march through any community, mouthing racist slogans and carrying racist placards.' *Socialist Challenge*, paper of the International Marxist Group, announced that Lewisham had been 'a victory for us, and a defeat for the police and government'.[27] Philip Kleinman penned one of the sharpest comments for the *Jewish Chronicle*, a paper hostile to the socialist left. Kleinman pointed out that the very purpose of the National Front was to stir up race-hatred. 'When it marches through an area with a large immigrant population, its purpose is precisely the same as that of Mosley's blackshirts – to stir up communal strife with the hope of reaping an electoral advantage.' He concluded, 'whatever their defects, the Trotskyists have the right attitude to the National Front and should not be left alone to stop its provocations'.[28]

It soon became clear that the main effect of the Lewisham protest had been to boost anti-fascists. John Savage, a historian of punk, describes how Rock Against Racism took on a new urgency, with the Clash now speaking openly against the NF: 'the National Front had "won on points" [in the press] . . . but Lewisham saw Rock Against Racism and the Socialist Workers Party winning hands down in pop culture'.[29]

Socialist Worker showed a front page of celebrating black youths, watching as the National Front were forced to retreat. 'We stopped the Nazis . . . and we'll do it again!' The paper also ran an interview with David Foster, whose son had been one of the original Lewisham 21:

> The National Front have done everything in their power to whip up hatred between black and white. They have brought racial violence and

destruction to a peaceful community.

On 2 July, when we marched for our children who have been arrested, the National Front showed who are the violent ones.

They attacked our demonstration; threw acid in the eyes of one young girl and broke the jaw of another.

I haven't heard anyone around here complaining about the violence on Saturday.

What they would say is: if the National Front had been allowed to march, there would have been much more violence in the community.

I don't agree with everything the Socialist Workers Party says, but they were the only organisation to stand up for the rights of black people here.'[30]

The Communist Party's paper, *Morning Star*, had been fiercely critical of the Socialist Workers Party in the run-up to Lewisham. In the aftermath, its attack was hampered by the fact that many Communist Party supporters had joined the second march. One article again condemned the organizers of the second demonstration while praising the 'courage and determination' of those who had taken part. Another article quoted a manual worker from the borough: 'The National Front won't be showing up here for a long time.'[31]

The socialist monthly *Women's Voice* interviewed Faith Foster, a West Indian woman whose son had been arrested as part of Operation PNH. Faith then attended the Lewisham demonstration, and described her feelings of joy when the police and the fascists were forced back:

The National Front couldn't march through Lewisham. We wouldn't let them. We stuck to our word, 'They shall not pass.' I caught the bus into Brookley with my friend to see the end of the march, as I couldn't go all the way; my daughter had only just come out of hospital after having her appendix out and couldn't be left for long. We walked down Ladywell Road and what I saw, my heart was laughing inside. I had not been happy for so long . . . I was really, really happy.[32]

One of the strongest arguments made, even at the time, was that physical confrontation had prevented the National Front from taking control of the streets. In 1976, the NF was able to turn out up to 1,500 members on its marches. By spring 1977, and Wood Green, the figure had fallen to 1,000. At Lewisham it fell again. Afterwards, the NF was never able to march again in significant numbers. The membership simply did not trust their leaders to protect them.

John from south London recalls a mood transformed: 'After Lewisham, the atmosphere changed. We intimidated them, for the first time. Now you could wear anti-racist badges in public, on the tube or at work. The atmosphere changed entirely.' According to Ian,

Lewisham raised the profile of the Socialist Workers Party enormously. We were denounced all over the place, but in my workplace that didn't rub off at all. If you just read the newspapers you would get the impression that SWP members wouldn't dare show their faces in the street, but I went to work with my badges on, and nobody batted an eyelid.

Jerry Fitzpatrick says that 'Lewisham was our Cable Street. We had in mind the slogan from 1936, "They shall not pass." It was our generation's attempt to stop fascism. It was rugged, scrappy. It got bad publicity. But it was a real success. The NF had been stopped, and their ability to march through black areas had been completely smashed.'

National Front News ran its own version of events, 'Red Rioters Fail', maintaining that the 'fine Police organisation' had enabled their group to march safely to Lewisham. The NF was 'now poised to inflict a savage revenge on Labour at the next General Election'. *Spearhead* also neglected to mention the breaking-up of the NF march, with Martin Webster writing that 'The NF column marched from New Cross in the northern part of the Borough to the prearranged open-air meeting place off Lewisham High Street at the southern end of the Borough', as if that was all that had happened.[33]

Gerry Gable gives a very different account:

> The Lewisham march marked a watershed for the NF. For as long as they could remember they could get away with murder when it came to street conflict with their opponents. Then after weeks of short engagements around the Lewisham street sales, the police moved in and arrested more Nazis than anti-fascists.
>
> A large section of the executive was opposed to going into the streets. They said it would end up with a head-on clash and as the police were already hostile in the area it might be a serious mistake to get on the wrong side of the law. Of course, they were now being challenged on the streets all over the country.

'A lot came of the events at Lewisham', writes Dave Widgery.

> The black community, who had successfully defended their patch, had had a glimpse of a white anti-racist feeling which was much bigger and more militant than the liberal community-relations tea-parties might suggest. A lot of ordinary people thought it was a Good Thing that the little Hitlers had taken a bit of a stick. Every little racialist was much smaller. Many people who had reservations about direct action found themselves regretting they had not been there too.[34]

'Two-thirds of the people who marched with the NF at Lewisham', claims Red Saunders of Rock Against Racism, 'never marched again. Lewisham pulled back the Union Jack to show the swastika underneath. If you're not ready for physical confrontation, you never come again.' According to the paper *CARF*, such was the scale of the setback that 'if I was a National Front member I'd be hitting the bottle by now'. The fact that the size of the NF contingent had sharply fallen between Wood Green and Lewisham was taken as evidence that opposition was working: 'many NF members are bloody angry with the leadership for putting them at risk'.[35] It really was a terrible defeat for the Front.

5

Even God has Joined the Anti-Nazi League

Through 1976 and 1977, a number of attempts were made to form anti-racist alliances. Rock Against Racism was one of many to get started at this time, although even RAR only took off in 1978. The Communist Party had its own All-London Campaign Against Racism and Fascism, which played a part at Lewisham. Another coalition was the All-London Anti-Racist Anti-Fascist Co-ordinating Committee, set up after the protests at Haringey.

In 1977, Danny was working at the Institute of Race Relations. A former member of the International Socialists, he threw himself head first into the campaign against fascism. Danny remembers this period as one of growing struggles and occasional left-wing collaboration. 'Seventy-six was quite a turning point. You had Grunwick, the Notting Hill Carnival riots, and Enoch Powell's speeches. You had the National Front and the National Party demonstrating all over the country. In every area, local anti-racist groups were formed. Sometimes the initiative came from political parties, sometimes informally from local youth groups or meeting halls.' The first chance for this collaboration to succeed came, Danny argues, in Haringey, with the preparations for the Wood Green protest. 'We worked together well in Tottenham. People came from all different backgrounds and for a time there was good co-operation.' Then in May 1977, 23 anti-fascist committees in London came together to form an All London Anti-Racist Anti-Fascist Co-ordinating Committee (ALARAFCC), which adopted *CARF*, the paper of the Kingston Campaign against Racism and Fascism, as its bi-monthly journal.[1] Members of the Socialist Workers Party and other left groups took part in this initiative. Danny became the first secretary of the campaign.[2]

As far as Danny was concerned, the immediate task was to build a national movement.

> We tried to organize a big conference at Middlesex Poly. Loads of people came, but somehow it didn't gel. Perhaps we were too liberal. We allowed resolutions from all over. There were so many motions, compositing, it felt like student politics. There were lots of different elements represented, old Communist Party, trades council types, women's groups, and the gay

movement, which was very hostile to the left. Everyone was trying to come together, but the movement was too disparate. We needed to have a healthier pulling together before that could happen.

So why did the conference fail? Even now, Danny is unsure what went wrong. 'We were trying to organize from the bottom up. We were local groups with scant resources.'

If ALARAFCC and *CARF* failed to create a single, unified campaign, then this failure was not apparent at the time. Instead, it only became evident with the rise of the Anti-Nazi League, the one organization that did establish a national profile in the campaign against the National Front.

From protests to organization

'After Lewisham', recalls Roger Huddle, 'it was obvious that an organization as small as the SWP was incapable of stemming the tide. So we set up a united organization, which anyone could join. It had a single demand. The Anti-Nazi League mobilized tens of thousands of people, Rock Against Racism could mobilize thousands of young people on one issue alone – stopping the Nazis, that's what it was all about.'

The idea of another, bigger anti-fascist alliance had first been mooted a fortnight before Lewisham in the Stoke Newington back garden of Jim Nichol, then the National Secretary of the Socialist Workers Party and since then a successful campaigning lawyer. Events at Lewisham clearly gave the discussions a new urgency. Nichol carefully sounded out a range of activists and politicians in order to gauge the potential of this new movement. Dave Widgery takes up the story:

> Nichol went first to the late Douglas Tilbey, Quaker Labour Party member, magistrate and OBE, 'a really nice guy, very principled on the question of race and always had a bit time for the SWP'. Tilbey thought it was an excellent idea. Then Nichol put the scheme to Tassaduq Ahmed, a middle-of-the-road Bangladeshi who had been in Britain since 1963 . . . Tassaduq relayed to him the concern he also felt about the number of factions that existed within the black communities. The next barometer was Michael Seifert, the lawyer and Communist Party member, because of his links with trade-union bureaucracy people like Ken Gill, George Guy and Alan Sapper – whose blessing was also going to prove essential. Nichol recalls, 'I said, "Mike, this is only really going to work if it gets the support of the CP and the left TU leaders. What do you think?" Mike said, "I think it's a bloody great idea. But I'm sorry, the CP won't, they'll crucify you. So I'll not mention it to anyone."'[3]

But Nichol was determined that the alliance should be established. And as the anti-Lewisham hysteria subsided in the press, so the conviction grew among all parts of the left that further confrontations were required.

Paul Holborow, recently the Socialist Workers Party's district organizer in east London, and described by Dave Widgery as combining 'the
Charterhouse air of clipped command with the concern for accuracy of an
artillery officer',[4] approached two members of the Labour Party, Ernie
Roberts, the trade unionist, and Peter Hain,[5] the anti-apartheid activist, in
order to establish a leadership for the new movement. Hain originally declined, pleading time and other commitments. But he was soon
persuaded. Together, Hain, Roberts and Holborow agreed to launch the
Anti-Nazi League. Holborow himself takes up the story:

> The aftermath of Lewisham was the essential catalyst for the formation
> of the Anti-Nazi League. Lewisham received absolutely saturation cov-
> erage. It was the silly season, and there wasn't anything else to put in the
> papers. Michael Foot was the Deputy Prime Minister and he condemned
> us. There was blanket publicity, plus our strategy of uniting the left and
> the anti-racist organizations. Imagine the SWP National Office. The
> phone never stops ringing with people saying, 'I want nothing to do with
> the SWP, but you're completely right to be taking on the Nazis.'

What was the role of Jim Nichol?

> Jim was not just National Secretary of the SWP; he was also manager of
> the *Socialist Worker* print shop. He knew people with whom we had
> printing contracts, who were sympathetic, but who didn't want to give
> money to the Socialist Workers Party. Jim put the scheme to me, and sug-
> gested that Nigel Harris and I should be central to it. Jim also coined the
> name, Anti-Nazi League; it played on the traditions of the labour
> movement.

Peter Hain was another key figure. 'He had an excellent reputation for
fighting apartheid', Paul Holborow recalls,

> and was a bridge to the left Labour milieu. Peter brought a vital dimen-
> sion; he opened up doors to the Labour Party. He also brought experience
> of running a press campaign – which we didn't have at all. He had excel-
> lent antennae. He and I got on extremely well. He taught me the
> importance of making your formulations exact. He and I drew up the
> founding statement.

In 1977 Peter Hain was a trade unionist and anti-racist in his late twenties.
He had first arrived in Britain some 11 years earlier, as a young exile from
apartheid South Africa. As a student, he became one of the best-known activists in the Stop the Seventy campaign against the touring South African
rugby side. He was also for several years a leader of the Young Liberals. In
September 1976, he had begun working as a research officer for the postal
workers' union (today the CWU). A year later, he had joined Labour, and it
was in the days immediately following that Hain was invited to join the
Anti-Nazi League. 'If I hadn't joined the Labour Party,' he reflects, 'I

doubt I would have been approached. The labour movement was key to the strategy of the League.' Why did he join the ANL?

> My view was that we had a big problem. With the decline of the Labour government, the National Front were pushing the Liberals into fourth place. There was a lot of concern about racist violence. For some working-class youth, the skinheads, the National Front were becoming fashionable. We had to go into places that no party could reach. If the Anti-Nazi League hadn't been launched, the National Front could have made real advances among youth in particular.

After Peter Hain, Paul Holborow's next contact was Ernie Roberts.

> I met Ernie at Centrepoint in Hackney. He had been assistant general secretary of the engineering workers' union for 30 years. He had always been interested in the political dimension of building the rank and file. He had cut his teeth in the Coventry tool-room disputes of the 1940s. He had an immense following on the left. For years, he had been editing *Engineering Voice*, which functioned as the broad left in the industry. He was never in the Communist Party, and never identified with the Soviet Union, but worked closely with the Communists. He took the statement to the Labour Party conference in 1977, and signed up 40 Labour MPs and many trade union leaders. That was our arrival.

Many left-wing Labour MPs signed up to the League, as did well-known anti-fascists such as Maurice Ludmer, the editor of *Searchlight*, who later joined the League's national steering committee.

A launch meeting was held in November 1977, at the House of Commons, with various sponsors. An ad hoc steering committee was elected, and the three executive positions of organiser, press officer and treasurer were taken by Holborow, Hain and Roberts. Of these, Holborow was the only full-time salaried official with the Rowntree Trust pledging £600 a quarter until the general election.[6] Jerry Fitzpatrick, who became national secretary, comments that 'Paul Holborow was a very cool organizer. He could be very inspirational and politically courageous. He did come from a public school background, and had a manner that could be austere. He followed the party line closely but was prepared to be flexible.' Paul didn't follow music like the RAR people, but he had the modesty to bring in others when required. 'He really was a good leader. He was the nuts and bolts of the Anti-Nazi League.'

Other members of the committee included four MPs, Martin Flannery, Dennis Skinner, Audrey Wise and Neil Kinnock, former Young Liberal Simon Hebditch and Maurice Ludmer of *Searchlight*, as well as Nigel Harris of the Socialist Workers Party and the actress Miriam Karlin, who had made her name playing working-class Jewish women in sitcoms.[7] A seat was also reserved in case the Communist Party decided to join.[8] Peter Hain describes the different individuals involved:

I had lots of contacts with local Labour parties. Ernie Roberts was linked to the traditional labour movement. He was close to the Communist Party, that tradition in the labour movement. Neil Kinnock had a very non-sectarian approach – he didn't want to spend ages debating racism. He wanted the movement to work. Dennis and Martin brought the Tribunite MPs. Audrey completely threw herself into the movement. Miriam was very important in the Jewish community. She was completely frustrated by the sectarianism – you don't just see it in the left parties, it was there in the Labour Party, in the Jewish community.

Peter Hain explains how the committee began as a small group with common purpose.

> We didn't start off by calling a conference. We would have just paralysed ourselves with argument. Debate is important in its own right, but not when it stops you from acting. We had to get together a group of people who were politically sussed. You build support from there. We wanted to get away from that sectarianism, when people only defend their own position. We made the focus action.

Holborow agrees:

> It was a very hands-off steering committee, more a point of reference than a decision-making body. The key decisions were taken in face-to-face meetings with myself and Peter and Ernie. I always took great care to make sure that Peter ratified everything I wanted to get done. I think he found it quite exciting, in contrast to the anti-apartheid movement, which was now slow and cumbersome and unimaginative.

Mike was a member of the 7/84 theatre group, and often unemployed. Shortly after the launch of the Anti-Nazi League, he was invited to work in its office with Paul Holborow. 'I was largely responsible for distributing leaflets. Soon we were having so many calls for leaflets that it became a kind of despatch room, packing leaflets, tying them together with string. There were just three of us in the office.' What was it like, working there? 'Paul was very easy to work with, very clear in what he was doing, giving roles, but you could always talk to him.'

Roger Huddle argues that Holborow's great strength was a grasp of spectacle.

> Paul had a fantastic ability to organize. I remember one time, we were in Walthamstow, it must have been '77 or '78. The NF called a demonstration against the local mosque. Paul got us all there, with banners, strung out in a great long line. He went into the mosque, and persuaded them not to be afraid, but to turn out too. It was a long line, very long. As the NF turned round a corner, marching towards us, suddenly they realized how many of us there were. They just turned and ran.

Paul Holborow recalls with gratitude the work done by the Anti-Nazi League's two full-time office workers, Joan and Mike. 'I must have been hell to work with. I did no administration ever. I used to bark orders at Joan, write this letter, do this, do that. It was so completely helter-skelter; there was just no time in the office. Joan was absolutely brilliant, and Mike as well. They in turn organized large teams of volunteers.'

Nigel Harris was research director for the League. An academic and journalist, he attempted to persuade the well-known faces of the left to join the campaign. Some of those he approached were supportive, while others were hostile. It was hard to predict who would go which way. Among other targets, Harris wrote to Edward Thompson and John Saville, the two former-Communist historians who had launched the first New Left in 1950s Britain. 'Thompson wrote back saying, "This whole thing is a front for the Socialist Workers Party, and you must think I'm an idiot to ask me." Saville wrote back, "Of course it's a front, but it's a good cause, and its alright by me."' The greatest hostility that Harris remembers came from the chair of the Jewish Board of Deputies.

> I went to see him, to talk him round. He was a hard nut. He kept on coming back to the point that the SWP did not support the state of Israel. I said that Israel was not going to be an issue for the ANL. He told me, 'We are as likely to support the National Front as the Anti-Nazi League.'

Nigel Harris recalls his colleagues vividly. 'Kinnock was a left shadow rider.[9] Hain had just come from the Liberals on a very militant campaign against apartheid. Roberts was part of the old order and would back anything.' But what was the glue holding together this diverse set of personalities? The crisis of the times clearly impelled people to work together. But Harris goes further, singling out the role played by Paul Holborow for special praise. 'Paul was very presentable, smooth, charming, very good at relating to different occasions. I don't remember any great divisions. Paul was a great operator, good at talking to people before meetings and securing consensus. There was never any embarrassment; the worst it ever got was the threat of embarrassment.'

The launch of the Anti-Nazi League was recorded in the *Guardian* newspaper. Neil Kinnock was interviewed, saying that it was no longer true that the National Front would go away if it was ignored. 'The popular belief that their support would dwindle is not true, and the silence of democrats can only help it. We have to give up our silence.' Peter Hain stressed that the League would be broad-based, recruiting from all sides of the political spectrum. 'We hope to extinguish their potential. I don't think banning them is the whole answer. Hitler was banned. Our major aim is to make the public aware of their Nazi credentials.'[10]

Many existing anti-racist activists felt wary of the new campaign. Danny of Haringey CARF was wary of SWP involvement in the new campaign. 'You've got to remember that lots of lefties were already alienated, not just politicos but black activists and gay activists in the movement.' David L had been a member of the International Marxist Group for about five years. By 1977, he was mainly active in Islington

Campaign Against Racism and Fascism. He felt protective towards the campaigning links that his group had already established, and was (like many of his friends) very suspicious of the new movement.

> It took me by surprise. At the time of Lewisham, the Anti-Nazi League hadn't been formed. It was only set up soon afterwards. I didn't know it was going to happen. I realize now that the SWP had played an important role at Lewisham, but that wasn't at all clear at the time. Other groups took part in Lewisham, women, lesbian and gay organizations. Then suddenly there was the Anti-Nazi League. I think we were a bit fed up, really. There was a lot of rivalry between the different groups. Some of it was a bit silly. Islington Anti-Nazi League broke up fascist paper sales at Chapel Street market, but we in Islington CARF didn't really get involved. There were lots of people who should have been working together. But there was too much suspicion.

The magazine *CARF* was guarded in its welcome of the new movement.

> There have been certain fears expressed by local anti-fascist campaigns that such a large national body might swamp local activity and initiative. But since the Anti-Nazi League is specifically geared towards fighting fascism at elections and will most probably dissolve after the next general election, the aims of local campaigns seem to complement rather than compete with the aims of the Anti-Nazi League . . . Campaigns can in fact take this opportunity to make full use of the propaganda available from the Anti-Nazi League. It is after all the local campaigns which will have to stand the test of time.[11]

Nigel Harris insists that groups like the Campaign Against Racism and Fascism had nothing to fear from the League.

> There were always tensions with the anti-racists. They could feel a bit like the dog in the manger, slogging away for years, horrified as the new flashy car of the Anti-Nazi League took over. They thought we were taking away their audience, but the reality is that the League brought new people in. Long after the Anti-Nazi League was wound down, their campaigns would continue.

In autumn 1977, it was by no means clear that the ANL would overcome the sectarianism that had long shaped the British left. If that happened, and this book suggests that it did, the change only became clear later, once the new movement had been fully established on the ground.

Designing the movement

Although the Anti-Nazi League was founded on the initiative of members of the Socialist Workers Party, it received the support of around 40 Labour MPs and sections of the broader left. Prominent members included Tariq Ali of the International Marxist Group and Arthur Scargill of the National Union of Mineworkers, as well as Hain, Roberts and Kinnock. The League's founding statement was sent to the press in November 1977.

> For the first time since Mosley in the thirties there is the worrying prospect of a Nazi party gaining significant support in Britain . . . The leaders, philosophy, and origins of the National Front and similar organisations followed directly from the Nazis in Germany . . . They must not go unopposed. Ordinary voters must be made aware of the threat that lies behind the National Front. In every town, in every factory, in every school, on every housing estate, wherever the Nazis attempt to organise they must be countered.[12]

Bernie was then a young activist in the Socialist Workers Party. Having cut his teeth on the Right to Work marches in Manchester, he wondered what this new movement would be like. 'The Anti-Nazi League all kicked off with a signed ad in *The Times*. It looked so boring, just MPs and worthies signing up. But from that, it mushroomed. Within a few months, everywhere you went people had the badges on, the Anti-Nazi League became part of the fashion, everyone I knew got involved.'

The organizers of the Anti-Nazi League wanted to sign up as wide a range of people as possible, to show that a majority of people actively despised the National Front. Crystal Palace manager Terry Venables signed up, with Nottingham Forest's manager Brian Clough, playwright Arnold Wesker and writer Keith Waterhouse, and several hundred trade unionists, community activists, musicians and other celebrities. Warren Mitchell, who played the bigot Alf Garnett in the sitcom *Till Death Us Do Part*, joined in, as did Compo from BBC's *Last of the Summer Wine*. Dozens of local Anti-Nazi League groups were set up, including 'Vegetarians and Football Fans Against the Nazis'. Patrons of a pub in Rusholme, Manchester, even set up their own group, 'The Albert Against the Nazis', with a badge and banner. Badges also proclaimed 'Aardvarks Against the Nazis', 'Skateboarders Against the Nazis' and so on. This was a remarkably diverse movement, which attempted to undermine NF support in all spheres of life.

One of the tasks was to come up with a visual language that would mark this movement off from the routine tradition of left-wing protests, and show it to the world as something new. Dave King drew up the blueprints for many of the Anti-Nazi League leaflets and stickers. A graphic designer who worked for the *Sunday Times*, he was also a long-standing, independent activist on the left and a collector of Soviet-era photographs and images. It was Laurie Flynn, editor of *Socialist Worker*, who suggested King. Paul Holborow emphasizes King's contribution:

> Another crucial part of the movement was the quality of the propaganda. Dave King was the editor of the *Sunday Times* colour supplement, and an

extraordinary designer. He taught us about over-printing in different layers, to give a real depth to the colour. I was always dropping in to his house to see how the latest leaflet was being developed.

King designed a number of posters with a deliberate montage effect, modelled on the style of John Heartfield, the anti-Nazi artist. He also designed the Anti-Nazi League arrow, which was also based on the historic symbols of German anti-fascism. The earlier image had been three arrows, a symbol invented in 1932 by Sergej Tschachotin and Carlo Mierendorff to link the struggles against capitalism, fascism and reaction. The German anti-fascist Iron Front, an alliance between SPD, free trade unions and the SPD's Reichsbanner, employed the image. Austrian Social Democrats also used it before 1934.[13] The Anti-Nazi League designers took the older symbol of the three separate arrows and abbreviated it, producing the new symbol of one arrow with three quills.

King's other innovation was the Anti-Nazi League yellow 'lollipop', unveiled at the first Rock Against Racism carnival in summer 1978. King saw these placards as a deliberate attempt to get away from the traditional black-and-white rectangles carried by the left. Different stories explain the image. Some thought King wanted to copy old CND symbols; others that the idea went as far back as Russia in the 1920s. Whatever their origin, the lollipops helped to give a visual sense of the League's novelty.

Where did the ANL's name come from? Paul Holborow credits Jim Nichol with the inspiration for the title. The idea was to remind working-class people of the reality behind the NF. According to Roger Huddle, 'It was necessary to remind people of the history in Germany. No one had said that they were Nazis till we did. If it had been called the Anti-Fascist League, it wouldn't have had the same impact.' To call the NF Nazis was to point to genocide as the goal of their movement.

Elections

Although the National Front was never simply an electoral party, there was a sense in which elections acted as the main barometer of its growth. The Anti-Nazi League was forced to respond, covering local areas with leaflets warning of the NF threat. The first test came in November 1977, with the by-election at Bournemouth East. Paul Holborow takes up the story: 'The president of the students' union at Bournemouth College of Education was brilliant; he turned out significant numbers. Two east London businesses donated paper to the campaign: it showed up by the lorry-load. Alexis Grower and Michael Seifert organized meetings of Jewish groups. We produced 50,000 leaflets. The Nazis' vote was derisory.' Kenneth McKilliam of the NF secured just 725 votes.

Another test came during the by-election at Ilford in spring 1978. According to Holborow,

> The Nazis were going to march, but they were banned. We too were banned from marching. This was a big test for us, and for Peter Hain. Traditionally, the Socialist Workers Party would have defied the ban. This time, we accepted it. But we took 2,000 people and leafleted the entire constituency. Peter was with me the entire afternoon. A steward with maps had responsibility for each ward. He was very impressed by our capacity to mobilize people, and also by our discipline. By then, the ball was rolling.

The Anti-Nazi League was now up and running, but the National Front was far from defeated: its candidate won over 2,000 votes.

Anti-Nazi League paint-out: London 1978

Exposure

Anti-Nazi League leaflets and stickers consistently exposed the fascist politics of the National Front. The strategy of the ANL was to focus on the most extreme expressions of racism, in order to demonstrate that racism of all sorts was wrong. Dennis Potter's play, *Brimstone and Treacle* (1978), explains this method in a dramatized form. A suburban family, Mr and Mrs Bates, are visited by a stranger, Martin. Mr Bates dwells longingly on the England he used to know, and admits his membership of the NF. Martin responds by suggesting, and it seems innocently at first, that blacks should be placed in special camps. Mrs Bates says 'like Butlins'. Then Martin continues,

> Camps. Any camps for the time being. Oh think of it! . . . Hundreds of thousands. Millions. Rounded up from their stinking slums and over-crowded ghettos. Driven into big holding camps, men, women, picconinnies . . . You'll see England like it used to be again, clean and white. They won't want to go . . . They'll fight, so we shall have to shoot them and CS gas them and smash down their doors . . . Think of all the hate we'll feel when they start killing us back. Think of all the violence! Think of the de-gra-dat-ion and in the end, in the end, the riots and the shooting and the black corpses and the swastikas, and the . . .

Bates begs him to stop, promising to leave the NF. Uncomfortable, con-fronted by the end results of racism, he is compelled to rethink what he believes.[14] This is how the Anti-Nazi League tried to work.

When it came to exposing the leaders of the National Front, the support of the anti-fascist magazine *Searchlight* was invaluable. Its editor, Maurice Ludmer, had been seconded to the War Graves Commission and visited Belsen concentration camp in 1946. According to one report,

> It was a year after the liberation, the place had been cleaned up, but there was still more than enough evidence of the unbelievable atrocities that had happened there, in the heart of Europe, in the middle of the twentieth century. And there and then, the young soldier pledged him-self, wholeheartedly and irrevocably, to seeing that this could never happen again.

Maurice was a founding member of the Anti-Nazi League, along with an-other *Searchlight* stalwart, the journalist Gerry Gable.[15]

Searchlight archives held an enormous quantity of material on the leaders of the National Front, going back to the 1950s and 1960s when many had been members of openly Nazi parties. John Tyndall was shown on leaflets wearing a Nazi uniform and swastika. Tyndall and Martin Webster were exposed through the words they had used. Martin Web-ster's article, 'Why I am a Nazi' was used against him. '*Mein Kampf* is my doctrine', Tyndall had said, and he was reminded of it. Other ANL arti-cles described the history of Nazi Germany and what life was like there for women or for Jews. The point of these articles was not simply to dig up the history of the 1930s, but much more to demonstrate what the NF stood for in Britain, 40 years on.[16] Yet ANL activists did not assume that exposing the supporters of the NF as fascists would be enough to ensure that movement's decline. As Malcolm Cottram, an experienced anti-fas-cist from Sheffield, pointed out, many members of the NF were comfortable with the tag 'Nazi', and it took more than that to discredit their politics. 'Yelling "Nazi scum" and "Sieg Heil" may bring home to passers-by that the NF have affinities with Hitler and are therefore nasty, but this doesn't deter the Front – it only hardens them.'[17]

Having exposed the fascist pedigree of the National Front, Anti-Nazi League leaflets went on to show that the NF's 'solutions' were lies. Typically, they argued that black people were not the cause of unemployment, bad housing and crime, but the victims of them. 'It is not black people who caused 300,000 building workers and 8,000 architects to be unemployed.' The crimes of the system were blamed on capitalism, and a message of class unity was argued in place of racial division.[18]

Students Against the Nazis

As the Anti-Nazi League grew, it quickly developed spin-off campaigns, involving particular groups of people depending on where they lived or worked. An impressive list of student unions affiliated to the Anti-Nazi League. They included Bedford College, Bradford University, Bristol University, Ealing College of Higher Education, Edge Hill College, Essex University, Exeter University, Liverpool Polytechnic, Loughborough University, Manchester Polytechnic, Newman College, St Peter's College in Oxford, Central London Polytechnic, the Polytechnic of Wales, the School of Oriental and African Studies, the University of Surrey, Sussex University and Teesside Poly. Twelve national student societies also affiliated, including the Union of Liberal Students, the Union of Jewish Students, the National Organization of Labour Students and even the Federation of Conservative Students. The FCS endorsement was certainly unwelcome. Most Anti-Nazi League activists judged that the racism of the National Front found its echo in the policies of the Conservatives in Parliament. The Federation was never denied membership, but when its subscription came up for renewal, the FCS was encouraged not to reapply.

How did student activists build a base for the League in their colleges? Chris and Simon, members of the Socialist Workers Party at Bristol University, helped to set up an Anti-Nazi League group there. First they contacted the Anti-Nazi League national office and ordered enough badges and posters to distribute. They organized stalls and raised the campaign in student union meetings. Then a proper founding meeting was called, at which a team was elected to co-ordinate the League's activity between larger meetings. 'From the beginning, we emphasized the activity orientation of the ANL. From the first meeting we elected a small co-ordinating committee, a non-decision-making body. We distributed 4,000 leaflets around the university and involved large numbers of people in this. We contacted lecturers in several departments and got their financial support for the ANL nationally.' One of the important jobs done was to help set up the Anti-Nazi League at other colleges by taking displays and propaganda to them and talking to other students. 'We have contacted two Tech colleges so far in this way. We have also arranged to give 500 ANL school student leaflets to [the National Union of School Students] in Bristol and to work with them . . . The ANL sent a coach to counter the

Nazi Youth rally at Birmingham, and has mobilized a militant picket against the racist Monday Club MP, Jonathan Guinness.'

David R was a member of Leeds Students Union: 'I worked on the ANL stall which we put on frequently in the Union building. Our main job was to sell badges and promote the ANL literature. Students were generally very receptive.' Students from Leeds University also took part in leafleting the football ground and the town centre.

Einde was on the executive of the City University Union Society. 'We won affiliation of CUUS to the ANL right from the beginning, despite opposition from some of the Broad Left members of the executive and some leading members of the Jewish Society – they weren't happy about the SWP's anti-Zionist position.' Most students were friendly to the Anti-Nazi League, Einde recalls. Indeed, without an atmosphere that was generally supportive, they would not have won affiliation from the City University students' union. 'It was a predominantly a technological university with a large number of traditionally apolitical engineers and scientists and a much smaller number of social scientists who tended to be more progressive. There was little overt hostility, except from the real right-wing Tories, who were died-in-the wool racists anyway.'

John helped to organize the Manchester carnival from offices in the students' union. Although not a member of the Socialist Workers Party, he was a supporter of its student group, NOISS. 'At one meeting of the Poly branch of the ANL, members of the International Marxist Group showed up, to argue about tactics.' The IMG members were guardedly critical of the Anti-Nazi League, arguing that as much energy should be devoted to fighting all forms of racism, not just fascism. 'The debate was had. It

Marching to the Manchester carnival: Paul Holborow is standing on the truck

wasn't a foregone conclusion. It was important to understand why the Anti-Nazi League and not something broader. There is a need to oppose all forms of racism, but when the far-right are organizing you *must* do something about that.' What convinced him that the IMG was wrong? 'I was at a meeting, which was attacked by the NF.' Having seen the National Front at close hand, John was persuaded that the left needed to defend its own spaces, and the only way to do that was by confronting the NF head on.

Football Fans Against the Nazis

As the Anti-Nazi League grew, it quickly developed spin-off campaigns, involving particular groups of people depending on where they lived or worked. The National Front had long been targeting football supporters. John Berry of the magazine *Leveller* describes attending Spurs games at White Hart Lane. Berry described hearing chants of 'TIN-DALL . . . TIN-DALL' – 'a regular feature on Saturday afternoons.' Berry interviewed 'Martin', an openly identified NF supporter on the terraces:

> Martin H is twenty-one. Half of that time has been spent in children's homes, detention centres, community school and Borstal. His parents are divorced. He never went to school except when he was in care and barely able to read. Most of the time he reads war comics in which gigantic and heroic British army sergeants single-handedly decimate battalions of Huns to whom they frequently refer as 'Nazi scum'. Martin wasn't recruited at a football match. He joined the NF about 18 months ago with 'a friend' but admits to persuading several mates to join at matches and that is something which is generally encouraged. In his own words Martin joined because 'the Front stands up for English people. The socialists want more niggers and Pakis here because they vote for them. We kick the fuck out of the wogs. The reds are always stirring up trouble. Someone's got to stop them.[19]

Tottenham Hotspur was not a major NF base. Far from it: the club had its heartlands in south Tottenham, which included Jewish areas like Stamford Hill. Spurs fans termed themselves 'Yids' or 'Yiddos'. The club became the launching pad for an anti-fascist campaign.

The original Football Fans Against the Nazis group was set up in Tottenham, on the initiative of John Deason, a member of the Socialist Workers Party central committee, a Spurs fan and secretary of the Right to Work campaign. The first Spurs Against the Nazis leafleting took place on the High Street in Tottenham, and only later outside the Spurs ground. The first time they went, many activists were nervous. Richard was a young architect and Spurs fan. He remembers the fighting that took place, the second time the group put out a leaflet: 'There was a group of National Front supporters leafleting outside the ground as well, and there were a lot more of them, than there were of us. We had all these old Jewish men walk up to us, and say "You're doing a really good job, lads", and then walk off.' It was worrying until 'we saw a crowd of about fifty teenagers, quite young, they were running towards us. We were really scared. But they ran right past us, charged into the National Front lot, and kicked them off their pitch. After that, it was fine.'[20]

The leafleting was a great success. Sixty people attended the first public meeting. The editor of the *Hornsey Journal* was the father of Kim Gordon from Lewisham, and he gave the group publicity, especially when Spurs' directors attempted to sue the group for breach of copyright, for using the Spurs' logo in its leaflets. Spurs Against the Nazis also celebrated the arrival of Oswaldo Ardiles and Ricardo Villa, as a victory against immigration controls, 'Ardiles and Villa – You're Welcome Here'. The group also organized a five-a-side football competition, in October 1978, which involved some 44 teams, including one from the band Aswad, and which was won by a group of workers from Tottenham bus garage, while Peter Cook and Bill Oddie were referees.[21]

Football Fans Against the Nazis (FFAN) was established out of the success at Spurs. Around 15 local groups were set up, including groups of fans at West Bromwich Albion, Swansea, Oxford, Barnsley, Coventry, Everton, Manchester United, Manchester City, Sheffield Wednesday, Norwich and Arsenal. Simon of Owls against the Nazis described the work of the group in Sheffield:

> There was good reason to launch the campaign at Wednesday. Racist chanting was becoming common, and an NF slogan painted up right next to the players' entrance had remained untouched for nearly a season. Meanwhile [pro-National Front] badge sellers outside the ground were doing a roaring trade in a badge saying 'Sabella is a Paki' (Sabella is the Argentinean whizz-kid signed recently by rival Sheffield United). Ninth December was the first leafleting, and despite a shortage of bodies, a group of about a dozen of us got an excellent response from the crowd. People took the leaflets, read them and came back for a badge. 2000 leaflets and 200 badges went on that first Saturday.

The majority of fans supported Owls Against the Nazis. Indeed, the only problem that Simon could find to report was the attitude of the club itself. Although manager Jack Charlton had publicly backed the Anti-Nazi League, Wednesday refused to let their fans sell anti-racist badges outside the ground. Even the club programme contained warnings to leave anti-Nazis alone.

Meanwhile, Leeds Supporters Against the Nazis was established in September 1978, and involved a regular group of between 40 and 100 people in leafleting outside Elland Road, through the winter of 1978–9. The local activities of the different groups were featured in *Time Out*, *Socialist Worker* and the *Morning Star*, whose sports editor Richard Weekes welcomed the Anti-Nazi League as a 'positive force' that 'attempts to unite [fans] against the divisive racists and chauvinists'. In Nottingham, there was no permanent group, but as Bev remembers, 'signing up Brian Clough and Peter Taylor [to the League] was seen as a terrific coup. I remember SWP comrades being more excited about this than any number of politicians or "serious" public figures who joined.' Richard from north London suggests that Football Fans Against the Nazis played a part in refocusing the anger felt on many terraces: 'It helped to turn racist football hooligans into anti-capitalist football hooligans.' He also stresses that FFAN was part of a wide range of ANL activities: 'everything was linked. It wasn't just about football. The Anti-Nazi League had a massive impact on youth culture at the time. Our slogan was "NF = No Fun", all our activities were based around that.'[22]

After football supporters and young music fans, another important area of anti-Nazi activity was among school and university students. Joe Pearce of the National Front had established an NF youth paper, *Bulldog*, and the Anti-Nazi League was determined to counter the media claim that young people were turning towards the racists. A group called School Kids Against the Nazis (SKAN) was established. Its paper sold 8,000 copies per issue, and readers' groups were set up in Sheffield, Enfield, Reading, Canterbury, Brighton and High Wycombe.[23] The magazine published articles, poems and letters, one from Cathy, a 15-year-old former NF supporter from Derby:

> I do not like their violent ways of dealing with people and their rules set down. I wouldn't like to see everyone in uniform or going into the army upon leaving school. I like people who like to be individuals, in clothes and mind. If everyone followed the NF Nazis we would be like cabbages, doing everything the same as everyone else . . . PS If the NF took Football or Punk away, I'd commit suicide.[24]

SKAN was closely allied with the National Union of School Students, and prominent members of the NUSS also played a role in SKAN. One was Rehad Desai, a young activist whose father had been a leader of the Pan African Congress in South Africa. Cait from Leeds remembers designing a 'Dennis the Menace and Gnasher against the Nazis' badge for the NUSS. The campaign also persuaded him to support his dad's club Liverpool, rather than his home team. There were 'too many nasty fascists at Leeds for my eight-year-old brain'. SKAN teams took part in the Spurs Against the Nazis tournament. There was an even larger campaign among university students.

No more normals any more

The strategy of the Anti-Nazi League was to demonstrate the consequences of racism. Although the League was primarily an anti-fascist movement, it did see itself as more than just a defensive process. In demonstrating that the bigotry of the National Front was abhorrent, the ANL hoped to show that all forms of prejudice were wrong. If racism was to be

smashed, and all the racists with it, then the fight against fascism would
have to be broadened out until it became a fight against the racist institutions of capitalism as well. Dave Widgery made this point in an article,
published in the first issue of *Temporary Hoarding*.

The problem is not just the new fascists from the old slime, a master race
whose idea of heroism is ambushing single blacks in darkened streets.
These private attacks whose intention, to cow and to brutalise, won't
work if the community they seek to terrorise instead organises itself. But
when the state backs up racialism it's different. Outwardly respectable
but inside fired with the same mentality and the same fears, the bigger
danger is the racist magistrates with the cold sneering authority, the immigration men who mock an Asian mother as she gives birth to a dead
child on their office floor, policemen for whom answering back is a
crime and every black kid's pride is a challenge.

In the opinion of many Anti-Nazi League activists, immigration controls were a similar problem to the racism of the National Front. In the
words of Bob Pennington, 'there is an inescapable conclusion, once you
accept the need for immigration controls, and that boils down to the argument that there would be more jobs, more houses, better schools and
better hospitals, if black people did not come to Britain'.[25] Popular racism
fed state racism and state racism fed popular racism. Both were wrong.
Miriam Karlin, interviewed by Women Against the Nazis, criticized the
press and the Conservative Party, as much as the NF. 'It's like a dustbin
where you know there are maggots. It's better that people know it's not
acceptable for them to make racist remarks, that they won't be tolerated.
"Bringing it out in the open", as Margaret Thatcher claims to be doing,
really means making racialism respectable.'[26]

Rock Against Racism and Anti-Nazi League publications did not limit
themselves to a language of mere anti-fascism, or even mere anti-racism,
but went out of their way to protest against all forms of oppression. Some
of the range of RAR's interests can be gathered by looking at its magazine, *Temporary Hoarding*. A typical issue features an interview with
Benji Arambi, an article about homophobia, an interview with Polysty-
rene of X-Ray Spex, an account of the murder of Steve Biko, three pages
of letters, an interview with the Tom Robinson Band and a feature on
Wolf Biermann, the dissident East German poet and songwriter. The
middle of the Tom Robinson interview was a collage of cinema-reel photographs of gay men holding hands, Windsor Castle, two hands in chains,
and a banner proclaiming 'no return to back street abortions'. Tom Robinson himself was quoted defending the Lewisham march, but also
insisting that the greatest threat came from the 'grey forces of the right',
as he put it. 'The National Front are evil which is why we do RAR gigs.
But they are not the real threat to our liberty. I think the Conservative
Party is, the right wing of the Conservative Party.'[27]

Other supporters brought their own concerns into the Anti-Nazi

League's work. Plenty of lesbians and gay men, including Tom Robinson, took part in the anti-racist movement. As well as Gays Against the Nazis, there was also Gays Against Fascism, based around the North London Gay Socialist Group. This group argued that fascism was only one extreme symptom of a violently homophobic society. At least nine gays were murdered in hate attacks between January 1977 and February 1978, and for Gays Against Fascism, the National Front represented simply 'the most oppressive form of male heterosexual society imaginable'.

Vegetarians Against the Nazis launched at the 1978 meeting of the Hunt Saboteurs Association. Within a year it had sold 4,000 badges, and recruited similar numbers of anti-fascists. It could boast the support of the Young Indian Vegetarian Society and the Gay Vegetarian Society. Given space in the Anti-Nazi League's first *Newsletter*, members of the group were proud to advertise their activities. 'Why not invite VAN to your meetings? We can help you with details of diet or even just good eating-places. Ask us if you want to sabotage a foxhunt. If you are expecting pale faced sandal wearers who wouldn't say Boo to a Nazi, forget it!'[28] The energy released by the Anti-Nazi League can be seen to have sparked the interest of the broadest possible left.

Storming sexism

There were also discussions within the Anti-Nazi League about how to link this campaign to the fight against sexism. Having grown for the first time in the early 1970s, the women's liberation movement had been revived in the mid-1970s by the campaign for abortion rights. This movement was now at its height. The organizers and supporters of anti-fascist events took it for granted that crèches would be put on to allow women to participate fully in the movement. Danny was then six years old, a child of activists who took part in demonstrations at Wood Green:

> I was taken off to [another] house where everyone had gathered to put flour, tomatoes and eggs into brown paper bags. Some select cadre were going to hide in the crowds and pretend to be passers-by rather than join the counter-demonstration and then launch their attack on the NF from the sidelines. Some of the tomatoes and eggs might even have been rotten . . . After they'd all been on the demo and come back I heard that my Mum had thrown a bag of flour towards the demo and it had landed on a shop canopy, rolling down and hitting another counter-demonstrator. I'm sure that even at six I could have done better than that.

The magazine *Women's Voice* aimed itself at a milieu of young women workers radicalized by networks such as Women Against the Nazis. One issue featured an interview with Carol Grimes, who had played at the first Rock Against Racism gig in November 1976. The structure of this piece was typical. Rather than focusing simply on the immediate issue of anti-racism, Grimes was asked about broader issues relating to her position as a woman in the male-dominated music world.

> When I did a gig at a Poly lately we were promised cash. When it came to it the union officials said that it was against their rules to pay out cash . . . When I said that we would have to sit in the bus station all night one of these guys said, "Well you can have a good time can't you dear", meaning me and the other ten blokes. What sort of attitude is that?

In the run-up to the Lewisham protest, Jane Hardy wrote an article for *Women's Voice* on 'Women and Fascism'. Her piece described how Hitler's Germany had forced women back into the home. Next she gave examples of fascist speakers defending a sexist vision of women's role in society. Then Hardy showed that these right-wing ideas had come back to haunt the present day. 'It is not so very different from what we hear every day; women should give up their jobs, the 1967 Abortion Act should be tightened or restricted or abolished . . . It is a thin line that divides conservative ideas from those of the extreme right.'

In July 1978, the magazine conducted a series of interviews with Josie, Karen and Doreen, three black and white school students who had set up their own School Kids Against the Nazis groups in Walthamstow. 'Our school may not have different sexes in it, but we do have different races and we all got along well together. There was no way the Front were going to destroy that.' In April 1980, *Women's Voice* featured a long interview with Anna Boguslawski, a member of the socialist underground that had opposed the Nazis in Poland in the 1940s.[29]

Another anti-sexist network was Women Against Racism and Fascism, who took part in the protest at Lewisham.[30] WARF was often critical of anti-fascist tactics, arguing that the Anti-Nazi League strategy of militant confrontation with fascism had a tendency to exclude women.

It was within the active movement that the sharpest debates took place. In June 1978, a Rock Against Racism concert at Brighton Polytechnic ended with a set by a local band who went by the name of the Fabulous Poodles. The band proceeded to play a number of supposedly ironic sexist songs, including one with the chorus, 'Tits, tits, tits.' *Temporary Hoarding* published a letter from eight members of the audience, furious at the songs, and angry also that the band had refused to discuss or admit their sexism. In response, the editors admitted that RAR could perhaps do more to root out sexism, and gave feminists and others carte blanche to subject any of their bands to the criticism they deserved.

> If anyone wonders why RAR doesn't simply ban all bands which are in the slightest bit sexist, the answer is (1) we would hardly have a band left on our books! (2) we hope that bands who don't normally have their sexist material challenged at ordinary gigs will benefit from doing a RAR gig and being confronted with feminist opposition. They deserve all they get!

One part of Rock Against Racism evolved into a sister organization, Rock Against Sexism, which was originally established by Lucy Toothpaste,[31] a member of the RAR standing committee in London.[32] In an article on Wilhelm Reich, a radical anti-fascist psychologist from Weimar Germany, Lucy Toothpaste attempted to demonstrate that the reactionary politics of the British right represented an onslaught against sex both in the 1930s and since:

> In case all that lot seems a bit far-fetched to you, we couldn't resist giving you some living proof of the connection between authoritarianism in the home and in the state. 'Love and discipline went together. My father sometimes took his pit belt off and leathered me. I shed tears, but I knew he was right and I was wrong.' That's what James Anderton said in an interview in the *Observer* in February. It was a belief that right and wrong were as distinct as black and white that reinforced his one and only ambition 'to be a policeman and if possible the biggest policeman of all'.[33]

By 1979, Anderton's goal had been achieved, as Lucy Toothpaste recalled. 'Well, he grew up to be a policeman alright, the chief constable of Greater Manchester to be exact, the second most powerful cop in the country.'

Eventually Rock Against Sexism established its own fanzine, *Drastic Measures*, its first issue titled, 'Love sex, hate sexism':

> Women in music are under constant pressure from the record companies to flaunt their bodies, both in performance and in adverts, in order to sell more records. If they succumb – and after all they have got a living to earn – hypocritical rags like the *NME* who think it's hip to pay lip-service to feminism, while making sure there's a neat snap of Debbie Harry in every edition, accuse them of exploiting their sexuality.[34]

Among its supporters, Rock Against Sexism counted Carol Grimes, the Mekons, Gang of Four, Crass and Tom Robinson; also such less well-known bands as Pam Nestor, Oxy and the Morons, Spurts, Tronics, Jam Today, The Raincoats, and The Resisters. *Drastic Measures* continued at least until 1981. Modelled like *Temporary Hoarding* on the punk fanzines of the 1970s, it spurned all traditional values, not just the sanctity of the family and women's place in the home, but the value of empire and the impartiality of British justice. One typical centre-page spread showed photographs of men in official uniforms (morning dress, suits and bowler, police and army uniforms). These were then placed against boxes of dialogue, similar to the gushing tones of the standard fashion press. Against a photograph of a chief constable, for example, were the words, 'Deliciously sexy uniform with seductive side-slits in pure dark cotton ravishingly adorned with glittering silver sequins. Matching overcoat and belt tying in front. Prices start from £230. Also available in pink.'[35]

A political milieu was created, in which Anti-Nazi League activists learned to oppose not just one but all forms of discrimination. Those who joined because they wanted to fight fascism were encouraged to see beyond the limits of the immediate campaign. Socialists within the League called for a generalized struggle, against immigration controls and racist policing, against sexism and homophobia, and for a society in which all forms of oppression were removed.

Critics

Not all feminists identified with the politics of anti-fascism. Another group arguing for non-violent opposition was the circle of activists around *Peace News*. A number of articles in this magazine defended a strategy of sit-downs to block the road against fascist marches. When asked what would happen if anti-fascists were attacked by the National Front, Judith Watson and others insisted that the dynamics of the situation (with the NF exposed as the real aggressors) would force the police to come to the defence of moderate anti-fascists.[36] Another piece claimed that the Anti-Nazi League tactic of calling for bans on fascism risked making it easier for the state to outlaw the left in future.[37]

The arguments of the Anti-Nazi League were in fact a little more nuanced than such criticisms suggested. The most coherent position was that of the Socialist Workers Party, which argued that trade unions, student unions and other democratic organizations should give no materials or other assistance to the National Front. This policy of 'no platform' was not extended to call for an all-out state ban on fascism, for the very same reason that the state or the police could not be trusted to ban fascism, but having taken on such additional powers, would be sure to use them against other parties as well. This was a position of free speech – for everyone apart from the National Front.[38] Other groups held different positions, with sections of the Communist Party and Labour left calling for a simple state ban. Meanwhile, whatever the arguments of the various factions, any position had to be applied locally. According to Pete Alexander, 'I remember Peter Hain calling for a ban on one occasion, which caused a bit of a stir. I think his view was that he had been mandated to do so by the steering committee. There may have been a degree of opportunism, but I suspect he actually spoke fairly quietly about the ban.'

The organizers of the Anti-Nazi League were attacked at different times from other points as well. Given the radicalism of its politics, it is not surprising that some potential allies chose to steer clear of the ANL. One dispute involved the Jewish Board of Deputies. Writing in *The Times*, William Frankel described the Board's hostility towards the Anti-Nazi League's demonstrations, 'which, they say, [lead] to "punch-ups" and to the publicity on which the National Front thrives'.[39] The *Leveller* magazine navigated between both sides:

> Officially non-partisan, the Board is inherently conservative – even if only with a small c – and strongly Zionist. The formulation 'Zionism

equals racism' has led to campaigns on some campuses which, Board leaders believe, has spilled over into anti-Semitism. On top of that the belief of the left that racism is built into capitalism this has meant a general political stance unacceptable to many of the Board's supporters in the Jewish community. Both sides in that particular row have, after much anguished discussion, agreed to peaceful co-existence. SWP supporters, like ANL full-timer Paul Holborow, play down their anti-Zionism in ANL public meetings while Jacob Gerwitz, director of the Board's Defence and Group Relations department says: 'We have a sincere feeling that the public argument wasn't very healthy. We accept that they are there to fight the Nazis. Our sole worry is the SWP control.'

The article went on to dispute that the SWP had ever 'controlled' the League. 'That control was always something of a myth, so spontaneous and overwhelming was the support the League built up.'[40] Peter Hain recalls of this period,

> When I first joined the Anti-Nazi League, the politics was quite difficult. There was a swirl of pressures. Many people in the Labour Party wanted to see the job done, but there was lots of hostility to the SWP. There was concern also within the Jewish community, and *Searchlight* played a useful role as a link between different groups. The conflicts lasted until the ANL got going. Once it was established, the sniping reduced.

From within the parliamentary Labour Party, meanwhile, many of those who had criticized the Socialist Workers Party at Lewisham felt nervous about then endorsing an alliance that took in leading members of the SWP. Yet by no means all Labour supporters were prepared to go along with the argument that the League was worthless, or merely an SWP-run 'front'. The *New Statesman* magazine, one traditional voice of the Labour left, ran a front page 'In defence of the Anti-Nazis'.

> Its National Secretary, Paul Holborrow [sic], is a member of the SWP. But most of the other members of the steering committee, Peter Hain, Neil Kinnock, MP, Audrey Wise, MP, Ernie Roberts et al. are scarcely Trots, whatever else they may be. Suppose that Mr Holborrow and his SWP friends were, with manipulative cunning, to try and turn the ANL away from its simple anti-racialist platform and towards some sinister purpose of their own – nationalising the mustard-factories perhaps, or substituting Vanessa Redgrave for the Queen – is it really plausible that they should succeed? It is a long time since the Comintern days when 'fronts' really were marched and counter-marched with clockwork precision.[41]

The large number of Labour MPs who continued to back the League, including Tony Benn, Dennis Skinner, Martin Flannery and Gwyneth Dunwoody, suggests that the *New Statesman* was right.

6

The United Front

Several of the people who wrote about the Anti-Nazi League at the time maintained that it was simply a front for the SWP. The National Front paper *Bulldog* had its own strange version of this story, claiming that Mike Kidron, Tony Cliff's brother-in-law and a Jewish refugee from apartheid South Africa, was secretly bankrolling the League. From a Cold War perspective, the writer John Tomlinson also maintained that the League operated to a hidden agenda: 'For motives of its own, the far left Socialist Workers Party in Britain has through its sponsorship of the Anti-Nazi League launched a recruitment drive avowedly against racism and fascism, but also by its own ideological implication, against state racism and state fascism, and ultimately against the state itself.' For such writers as Tomlinson, the SWP was incapable of fighting racism for anything but dishonest motives.[1]

Ernie Roberts, the Labour MP, disagreed with such claims. 'There grew to be some foundation to the contention that the SWP "controlled" the League, mainly because a steering committee of busy politicians cannot run an organisation on a day-to-day basis.' Because the prominent sponsors could not run a grassroots campaign, he wrote, responsibility fell 'upon those who [were] prepared to beaver away at the practical jobs beneath the surface of top management'. Roberts attempted to interest Labour branches in this important work, but to no avail. Still, he maintained, it was Labour supporters who provided the Anti-Nazi League's numbers. 'The ANL was built on the impetus and support of those Labour Party members who took up its cause.'[2]

The Anti-Nazi League was a movement of hundreds of thousands, if not millions. There is no way that the three to four thousand members of the Socialist Workers Party would have been able to stamp their will on the movement, if they had not been able to work in alliance with other forces. There is no way that the League would have survived if the members of the SWP had determined to shift it in directions that the majority opposed. Yet the truth remains that the Anti-Nazi League was an initiative launched by the members of the SWP and adopted some of the political style of the older body. So far, this book has discussed both Rock Against Racism and the Anti-Nazi League, without yet saying much about how they fitted into the history of the International Socialists and the Socialist Workers Party.

Situating the SWP

The Socialist Workers Party was and is a Trotskyist group, claiming continuity with the Marxism of the First, Second and Third Internationals – with Karl Marx, Frederick Engels, Rosa Luxemburg, Vladimir Lenin, Leon Trotsky and the Russian Revolution. Leon Trotsky was the leading propagandist of the revolution, the organizer of the insurrection, and the founder of the Red Army, which secured the survival of the Soviet state after 1917. Yet Trotsky grew increasingly critical of the bureaucratization of the revolution, explaining this weakness in terms of the isolation of the USSR. If the revolution spread outside Russia, it had a chance. If it did not spread, then the result could not be socialism. Leon Trotsky was exiled from Russia and established a Fourth International to bring together revolutionaries in opposition to both capitalism and the degenerated workers' state. The Socialist Review Group (the parent to the SWP) was established in the late 1940s from a small current of around a dozen socialists who were critical of orthodox Trotskyism.

The Socialist Review Group distinguished itself in several ways from other parties on the revolutionary left. It argued that Russia system was a form of state capitalism,[3] and that there was nothing about Russia that socialists should defend. In the midst of the Cold War, this was an important argument – separating the group both from the Cold War pro-Americanism of the Labour Party, and from its obverse, the Soviet loyalism of the Communist Party. Tony Cliff, the founder of the Socialist Review Group, and his allies were also critical of their rivals on the British far left. They saw the various Trotskyist groups as grandiose, proclaiming themselves a Fourth International when the forces they represented were tiny. In the 1950s, the Socialist Review Group also tended to argue that Rosa Luxemburg's ideas on organization had as much to offer as Lenin's. This emphasis on spontaneity placed them at odds with larger forces on the Stalinist and Trotskyist left.[4]

The Socialist Review Group mutated into the International Socialists. Through the 1960s, the IS remained a propaganda group of between 100 and 200 members. The party then experienced an extraordinary year of growth in 1968, the year of the Paris student and worker revolts, attaining a momentum that would last it through to 1974. By the time of that year's elections, the IS had 3,000 members, many of them organized in factory branches. The newspaper *Socialist Worker* was selling up to 50,000 copies a week. Although it was far smaller than the Communist Party of Great Britain, which had around 20,000 members and remained the largest party to the left of Labour, the CP was in decline, and the members of the IS expected that their party would soon become the largest on the far left. More and more the comrades saw themselves not just as one part of the left, but as its most dynamic component. A shift away from the previous emphasis on spontaneity, the idea that 'the movement' could deliver, was represented in Tony Cliff's three-volume biography of Lenin. The comrades began to see party building as an urgent task.

Many members of the International Socialists were recruited in the early 1970s, at a time of increasing trade union struggles. Edward Heath's Tory government was challenged by wave after wave of protest. The miners, the dockers, the building workers all took on the state and won. For activists living through these years, it was easy to imagine that each protest would be a followed by a further demonstration, each demonstration by a further strike, each strike by a further occupation, and so on until the workers' movement was strong enough to challenge for power in its own right. This seemed to be the experience that was unfolding before their eyes. Yet once Labour had taken office on 1974, the movement began to decline. The trade unions accepted a policy of wage restraint, the 'Social Contract'. The number of protests and strikes reduced sharply. Tactics of struggle that would have succeeded against Heath failed under Wilson. The political climate changed. Contrary to expectations, six years of rapid growth were followed by five years for the locust.

From 1974 until 1976, the International Socialists was an organization in flux, trying to make sense of the new period, and without the certainty of earlier times. The chapter of Tony Cliff's autobiography that deals with our period is titled 'From beautiful spring to freezing winter'.[5] One moment it describes is a deep split that weakened the group between 1974 and 1976. The party's former National Secretary Jim Higgins and the editor of *Socialist Worker* Roger Protz both left.[6] The International Socialists' industrial work around groups such as the National Rank-and-File Committee was also reduced, as the strikes came to an end. Yet while the IS was in flux, so were the other socialist groups. Some signs pointed towards a decline in the struggle; others suggested a new generation emerging on the left.

To read *Socialist Worker* in the years of the Labour government is to be reminded of a series of campaigns: the struggles of the unemployed, of women's organizations defending abortion rights, of strikes by dockers in Liverpool, engineers in Cheshire and on Merseyside, of the Grunwick campaign, anti-apartheid and movements in defence of the Portuguese revolution. Students occupied their colleges and universities. 'The movement of 1976 and 1977 was actually much more extensive than 1968,' recalls Pete Alexander, 'and in most colleges we provided the leadership. Places like Lancaster were able to bring a coach of delegates to [the IS student] conference . . . What drew me to IS was that it related to students and workers, and to ideas as well as activity.' Membership of the International Socialists rose to 4,000. People began to speak of outstripping the Communist Party – or of more ambitious demands beyond. 'We wanted to outstrip Labour,' recalls Steve Jeffreys, then the SWP's industrial organizer. 'We wanted to challenge Labour in the workplaces, and at elections.' The group's name changed. The International Socialists became the Socialist Workers Party in January 1977.

There were still many other left-wing groups active at this time. So why did the Socialist Workers Party contribute disproportionately to the anti-fascist campaign? The Labour and Communist parties retained widespread support. Even assuming their failure, there was no iron law that stated that any one group would appear most vibrant in response to any one issue. In the 1950s, another group, the Trotskyist Socialist Labour League, had gained more than any of its rivals from splits in the Communist Party. In the late 1960s, the International Marxist Group grew quickly by recruiting students. In the 1980s, Militant would profit more than the SWP from the left mood within Labour. But in the 1970s, none of these groups was able to play a leading role in the anti-fascist campaign. The Communist Party had the numbers to build a mass movement, but many of its activists still believed deep down that rock music was a US weapon in the Cold War. The theory of state capitalism protected SWP members from the kind of knee-jerk anti-Americanism that the CP encouraged. In addition, the SWP's emphasis on the rank and file made it more open to the militant activism exemplified by Rock Against Racism and the Anti-Nazi League.

A former designer in the SWP print shop, Ian Goodyer argues that the style of the Anti-Nazi League demonstrates the enduring influence of Rosa Luxemburg on the Socialist Workers Party. Luxemburg had been a constant exponent of the power of struggle as a school of experiences – in contrast to other socialists, such as Lenin, she had placed more emphasis on struggle, and less on the revolutionary party, as such. '[Tony] Cliff thought she had a lot to offer on questions of organisation. He obviously revised his views in light of the party's experience during the 1970s, and this was expressed in the first volume of his biography of Lenin, but this didn't amount to a complete rejection of Luxemburg's example.'[7] Tony Cliff's belief in spontaneity is expressed nicely in two anecdotes. According to Roger Huddle, 'If Cliff had had to book the music for the Carnival, he would have booked the Bach string quartet, and no one else.' Yet although he rarely attended demonstrations, Cliff spent the first Rock Against Racism carnival at the back of the crowd, watching. He was already aged 60 and the music was hardly his own, but he loved every moment.

When Dave Widgery reviewed the third volume of Cliff's biography of Lenin in 1975, he titled his review article 'Alternative Lenin'. The article was a spirited vindication of the Luxemburg–Lenin synthesis, as much a general defence of the rebellious values of 1968 as a straight reading of Cliff's Lenin. Nigel Harris, an early member of the International Socialists and then the Socialist Workers Party, now on the outside of the party, takes an Olympian view.

> Many people on the left get stuck in rigid formula. But at its best, the SWP combined opportunism with organizational flair. I remember in 1968, Mick Jagger was arrested for smoking pot. At York University, the students stuck up posters in his defence. For the organized left, with their fixed concerns, this appeared opportunistic. Tony Cliff could indeed be

opportunistic. But the flair of the Socialist Workers Party enabled it to relate. By the mid-1970s, we had 20 rank-and-file groups for organized workers. And the tail end of that upsurge was the Anti-Nazi League.

Harris uses the word 'opportunism'. Other members of the SWP might have used a more positive term, such as 'flexibility'. Either way, the point remains: the SWP in 1977 was looking for a campaign, and once it had found it, the organization threw into it every resource it had.

Marxists in face of fascism

The Anti-Nazi League was not the first International Socialist or Socialist Workers Party initiative against fascism. Instead, it drew on the experience of several decades of anti-fascist work. Members of the IS had first discussed the subject way in 1962, following a fascist rally in Trafalgar Square. The IS-backed student paper, *Young Guard*, covered the rally on its front page, while the organization's magazine, *International Socialism*, ran an editorial, 'Fists Against Fascists', insisting that fascism could only be stopped 'physically and directly'. This approach was then criticized by one comrade, Peter Sedgwick, who wrote a reply insisting that Mosley should have been allowed to speak, if only to appear ridiculous. 'It was far better when Mosley spoke in Trafalgar Square only to the pigeons.' This was, however, a minority view within the IS. The majority wanted to fight fascism, and as the National Front prospered, Sedgwick came round to their view.

Members of the International Socialists disrupted fascist meetings in the 1966 election, including meetings in Southall and Islington. Two years later in 1968, following Powell's racist speech, the IS again took the threat seriously. Terry Barrett, the sole docker in the IS, signed and distributed a leafleting calling on London dockworkers to resist Powell's racism. Barrett complained that the supposedly unplanned march wasn't spontaneous at all. 'Not only did the small group of fascists who normally had no influence play on the dockers' fears about their jobs, but they didn't lose their pay when they went down to the House of Commons.' By contrast, neither the Labour Party nor the Communists made any serious attempt to oppose Powell. That summer also saw a fascist-organized pro-Powell march in central London, which was physically attacked by members of the Jewish 62 Group, with support from the IS.

Again in 1968, the International Socialists issued 'The Urgent Challenge of Fascism', an appeal to other left groups for unity around four issues of principle, one of which was 'Workers' control of society and industry as the only alternative to fascism'. Between August and November 1969, *International Socialism* printed selections from Trotsky's writings on German fascism. In 1970, the magazine published a Peter Sedgwick article, arguing that Hitler should be seen not as 'a front-man for business', but as the pioneer of state capitalism and corporate planning. The success of Nazism was explained with references to a general trend towards state ownership and control, in the aftermath of the Wall Street Crash, which shaped developments in Britain and the USA, as well as Germany.[8] Through the late 1960s and early 1970s, a number of articles by members of the IS or its supporters attempted to relate this general analysis to the specific conditions in Britain at the time.[9]

If the kids are united

One further influence may have been the Right to Work campaign. In the early 1970s, the IS had organised among employed workers, setting up Rank-and-File committees in engineering, mining, among teachers and transport workers. By the mid-1970s, more emphasis was put on organizing the unemployed. Various Labour MPs supported the Right to Work marches, including Eric Heffer, Harry Selby, Brian Sedgemore and Maureen Colquhoun. Several dozen trade union branches also gave their backing, as did Ernie Roberts of the engineering workers' union and Harry McShane, who had led the unemployed struggles of the 1920s. The first Right to Work demonstration took place in March 1976. It was called to protest against wage freezes, social services cuts and unemployment figures of over one million.[10] Nearly 570 marchers participated, walking 350 miles from Manchester to London. After marching for several weeks without arrests, the demonstrators were attacked by police as they approached Staples Corner in west London. Thirty-five marchers were arrested, along with nine local trade unionists who had come to welcome the marchers to London.[11] The next Right to Work march, from Liverpool to Blackpool for the Trades Union Congress in September 1977, involved 700 people. John Deason, the national secretary of the campaign, always insisted that the marches were not hunger marches. 'It is more of a flying picket,' he said. 'Our job is not only to remind workers of the desperate plight of the unemployed. It is also to encourage employed workers to throw their strength behind policies which can stop unemployment.'[12] Some workers did come out on strike or occupy their plants to stop redundancies after encountering Right to Work delegations, including workers at Ainslie Wire. Elsewhere, Right to Work marches were prevented by police cordons from entering sites and addressing the workers.[13]

In Ian Goodyer's words, the Right to Work campaign 'signalled a shift in the SWP's perspectives, away from established union and political structures and towards the unemployed, who were disproportionately represented among the young working class, and who, when they did find work, lacked a history of engagement with organized trade unionism.' The radical shop stewards of the early 1970s were said to have been absorbed into bureaucratic positions. There was a new emphasis on the potential radicalism of the young. Pete Alexander sees the campaign as more of a continuation of the previous emphasis on trade union militants. 'Right to Work gave us the link to Ernie Roberts and to many union leaders, especially at the middle level. It also meant that we had experience of walking into work places and union branches and talking to people we didn't know. This was useful with the Anti-Nazi League. It also gave us some practical experience of united front work.'

The Right to Work campaign did not beat capitalism or bring an end to redundancies. The worst years of unemployment were actually to come later. But the movement did succeed in radicalizing a generation of activists. The people who contributed most to the Right to Work campaign were a layer of young workers and former students. According to Mike, an activist from Cardiff, 'The style of organizing was the same and the layer of youth was the same as that which was attracted to the ANL.' The Clash played their first political benefits not for Rock Against Racism or the Anti-Nazi League, but for the Right to Work campaign. This generation of activists would later give the ANL its edge.

It is also worth mentioning in this context one short-lived campaign from spring 1977, 'Stuff the Jubilee'.[14] *Socialist Worker*'s headline was one of its best selling ever. Some 30,000 copies of a badge carrying the same logo were sold. The slogan caught a generational mood of revolt against the monarchy.[15] The activists involved in Right to Work and Stuff the Jubilee were natural anti-fascists. They already saw the threat from the National Front. It was their presence that explains the organic character of the ANL. When there was a need to fight the fascists, these activists flocked to Rock Against Racism and the Anti-Nazi League. When the need subsided, they turned their energies elsewhere.

The united front

The Anti-Nazi League was conceived loosely along the lines of the 'united front', generally following Leon Trotsky's interpretation of such an alliance. Writing in the 1930s, Trotsky had warned the left of the dangers of standing still while fascism took power. His most famous articles had been penned between 1930 and 1932, in response to events in Germany. The theme of Trotsky's advice was urgency. The left must unite immediately to stop Hitler. Any delays, any prevarications could assist the right. Fascism represented an all-out assault, not just on the revolutionary left, but even on the reforms that workers had won through many decades of trade union struggle. Under Hitler, Trotsky warned, Socialists would be jailed, Communists shot, and the whole of society turned into a giant police state. Trotsky's advice was aimed above all at the leaders of the two German workers' parties, who insisted on marching apart and organizing separately. They were sleepwalking to destruction, he warned. They had to ally.

After 1933, Trotsky's arguments changed. Hitler did indeed seize power. Workers' movements were crushed first in Germany, then in Austria. But a powerful movement grew up, arguing for workers' unity to stop fascism. Ironically, the Communist parties, which had previously insisted on working in hostility to other groups on the left, now flipped round altogether, and began to argue for a new strategy of anti-fascist unity, involving not just other working-class parties but liberals and forces to their right, even up to the edges of the fascist parties themselves. This second tactic, the 'popular front', was attempted first in France and then in Spain. Trotsky warned against it. He argued that the popular front governments would inevitably cause frustration and disillusionment, even among their own supporters. For while left-wing parties might work together in defensive alliances, there was something different about unity with capitalist parties, representing very opposed groups of people and with quite different ideas about how society should be run. Trotsky's point applied not just to popular front governments, but to any alliance that was based on the tactic. By waiting on the capitalist parties, it would inevitably undermine workers' militancy and confidence.

In Trotsky's theory, then, a united front was a voluntary combination of pro-working class organizations. Building on Trotsky's theory, the Anti-Nazi League was advocated as a joint project. Members of the Socialist Workers Party took seriously the arguments that the ANL should be an independent project with a life of its own, and that it should involve forces to their right. They saw a division of labour between the revolutionary party and the anti-fascist alliance. According to one SWP pamphlet, 'If the Nazis go on the rampage, an organised force is needed to fight back. An organisation like the Anti-Nazi League can be enormously important in pulling thousands of people into the struggle. But because of the wide range of ideas within its ranks it cannot give clear and decisive leadership at every point in the struggle.' Only a revolutionary party could play that role: 'A party made up of people who have clarified their ideas in advance, who think along the same lines, and who can put forward a clear line of action to counter every twist and turn the Nazis make.'[16]

Dave Widgery's *Beating Time* admits that the alliance between the reformist parliamentarians of Labour and the Marxists of the Socialist Workers Party might appear 'incongruous', but argues that it was less so than it seemed. 'For a clear-cut common goal had been set – the decrease of the influence of the NF – even if the Labour Party's primary concern was the danger of losing marginal seats because of a high NF vote and the SWP's was to encourage people to consider the case for revolutionary social change by working-class direct action.'[17]

One place where the political character of the alliance was debated was at the League's July 1978 national conference, attended by over 800 delegates from across the country. Various motions were put, some of them with the intention of teasing out possible contradictions within the

League's positions. One debate concerned whether or not the League should publicly campaign against all immigration controls. The argument for was simple: the racism of the National Front did not emerge by chance. It drew on institutional factors: press racism, the hostility of the police and a racist system of immigration controls that were designed to prevent black people from moving to Britain. The argument against was more subtle: while 'objectively' immigration controls may have served this purpose, it was also true that most Labour Party supporters ran shy of calling for all controls to be lifted – such a demand seemed too radical to them. There was a fine line between a campaign that educated its activists in left-wing politics, and one that put up so many barriers to membership that no one joined.

The delegates did vote to adopt a policy of opposition to all immigration controls, but this was always treated as part of the Anti-Nazi League's policy, and not its activist programme. In other words, while the leading members of the ANL might argue publicly against all immigration controls, it did not make opposition to all controls a precondition of membership. The organizers did not want the League to be like those left parties so weighed down by policies that supporters were expected to pass an examination before being allowed to join.

Another motion called for the Anti-Nazi League to support the withdrawal of British troops from Ireland. The logic of this debate was similar. On the one hand, the British presence was described as an imperial venture: how could there be democracy in Belfast or Derry, when people were being shot on the streets? How could the British free themselves from racism and all the other legacies of colonialism, while they remained a colonial power? Opponents of the motion responded, what was the point of the League, to represent internally all the considered positions of the left or to challenge fascism? The motion was defeated. The League was not a political party. People would be attracted to it (or not) on the sole grounds of its success in fighting the NF. Its actions would count for more than its words.

A number of other questions came up at the same conference. These included the extent to which the League was against all forms of racism or merely an anti-fascist alliance, the issue of state bans, and the question of Israel and Palestine. Each of these points is addressed elsewhere in this text. It is enough to say here that delegates from the Socialist Workers Party argued with those other delegates who claimed to stand to their left that there was a political need for unity with people from Labour Party and other moderate backgrounds. The members of the SWP argued for a coalition in which the programme was short, but people learned through struggle the lessons of socialism. In the words of Paul Holborow, on the day, 'Unity in Action! Don't avoid debating what divides us, but fight around what unites us.'[18]

Interviewing leading members of the Anti-Nazi League in retrospect, it is striking how readily even non-SWP members endorse this stress on unity in action. The ANL national organizer, Peter Hain, is typical. 'You get on with action. The time to debate how many angels dance on the head of a pin, if that was ever much use, that time had passed. We had to set aside arguments which had bedevilled the movement for years.' When Peter Hain describes today the leading SWP members of the coalition, he does so with striking admiration.

> Paul Holborow was very good to work with. He was very shrewd, one of the best political activists to work around. His politics were very different from mine. The SWP is a very hard-line party, but Paul had an unusually non-sectarian approach towards broad-based campaigning. He brought their sense of dynamic campaigning and energy. They had designers, artists. They could print things overnight. The Anti-Nazi League was a fusion of music and confrontation. The SWP brought Rock Against Racism. Without the SWP, there wouldn't have been enough energy.

Holborow is equally effusive in describing Hain's role.

> I never took any initiatives without the closest consultation with Peter. I would phone him three or four times a week. He would phone me He was a very committed person. He was attracted to the élan of the SWP, its energy and decisiveness. And the ideas. Let's do it, we would say, and 24 hours later it was done.

Talking to Holborow, it is clear that he sees a contrast between the work of the League, and the Communist Party-dominated popular fronts that still predominated at this time. This, for example, is Holborow's reflection on the 1977 by-election campaign at Bournemouth East: 'A method had been established; a flavour of what the Anti-Nazi League was designed to do. It was a complete break from the other campaigns, which had been completely ruled by the pace of the most conservative groups. We were activists, we would do something quickly rather than deliberating and do nothing.'

Some left-wing parties including the Workers Socialist League and the Revolutionary Communist Group, argued at the time that the Anti-Nazi League's failure to adopt a full socialist programme proved that it was secretly a middle-class organization or, using the contemporary terminology, a popular front.[19] A true united front, they argued, should be equipped with a full programme that addressed all aspects of racism in Britain, not least the institutional racism of the press, police and courts.

Perhaps one lesson of the Anti-Nazi League is that unity can be too narrowly conceived. For an alliance to constitute a united front, that does not mean that it should open its membership only to card-carrying members of the proletariat.[20] What, for example, of the women's organizations or the black networks? Few of their members saw themselves in quite these terms. Nor is it the case that a united front must have a full socialist

programme, addressing every issue of present-day politics. More important than its sociological or political origin is the question of who leads
the alliance, and where it is heading. The character of a campaign is decided by the direction of its politics. Einde, one of the veterans of
Lewisham, makes this point well. 'The Anti-Nazi League wasn't a united
front, but it was a united front-type organization. It wasn't a pact between
mass organizations, but there was an alliance between reformists and revolutionaries, unity around specific organization demands which left the
organizations free.' The ANL may have involved more youngsters than
trade unionists, and it was a cultural as well as a political phenomenon.
For these reasons, it may have differed from parts of the original united
front formula. But it was not a party front and neither did it become a popular front dominated by the establishment parties.

Workers Against the Nazis

There were various ways in which the Socialist Workers Party's involvement helped to shape the Anti-Nazi League, influencing its character. One
of the most important was the emphasis on workplace roots. For decades,
the SWP had consistently argued that any better society would have to be
based on the most thoroughgoing working-class democracy. It followed
that any campaigns should be established on a similar basis; that they
should involve as many organised workers as practicably possible. This decision was a matter of tactics as well as strategy. If the National Front was
trying to recruit in working-class areas, there was no point opposing the
fascists from the outside, from parliament, or from the universities; the
campaign also had to be rooted on council estates and in the workplace. Of
course, such ideas were not merely the preserve of the SWP – they were
also common currency among much of the far left, and even in the Labour
Party. Even as late as 1978, for example, it was still Labour policy that all
Labour Party members were required to be members of trade unions.

According to a recent *Searchlight* pamphlet, 'The ANL won support in
industrial and white-collar unions both at a leadership and rank and file
level.'[21] In November 1978, Bill Dunn of the Communist Party reported
on the League's successes so far. Twenty union executives had voted to
back it. Six hundred workplace organizations were 'in direct contact'
with the Anti-Nazi League. 'Among them are ANL groups working in
massive factories like British Leyland Longbridge or Fords of
Dagenham, Yorkshire miners, civil servants and local government.' Bill
Keys, general secretary of the print union SOGAT, had addressed rallies
in northern England as well as marches in London. There were also ANL
blocs among the print workers of Fleet Street, and among technicians and
journalists working in television.[22]

Many supporters of the ANL worked in schools. The NF had made a
series of attempts to recruit school students, culminating in the

publication of a Young National Front paper, *Bulldog*. The Anti-Nazi League responded with groups for Skaters and School Kids. SKAN had its own 16-page magazine. The third issue ran an interview with reggae band Steel Pulse and a poem by Leon Rosselson:

> School taught me / To write my name,
> To recite the answers, / To feel ashamed
> To stand in corners, / To wait in line,
> To kiss the rod, / To be on time,
> And trust in God
> To make me a model citizen, / That was their goal.
> Well I don't know about that / But it was useful training
> For a career / On the dole.[23]

The group Teachers Against the Nazis wrote education packs against racism and fascism, establishing a tradition of anti-racist education that would continue at least into the 1990s. An ANL teachers' conference was held in Manchester in May 1978, with John Rowbotham speaking for the National Union of Teachers, alongside Colin Barker of Manchester SWP and London NUT activist Sean Doherty.[24] The follow-up conference in June 1979 was organized under the banner of the Campaign Against Racism in Education. Speakers included a school student from Soweto and A. Sivanandan of *Race and Class*.[25]

The first national education conference of Teachers Against the Nazis took place on 23 September 1978, the day before the second carnival. Many speakers were long-term anti-fascists, including Maurice Ludmer, the editor of *Searchlight*, and Joan Lestor, the Labour MP. Yet alongside traditional anti-fascism there was also space for a discussion of the broader issues of racism in education, with workshops on 'Asian girls in schools' and 'Why schools fail the black community'. Because the entire movement was seeking to understand and fight racism, you find many children's voices, not just in the educational materials but also in the literature of local anti-Nazi groups. The winter 1979 *Bulletin* of Merseyside Anti-Nazi League, for example, carried the following story, written by Fran from Netherley:

> At an early age I was made more aware that I was different. I was at school and my teacher was doing geography and she went all round the class asking where everyone's father was from. At that time there was only me and my friend Carol who were coloured in the senior year. She was lucky, as I thought at the time, because it was her mother who was coloured and her father who was white. Everyone was answering by saying 'Ireland, Wales or Scotland'. When it came to Carol, she replied 'Wales', then it was my turn and my nerves were shattered. I answered with an embarrassed 'Oh sorry miss, but I've forgotten'. I didn't have the heart to say 'the Gold Coast', because Ghana hadn't got their independence at that time. But I was made aware that I was different to anyone in the class.[26]

John T was then a young teacher, working in a Bradford comprehensive. The Anti-Nazi League failed to get the official support of his NUT branch, but it won support among individuals and union meetings. 'The badges were everywhere. I seem to remember that the head tried to ban them, which led to a good argument in a staff meeting.' While the atmosphere at work had been mixed before the ANL came on the scene, 'We never heard racist statements uttered in the staff-room after this period.'

As anti-racist teachers became better organised, so the situation in the schools began to change. Yuri was at primary school in 1977, 'and like a lot of Indian families, we left for a while and came back. Everything had moved on. I heard names I'd never been called before. I remember asking my parents. The National Front, if they win, does that mean we'll have to go to India for ever?' An older pupil Kate recalls, 'One thing about my school was that we had a very strict uniform and we weren't allowed to wear anything with it. Then one day, the R[eligious] E[ducation] teacher came in, and she was wearing an Anti-Nazi League badge. I remember feeling outraged, the way kids do. Why not us, why couldn't we wear badges? It turned out that the teachers had had a big meeting. There were young teachers, arguing with the old teachers, what would you have done, when fascism was growing in the 1930s. After that we were allowed to wear just Anti-Nazi League badges only with our uniforms.'

Important teachers' groups included Rank and File, the Socialist Teachers' Alliance, and ALTARF, All London Teachers Against Racism and Fascism. The Anti-Nazi League organized a teachers' conference where Teachers Against the Nazis education packs ('TANKITS') were distributed. As well as teachers, other groups of white-collar workers contributed to the ANL. Alan was a lecturer at a Transport and General Workers' Union summer school. He remembers signing up a number of shop stewards from there to the League. Ian moved the vote for affiliation at the conference of the lecturers' union ATTI (today NATFHE). This motion was eventually won, he recalls, thanks in part to the timing of the conference. In March 1978, the Communist Party, which dominated the ATTI executive, remained hostile to the Anti-Nazi League. After the Rock Against Racism carnival, however, the Communist Party reversed its line. The ATTI conference followed just days afterwards.

Support came from a series of unions. Following an arson attack on the Anti-Nazi League headquarters in London, the Civil Service Union gave a one-off grant of £500 to pay for repairs.[27] Ten national trade unions voted to back the League, and several more gave practical assistance to the anti-racist campaign.[28]

The Anti-Nazi League was not only successful within white-collar unions. In Manchester, Dave remembers that Larry Aitken and other members of the Fire Brigades' Union from New Mills Fire Station took part in protests and helped to raise funds for the campaign. Elsewhere, the technicians' union ACTT worked with the ANL in arguing that the National Front's broadcasts should be banned. Francis Wheen rang Alan

Sapper, general secretary of the ACTT, to suggest that such disruptive action would only make martyrs of the NF. 'Democracy is threatened', Sapper replied. 'We don't need to bother with philosophical arguments. We can discuss democracy until the concentration camps come in.'[29]

Some workplace ANL groups were little more than a badge, while others were able to establish an occasional paper or magazine. One example of this latter group was Rail Against the Nazis: members of the rail unions RMT, ASLEF and TSSA, with support in London and the north-west. Their banner showed a high-speed train knocking over gang of Nazis. Members of King's Cross ASLEF played a leading role. King's Cross had not always had a reputation as a left-wing depot. Many years before, it had in fact been a target for fascist infiltration. But by the 1970s, the depot was younger and more mixed. One member of the ASLEF branch, Leno Carraro, was arrested at Lewisham in 1977. The branch took great pleasure in paying his fine. When the ANL was established, a leading steward Steve Forey took a petition around his branch. Badges were sold and stickers put up. Forty people attended a meeting in the depot, to establish a local group. Members of the King's Cross branch took part in the protests against the National Front at Brick Lane. This activity then led to the formation of a national network.[30]

One member of Rail Against the Nazis in the north-west, Paul S, was an activist in the Labour Party. Another prominent anti-fascist in the region was Declan, a long-standing Irish socialist, then working in a booking office on the Altrincham line. He found it hard to build a base in his section, as there were only two or three other people working in his office. But he tried to win support for Rail Against the Nazis in the staff association and TSSA. 'There were three or four of us in the group, mainly from the National Union of Railwaymen. We organized fringe meetings at union conferences, and tried to isolate self-declared Nazis in the union.'

John from Wood Green was a young ASLEF activist working on the tube. He had been based in the depot for six months, but in all that time the branch had not succeeded in holding a single quorate meeting. 'We never had more than six.' He was also worried by the extent of National Front support in local workplaces, including some of the London sorting offices. One or two of the train drivers were seen wearing racist badges. He decided to kill two birds with one stone. 'One day, I put up a poster saying that at the next meeting we would affiliate to the Anti-Nazi League. About 50 people came, and there was a big row, but we affiliated. After that the branch never looked back.'

From spring 1978, the Anti-Nazi League attempted to move the campaign out of the schools and colleges and into the factories. Tony Cliff argued that 'The more the ANL is rooted in the workplace, the more the inter-connection between *all* aspects of struggle will be clear to everyone.'[31] This new line was successful in different areas. Mike was an unemployed engineer at the end of the 1970s. He worked briefly as a full-time organizer for the League in Preston and then in Nottingham. In Preston, the fire-fighters' union and the postal workers' union backed the League, as did the joint shop stewards' committee at Leyland motors. The convenor at Leyland's, Len Brindle, backed the Anti-Nazi League. In Nottingham, Mike remembers that the League received support from the white-collar union ASTMS, and the teachers' union. One of the most important members of the League in the city was Don Devin, an activist in the National Union of Hosiery and Knitworkers and a member of the Communist Party. Other local Communists were much less helpful: 'the Communists in the miners' union wouldn't back us at all'.

Elsewhere, Communists were more supportive, especially following the first carnival, which was the point at which their party decided to back this new movement against racism. In February 1979, 200 people attended a Miners Against the Nazis conference, held in Barnsley. Speakers included Arthur Scargill, Jonathan Dimbleby, Paul Holborow and Ashok Biswas.[32] Although the Socialist Workers Party did have around two dozen members in the mines, this sort of turnout was only made possible by co-operation with the much larger group of Communist miners and people drawn by personalities such as Scargill.

In Manchester, members of the Communist Party ran the engineering union. Consequently, Communist support was essential if a mass movement was to be built. After the first carnival, the trades council and the divisional council of the engineering workers' union both passed resolutions of support. At other times, the Manchester Teachers' Association, white-collar workers in ASTMS (Central Manchester) and nurses in COHSE (Ladywell Hospital) all gave their support. The district council of the National Union of Railwaymen affiliated to the League. Official recognition made life much easier when it came to organizing local actions. John was then an 'ageing hippie' living in the south of the city:

> I remember we did one cleaning of paint from buildings. The Nazis had been putting up slogans for some time. It had happened over years, so we organized a local paint-out. One local factory, there were about 20 people inside. We came in and spoke to the local steward. He was known locally as a strong Communist. He said, that was fine, he'd already been trying to get management to paint it out. The union provided a ladder. Several workers took badges. They all supported what we were doing. It was that kind of atmosphere.

Chanie Rosenberg, then an activist in the National Union of Teachers, describes some of the ANL's support:

> In Longbridge, 200 assembly line workers refused to work with a National Front supporter, who was moved elsewhere . . . A school NUT sent an NFer to Coventry; he eventually left. In Keighley, a National Front candidate was fined for window smashing and therefore sacked from his job as a busman. The National Front did nothing for him. He appealed through the union, and getting the full support of the Pakistanis, was

reinstated. He left the National Front and rejected racism. The [civil servants' union] CPSA took action in a number of offices winning the right to wear ANL badges, and getting a racist disciplined by union action. Railworkers succeeded in getting a ban on driving trains if they were daubed with racist slogans. *Hackney Gazette* journalists went on strike for three days to prevent the printing of a National Front advertisement. In International Harvesters a National Front member was strung upside down.[33]

Through the 1970s, the National Front had organized in a number of workplaces, but under the pressure of the anti-fascist campaign, even these former strongholds were lost. In 1979, Mark began working as a postman from the North Delivery Office in Islington. 'When I started, the NF ran the branch committee. They used to collect openly on the shopfloor. The collections paid the deposit so that the NF could stand in elections.' Already by 1979, however, the supporters of the NF had been removed from the branch committee. 'The people who took control of the branch were trade unionists, middle of the road Labour.' Yet the National Front retained some support among the workers. 'One day, soon after I started, I was in the toilets. This old guy came in and asked me for 50p for the NF. I'd come from a school in Hackney, it was black, Asian, Greek, Turkish. I thought he was joking, he was having a laugh. He cornered me.' Dolan pushed the older man back, and in the weeks afterwards he could see the balance of power change. 'Outside affected the inside. The Anti-Nazi League, the marches, Rock Against Racism, it had its weight in the workplace. Within a couple of years, the NF had gone altogether.'

Perhaps the most striking example of Anti-Nazi League success came on the docks. Early on, socialist dockers set themselves the task of undoing the defeat they had suffered in 1968, when they had marched in support of Enoch Powell's racist 'Rivers of Blood' speech. The port of London shop stewards' committee voted to affiliate to the League. Alongside Bob Light and Eddie Prevost, Mickey Fenn was another activist. Always at the front of the marches, he was arrested in June 1977 and accused by the police of assaulting fascists. In an important move, the London dockers provided the stewards for the first carnival – and also loaned to the Anti-Nazi League their famous banner from the 1972 campaign against the Industrial Relations Act, 'Arise Ye Workers'. It was a complete turnaround from just ten years before.

Populism in practice

Alongside the Anti-Nazi League there were other anti-fascist organizations, as we have seen. Some were close to the ANL, in inspiration or politics; others were genuinely based on a more cross-class alliance. Joan Lestor, Labour MP and former editor of the original *Searchlight* in the 1960s, was the central figure behind the Joint Committee Against

Racialism (JCAR), launched in December 1977.[34] It attracted support
from the Liberal Party, the British Council of Churches and the National
Union of Students. Another important backer of JCAR was the Jewish
Board of Deputies, which campaigned against the ANL, accusing it of
being a front dominated by the SWP. Difficulties were encountered in
agreeing to policies and JCAR's 'activity appears to have largely centred
around distribution of anti-racist literature'. Stan Taylor describes the
Join Committee rightly as an 'alternative to the ANL for moderates'.[35]

The house that Jack built

In the same way that the Anti-Nazi League cannot be reduced to the
single intervention of any one person or group, so its constituent parts
were themselves complex alliances. The real problem with the idea that
the SWP could secretly dominate the Anti-Nazi League is that it misun-
derstands the extent to which the SWP was itself a diverse space, an army
that rarely marched in time.

A previous chapter made the point that the Socialist Workers Party's
initial involvement in Rock Against Racism had been relatively shallow.
Some of the founders of that campaign worked in the SWP print-shop,
but their party left them alone to get on with the tasks at hand. The SWP
involvement in the Anti-Nazi League was much more systematic. Chapter 5 described the key role played in the formation of the Anti-Nazi
League by members of the SWP, including Jim Nichol and Paul
Holborow. Speak to such activists now, and they emphasize the importance of their political training in the SWP. Paul Holborow is typical.
Despite the role he played in leading the campaign, he is quick to place
the credit elsewhere. 'I have no delusions of grandeur. There was never
any doubt in my mind that my membership of the IS and the SWP was
quite pivotal to the campaign. It taught me lessons. It ensured that it was a
consistent and level-headed campaign. The method of the united front
was the method of the Anti-Nazi League.'

In 1977, Steve Jeffreys was the Socialist Workers Party's national industrial organizer. How did the Anti-Nazi League fit into the party's
strategy for working against racism?

> There were two strands, really. One was working in the unions, support-
> ing campaigns such as Grunwick. We wanted to show black workers that
> we had something to offer them. We found that many didn't speak much
> English, or wanted to organize separately. So often we had newspapers,
> first *Chingari* for Asian workers, then *Flame*, for black workers. With
> the Anti-Nazi League, we hoped to show that the SWP could play a lead-
> ing role against the Front.

'The initiative came right from the top of the party,' recalls another prominent SWP activist from the time, Pete Alexander.

Jim Nichol was the [SWP's] National Secretary. At that time, he was probably the second most influential member of the [party's] Central Committee, and it was he who, by deciding what went out to the branches and relating directly to key organizers, 'ran' the party on a week-to-week basis . . . The first ANL activities – collecting the signatures, establishing the steering committee and producing posters and badges – were handled centrally [by the ANL office]. But before long – certainly by the time of the first carnival – the whole party had been moved into action. At a local level this meant it was not just a few members sent off to organize a RAR gig, but everyone involved in filling coaches (and even trains), starting ANL branches and the various ANL 'sections', organizing local protests, winning affiliations, selling badges, fly-posting and so on. During 1978 we were pretty much the ANL party. I'd really have to stretch my memory to think about what else happened that year.

One of the ironies of the situation is that, despite its prominent role in initiating the Anti-Nazi League, the Socialist Workers Party was not the main beneficiary of the work put in. Instead, it was the Labour Party that reaped the rewards of the campaign. Ian Birchall suggests that the SWP concentrated on building the League at the expense of building out of it. The party watered down its own message, and failed to recruit potential supporters to Marxist politics – or, if it recruited them, it failed to retain them in the months afterwards. According to Birchall, 'the Labour Party probably recruited rather more members via the ANL than the SWP did'. More to the point, it was MPs later associated with the Labour right, including future Labour leader Neil Kinnock, who allowed themselves to ride this wave. Following Labour's defeat at the 1983 election, Kinnock took over as leader of the Labour Party. He drove his party to the right, paving the way for New Labour. In Birchall's words, 'For Kinnock, like so many reformist leaders before him, was elected by the left in order to lead from the right; his past with the ANL was undoubtedly one of the factors that enabled him to create his left image after 1983.'[36]

Keith agrees that the Socialist Workers Party failed to build a lasting relationship with the thousands of people involved in the Anti-Nazi League and Rock Against racism. 'The emphasis, correctly, was on activity and also a horror, again correct I think, of continuing a campaign for the sake of it once it had done its job. Yet the ANL never had its own paper and we simply forgot quite quickly many of the people who were involved if they didn't join.'

The evidence of membership figures suggests that both are right; Labour did grow off the back of the League.[37] Yet it is hard to see what else could have been done. The Socialist Workers Party formed the leadership of the Anti-Nazi League, but only a small proportion of its membership. The downturn in left-wing politics that began in Britain in 1974 would continue after 1979 with a vengeance. The defeat of the steelworkers, the miners and the Greater London Council (GLC) demoralized the generation of activists that had been part of the ANL, and although many remained part of the movement, there simply was not the space in society for a mass revolutionary party during the Callaghan or Thatcher years.

7

Carnival

Through 1978, the movement continued. The largest events were the Rock Against Racism carnivals. The strategy was to connect an anti-racist political message to radical music, to separate young people decisively from the National Front's politics. Peter Hain outlined the method in the Labour paper, *Tribune*: 'The carnival[s] point the way to a style of campaigning that is likely to win the emerging rearguard battle which must be waged against the National Front. In the longer term, of course, socialist solutions will be needed to pressed and fought for. But, in the shorter term, we desperately need to undercut the support of the new Nazis.'[1] This was anti-racism with a new emphasis, on pleasure, on self-activity and on spectacle.

The first carnival took place on 30 April 1978. The date was chosen to highlight the radical ambitions of the Anti-Nazi League. It was 130 years since the huge Chartist demonstration at Kennington Common, the closest that the British ruling class has come in recent times to facing an insurrection. The carnival was fully publicized by the left and in the musical press. Following the lead given by the *New Musical Express* over the previous year, all the music papers now carried regular features supporting both Rock Against Racism and the Anti-Nazi League. A year on from the launch of RAR, *Melody Maker* ran an interview with Syd Shelton and Roger Huddle, Shelton describing the purpose of the movement. 'We try and use popular culture which we all enjoy to mobilise people, not in a specific way, but just getting them to take a stand against the Front.' Shelton insisted that RAR's target audience was not the already convinced but ordinary kids on the estates. 'There are no jobs for them, they're living in cities and estates that are closing down . . . Conditions are right for the Front.'[2]

Who came up with the word 'carnival'? Jerry Fitzpatrick was given the job of organizing the events. 'I think it must have been Paul. Red Saunders was struggling towards the idea, something even bigger than the Rock Against Racism gigs and the tours. They wanted something to bring together the cultural and political lefts, like the fêtes organized by the Communist Party in France. But it was Paul who capped it.'

We started planning the first carnival in January 1977, at least three months beforehand. I remember booking the event through the GLC.

The form said that if you had more than 10,000 people, you needed portaloos, and all that. So I booked a mini-festival, for 10,000, not more. I knew we had no money. I wasn't expecting more than 20,000, tops. We made a deal to book the PA; we paid three thousand there and then, four thousand on the day. Paul drew the money out. I had to sew it into the lining of my leather jacket, so it wouldn't get stolen. There were scaffolders from Donegal who put up the stage. Red and Roger booked the bands. Tom Robinson, Steel Pulse. Tom Robinson got X-Ray Spex. Two weeks before the carnival, we started trying to book the Clash. I went to a meeting with their manager Bernie Rhodes, then one with the band. Red and Syd [Shelton] were absolutely brilliant. But I remember Mick Jones flicking ash in my hair. Finally Joe Strummer spoke, and said, 'Fuck it, we'll show them!' That was just two weeks beforehand. The word went round the streets of London. After their songs 'White Riot' and 'Guns of Brixton', the Clash were huge. They brought the youth.

Local anti-fascists put out leaflets for the carnival. Mike from Preston booked coaches: 'Wherever you went, you sold tickets. Punk bands played gigs for the coaches, all sorts of people got involved. You really knew something was happening.' Eighty coaches were organized from Manchester. According to Geoff, 'I don't think that the left has organized a larger number of coaches to anything in London, ever, and most of those coaches were full.' Twelve coaches were sent from Sheffield, 25 from Leeds, a train from Glasgow. Keith remembers being stopped by a policeman flyposting for the first carnival on Tottenham High Road. 'We said we hadn't done that many and anyway it was for a worthwhile cause, and he just walked off and left us to it.' These young anti-racists were astonished when the officer left them alone to get on with sticking posters. 'This was not a usual occurrence!'

Marching to the carnival

The Manchester carnival

The carnival began with a march to Victoria Park, starting from Trafalgar Square, and going via the Strand, Fleet Street, Shoreditch, Bethnal Green Road and Old Ford Road. According to Dave Widgery,

> At 2 a.m. on the night before the demonstration, a group of RAR stalwarts including Tasmanian journalist Philip Brooks and the New York poet and club doorman Haowi Montag, who inhabited a labyrinthine eighth-floor squat on Charing Cross Road, began to hear crowds chanting through the downpour. And by 6 a.m. the following morning there were already 10,000 people in Trafalgar Square.[3]

The organizers deliberately avoided placing the carnival in London's Hyde Park, the traditional destination of such protests, choosing instead Victoria Park, which was situated between Hackney and London's East End. The march went close to Brick Lane, scene of many conflicts between left and right, and the main centre for Asians living in the East End. The area also had a resonance with the anti-fascism of the 1930s and especially the famous 1936 Battle of Cable Street, when Mosley's blackshirts had been prevented from marching. The National Front's John Tyndall had recently announced that he planned to stand in South Hackney, a constituency that included the park. On the day, left-wing Labour MP Ian Mikardo explained why Victoria Park had been chosen. 'In the East End, fascists have done their traditional work of dividing one group of workers from another group of workers. There are too many people in the labour movement who believe if you leave it, it will go away.' David R was a young socialist in Leeds: 'The first [carnival] was brilliant, but the most exciting bit was the march to Victoria Park where we were reclaiming the streets of the East End, which had been swamped by fascists at an earlier demo organized by local anti-fascist groups.'

Mike from the Anti-Nazi League office recalls some of the planning discussions: 'Roger Huddle from RAR came into the office to argue with Paul that there needed to be a bigger, higher stage for the carnival – thank Christ they did – they understood the need for security, which none of us did.' Roger Huddle himself would be stage manager on the day: 'The first band started, and the crowd rushed the stage. Four people passed out. We took them round the back, and just fortunately they came to. We were so naive, we didn't have security, we didn't have ambulances.'

A special issue of *Temporary Hoarding* was produced – an A1 sheet folded three times to A4 size. Inside was a giant poster of the main acts of the day, Steel Pulse, Poly Styrene, Tom Robinson, replete with anti-National Front quotes, including one from Mick Jones of the Clash, 'I'm half Jewish so I suppose the NF will try to send half of me back to Lithuania.' Another large poster asked, 'How did race hate happen?': 'when vote KKKatcher Thatcher makes speeches about the "threat" of alien culture; when Labour MPs sign a parliamentary report which recommends identity cards for all black citizens; when a Ku Klux Klan gang leader can shoot his mouth off on TV – race hatred becomes respectable. Don't let's be fooled. Race hate divides us when we most need to stand together – against the real enemy.'[4]

The march was led off by giant papier-mâché models of Martin Webster and Adolf Hitler built by Peter Fluck and Roger Law, the people who would later make *Spitting Image*, while the Tower Hamlets Arts Project provided clowns, stilt-men and street theatre. There were dozens of banners, ranging from old-style trade union signs that took four people to carry, to home made spray-painted sheets: 'Karen, Kate, Anna and Jill Against Racism, Fascism, Sexism.' There was a steel band, and thousands of people carried the Anti-Nazi League's distinctive yellow lollipop placards. 'They were so different from the usual placards you would see on demos,' remembers Geoff from Manchester. 'At the first carnival we were giving lollipops away; by July you could sell them.' Alongside the ANL lollipops were many more conventional *Socialist Worker* placards, blocks of text in Helvetica, against a background of green and purple swirls, 'Stop the Nazis, No Immigration Controls.'[5]

The march was due to set off at 1 p.m., but long before then Trafalgar Square was full, and the marchers set off under their own steam. Mike from the ANL had been given the job of making sure that the giant puppets of Tyndall and Webster were at the front of the march. 'We had to run through the crowd, to try and get the heads and get them out, and we were the organizers . . . There was an enormous degree of spontaneity.'

Einde had arranged to meet friends between the Strand and Trafalgar Square.

When we got there it seemed that tens of thousands of other people had also arranged to meet at the same corner. Eventually enough of us found each other and we unfurled our banner along with the thousands of other banners . . . We looked like a bunch of hippie desperados, to be quite honest – how could we wear such dreadful clothes? It was a glorious day and despite the long walk to Victoria Park I wouldn't have missed it, one of the most enjoyable demonstrations I ever attended and the music was great, too.

According to the report in the next Monday's *Guardian*, 'Police spokesmen said they were "astonished" at the size of the event. The tail of the march had still not left Trafalgar Square as the front reached journey's end at Victoria Park.[6]

'Outside a couple of pubs near Brick Lane', according to Dave Widgery's history *Beating Time*,

> there were a few Fronters with their mates, the sort of beer-gut and Page Three brigade who have an *I love virgins* sticker in the back of their off-brown resprayed Rover saloon and two kids whom they hit. They had come for a good laugh at the do-gooders. Three hours and 100,000 demonstrators later, the smiles were well and truly wiped off their faces and their bloated egos had evaporated into the swill at the bottom of their glasses.[7]

Peter Hain watched the crowd as it reached the park. 'I remember the whistles, everyone in the crowd had whistles, also the ANL lollipops, they were new. It gave me a bubbly feeling that I had last experienced eight years previously on the Stop the Seventy campaign.'

Red Saunders compèred, wearing a cap covered in Rock Against Racism badges and a 'Mr Oligarchies' cape, an outfit from one of the Kartoon Klowns' plays:

> The first carnival took place just a day or two after my daughter was born, and I was horrified that my beloved Nina wouldn't be able to make it. The equality of the sexes, wasn't that what we were supposed to believe in? Laurie Flynn, to his credit, made sure that all that day, whenever Nina wanted anything or needed anything, there was always someone from the SWP on hand to help her.
>
> By 8 a.m., I was waiting in Trafalgar Square, absolutely pissing myself. I'd been up half the night with the baby. Syd and Ruth had been staying at some squat, and they were absolutely stoned. I was worried about the weather – would it rain? I went for a bacon butty. By the time I came back, I saw the first coaches arrive, and disembarking these dusty-eyed punks. Where are you from, mate? Liverpool. It would be big, then, I knew! We had 10,000 whistles we gave out free, thanks to Tom Robinson. We had the papier mâché models of Tyndall and Webster – we stuck them by the lions at the bottom end of Trafalgar Square. The weather was lifting. By the time people were sitting off, it had lifted.
>
> At Victoria Park, we had the stage. It was very amateur compared to the ones you see these days – put up by a whole bunch of comrades

working through the evening. Paul Holborow and I drove down to the park in a white transit van. There was Jerry Fitzpatrick, still finishing the stage. You could see big Rastas chatting to very straight St John's ambulance men, all sorts of dialogues.

The park began to fill up. I ran on, and the first thing I shouted was 'This isn't Woodstock. It's the Rock Against Racism carnival!' and there was this huge cheer!

The Clash, Tom Robinson and X-Ray Spex played to an audience of at least 80,000 people. Pink Floyd loaned their PA to the organizers. The Clash agreed to play, despite their manager's protests. 'They can do it,' Bernie Rhodes said, 'if you let them buy a tank for Zimbabwe.' Publicity for the carnival put Aswad as the headline act, and Tom Robinson second. The Clash felt that they should have been given the best slot. But Robinson was higher in the charts. According to Roger Huddle of Rock Against Racism, 'The Clash threw a wobbly and refused to stop playing when their time was up. Red Saunders had to pull their wires.'

The carnival's platform included Peter Hain, Miriam Karlin, Vishnu Sharma of the Indian Workers' Association, and Ray Buckton, general secretary of the rail union ASLEF and a member of the TUC General Council. Another trade union leader, Ernie Roberts, remarked, 'None of the speakers could have addressed a crowd quite like this before. Dressed in an assorted garb of leather and satin, with hair of green or purple or pink, the teenagers gave them an enthusiastic welcome.' Tariq Ali told the *New Musical Express*, 'Lots of people will come for Rock Against Racism today and see that it should be Rock Against the Stock Exchange tomorrow.'

X-Ray Spex took the stage at 1.30, and were followed by the Clash and then Steel Pulse. Tom Robinson played his song 'Winter of '79', predicting the news if complacency got its way and the National Front was allowed to prosper, 'All the gay geezers were put inside / the coloured folks were getting crucified / a few fought back and a few folk died / in the winter of '79.' The threat of fascism was urgent, Robinson warned, 'but now they've got no chance'. The last song brought each of the bands back on stage, for a one-off Tom Robinson number, 'We Have Got to Get It Together'. The carnival was the lead story on that evening's ten o'clock news.[8]

John from south-east London had been arrested at the anti-fascist protests at Lewisham and sentenced to three months in jail. He was still in prison when he heard of the numbers attending the carnival:

> As the news came through of the numbers assembling in Victoria Park, our wildest expectations were exceeded. Ten thousand, then twenty, then thirty, then forty thousand. Earlier one of the fascist screws had jeered through the cell door, 'Where's your nigger friends now then, Johnny?' Now he was quiet. The other cons on the wing didn't support my ideas but they knew that something was happening against the system that

crippled their lives. Radios were our contact with the real world. Everyone was listening and with every new announcement they cheered. As the final numbers came through, we were told that 100,000 people, black and white, had marched from Trafalgar Square to east London. All the cons on my wing, many of them racist, cheered and banged on the pipes. It's a memory I will take to my grave.

Gavin Weightman described the carnival in *New Society*: 'There was something unreal about the sudden flowering in London of all the yellow and red anti-nazi propaganda – as if CND, lying dormant all these years, had bloomed again in different clothes and different colours.'[9] Richard from Football Fans Against the Nazis was 'flabbergasted' by the size of the event: 'We expected 10 or 20,000 people, which would have been excellent, a big rise in the numbers who came on the marches and the demos. But on the day there were tens of thousands of people there.' John S from south London was also 'utterly amazed at how big it was. No-one expected it to be so big.' Alex Callinicos of the Socialist Workers Party drew an upbeat conclusion, 'The Anti-Nazi League is more than just a campaign – it is a mass movement.' The historian Raphael Samuel, a member of the Communist Party from his early youth, described Victoria Park as 'the most working-class demonstration I have been on, and one of the very few of my adult lifetime to have sensibly changed the climate of public opinion.'[10]

According to Rock Against Racism's Sharon Spike,

> What was amazing was all the different people enjoying it; skinheads, punks, teds, Rastas, some old hippies, Greasers, disco-kids ands loads of middle-aged people and all. There were quite a few dogs. There was such a big turn-out that people at the back felt it hard to hear what the bands on stage were singing. But it didn't matter too much because it was all so interesting just to walk around. It is very hard to describe what it felt like. Not Love and Peace and all that rubbish. It was more than music. Feeling all together. Not being scared of one another. Making you feel strong in a good way.[11]

Socialist Worker was no less ecstatic:

> At dawn on Sunday in Victoria Park, the Anti-Nazi League and Rock Against Racism put the final touches to all their hard work. A young park-keeper watching the stage and tents and stalls going up said, 'We're expecting five thousand, but we're ready for ten.' And more came. Fifty thousand stretched from Trafalgar Square to Hackney. The kids had joined the march . . . Eighty thousand thronged the park, celebrating the rise against the fascists. 'We're black, we're white, we're dynamite', they sang. They stood in the sun together. Eighty thousand. No trouble. Magic. The next day the National Front held a walk through London's East End. Nearly two hundred attended. It was secret. It rained all the way. Even God has joined the Anti-Nazi League.[12]

Pop or politics?

Describing the carnival for the *Leveller* magazine, Ian Walker contrasted Rock Against Racism to the one-dimensional socialism of the left sects.

Some people are never satisfied. 'No politics at Carnival' was the puke-making headline in *Newsline*, daily organ of the Workers' Revolutionary Party. Where were they looking for the politics? If they didn't see it in any of the bands or the 80,000 people, they could have tried looking in one of the dustbins where leaflets distributed by the Workers' Socialist League [WSL] were there for takers. This leaflet denounced the Anti-Nazi League, denounced Peter Hain (who's he anyway?) and denounced the petty bourgeois reformism which had diseased the enterprise. The WSL issued a call for 'workers' defence squads' to replace the ANL. To be organised by who? The massed ranks of the WSL? Wakey, wakey.

Walker's article explains why punks loved the carnival. This time, they were in charge of the movement. Control was given right into the hands of the newest and most excited of activists. 'Victoria Park', he called his piece, 'what did you do there? We got high. We touched the sky.'[13]

Dave Widgery, Roger Huddle and others argued in a letter to the Socialist Workers Party's new monthly magazine, *Socialist Review*, that the magazine's coverage was inadequate. 'Atrocious articles on Carnival. Mr Calico Nickers wants to harness and channel the energy of "Youth" who have ten times more idea of what's going down than your pretty average Marxist Editor . . . Working class kids NOW are political and fun without having to make five minute speeches to prove it.'[14] 'Calico Nickers' was the *Review*'s editor, Alex Callinicos. The fact of the letter's publication suggests a certain willingness to tolerate divergent views.

The presence of creative Marxists like Huddle and Widgery was one factor that ensured the independence of Rock Against Racism, but the more 'orthodox' members of the Socialist Workers Party had strong points as well. What use were all the bands, without a movement putting up the posters and booking coaches? Who was supposed to sign up the activists, or would music alone do the trick? Without challenging the rank-and-file members of the Anti-Nazi League, and winning them to a more developed left-wing politics, how could any lasting movement be built?

In contrast to the activists from Rock Against Racism, other participants disagree that the success of anti-fascism could be put down to new art forms and punk language. John S believes that the success of the Anti-Nazi League was based on a simple message of united working-class action. 'Older trade unionists also played a part. That didn't have anything to do with alternative forms of communication – it was because the ANL was a United Front.'[15] Ronnie from Merseyside remembers a strong local League group, but not much of an independent Rock Against Racism presence:

> I can't remember a local RAR group as such and most things were really ANL organized. Even Merseyside Anti-Racist Alliance would have been a non-starter without the people who were members of the ANL too. We did the leg work, leafleting etc., but they had the names, David Shephard, Gideon Ben Tovim . . . In Liverpool at least, the ANL was an entity, whereas RAR was a badge a lot of us wore.

A similar idea was expressed in an article by Pat Stack, which appeared in *Socialist Worker Review* in 1986. Reviewing Dave Widgery's book, *Beating Time*, Stack complained that its author had exaggerated the success of Rock Against Racism:

> The first thing that struck me about the book was that the style of design and layout was dated, photographs thrown around the pages in chaotic style. A style, which like the fanzine, belongs now to another era . . . For most of those active at the time there is little doubt that the ANL was key to the growth of RAR yet Widgery tends to put things the other way around.[16]

When Ian Birchall considered Dave Widgery's *Beating Time* for the SWP's *International Socialism Journal*, he attempted to draw a middle line between Widgery, with his enthusiasm for a primarily cultural leftism, and the opposite view, which denied the same importance to art. Although Joe Strummer and Elvis Costello did pull the crowds to the Rock Against Racism carnivals, Birchall argued, the radical music was really a temporary consequence of the music industry's continuous desire for innovation. Punk music could build a movement, but did not provide a firm basis for any lasting process of politicization.

Pete Alexander remembers the process in similar terms. He argues that the Anti-Nazi League gave Rock Against Racism quite a boost.

> I suspect that in most localities, organizing a Rock Against Racism gig was seen as part of the Anti-Nazi League activity. However, in many localities the Socialist Workers Party built the ANL with contacts, experience and confidence gained from preceding Rock Against Racism work. With the carnivals, whilst RAR's contacts were key to getting the bands and the support of the music press, and Red [Saunders] did a terrific job as the lead man, the marches, political speeches and most of the mobilization was to down to the Anti-Nazi League (and the SWP).

Even in 1977, there was a tendency among the RAR activists to argue that the success of the Anti-Nazi League depended on their own cultural intervention. But outside London, it was the members of the ANL and often the SWP whose presence was far more obvious on the ground. Surely the real lesson of the movement was not the innate advantage of radical culture over a radical mass movement, but the possibilities that can open up when politics and creativity are combined.

Whose movement?

It is also useful to ask why the movement chose to call its largest events *carnivals*. The name conjures up ideas of music, alcohol, circus. It suggests the rough music of peasant societies, when men dress up as women, and the rich are humbled . . . but just for a day. In Britain by the 1970s, 'carnival' had become a 'black' word. *Race Today* wrote that in the West Indies,

> The Carnival festival is peculiarly Trinidadian, held annually on the Monday and Tuesday immediately preceding Lent . . . On the two days, small groups and individuals would disguise themselves and parade through the streets, mimicking their masters. The symbols of the event were the Calypsonian, the radical poet whose words would provide the event with its radical edge, and the steel band that accompanied them.[17]

The use of the word 'carnival' raises old questions about the relationship between black and white in RAR and the ANL.

In Britain, 'carnival' was associated with Notting Hill, an event that was still portrayed by the press as a dangerous occasion on the fringes of forbidden London. Claudia Jones had founded the Notting Hill Carnival. Her biographer Marika Sherwood describes the carnival as a successful challenge by black British people against white values. 'The black people who came to Britain have simply refused to be cowed into the kind of social and residential ghettos that have resulted from living beside white racist hostility in so many other societies.'[18]

Was the Anti-Nazi League replicating the ways in which white society has learned from black people, taking their ideas and taming them? This potential criticism is important because there was at times a division in the movement between black and white, as Ronnie from Merseyside argues: 'If I have any feeling of disappointment at all, it's that there were not more black people involved in the Anti-Nazi League. I don't know why we didn't appeal to them any more than why revolutionary groups still don't. I think there are lessons to be learned about this whatever socialist position we adopt.'

In Tariq Mehmood's novel, *Hand on the Sun*, this gap between black and white socialists is symbolized by the character of Hussain, a young Asian in Bradford who joins the International Socialists. Over time, Hussain finds the discussions patronising. He believes that while the socialists try hard to recruit Asians, they don't put in the same amount of time as with white youth. Hussain's politics begin to feel to him like slogans. He identifies more with his Asian mates than with the white left. Hussain's frustrations are brought out in friendship with another youngster, Jalib, who has none of his political knowledge, but seems to respond more freely to events. 'Whenever Hussain talked to people, he always talked about politics and about struggles that were taking place in various parts of the world. He felt that Jalib, unlike himself, did not gloss over the reality of black people's lives with empty phrases.' In the novel, a breakaway group is established for Asian socialists, 'Somage', and Hussain joins that instead.[19] This incident is hardly fictional. In 1976, there was a small split from the IS and it published a paper titled *Samaj in Babylon*. This fell apart by 1977. At least some of its members returned to the Socialist Workers Party. Meanwhile, Mehmood was himself a member of the local Asian Youth Movement, a group with links in some areas to the IWAs and in others to the Marxist left, but which evolved politically, reappearing in various guises through this period.

In racist myth, all black or Asian people think the same. In lived history, different people could draw all manner of conclusions from the same events. Tony Bogues argues that events at Lewisham were shaped by the history of black south London. 'The fascists were taking up race, using it against black people.' But for a long time, he insists, there was very little collective response. 'Blacks and Asians didn't always experience racism in the same ways. It was the Asian community that often took the worst beating. There was a feeling that they were prone to be meek. Nobody would attack the black community.' In different hands, such arguments could represent confidence or bluster, apathy or some mixture of all them combined. So racism's victims were not 'naturally' anti-fascist: their politics were shaped by arguments within and between political groups, within and between friends, their sense of whether resistance was possible, their feelings also about whether white anti-racists were taking rebellion far enough.

Even within the second generation, some people joined or sided with the political left, while others moved towards ideas influenced by black separatism. Even among the community organizations, there were differences between the people looking for careers and those looking to fight. Balwinder Rana, the chief steward at Southall, knew Tariq Mehmood, but his politics were evolving in the opposite direction. He argues that the League's strategy of black and white unity was the best way to win real gains for Asian workers. His proof is in the invisibility in the years after 1981 of those community activists who had spoken in 1977 or 1978 of the need for black unity.

> There was a lot of bullshit talked by the black nationalist leaders thrown up in the struggle. Almost every one of them became a full-time official in some campaign. They had no conception of solidarity, of class struggle. In struggle, all the [nationalist] ideas are useless. If you're in a trade union situation, you strike together. They were bought off very quickly. Following the riots in 1981, that was the idea – buy them off, give the people grants. They all disappeared.

But Balwinder Rana also acknowledges the frustrations that made black nationalist politics feel relevant to many people at this time. 'Where they came from was the lack of struggle within the working class. There were

groups like the SWP trying to fight, but most of the labour movement ignored racism and fascism. People felt they had to do something
themselves. If the trade union movement had been in the forefront, it
would have been much easier.'

There was a black political milieu in which all sorts of ideas, back to
Africa, anti-racism, socialism and black separatism mixed and fused. The
most sustained critique of the Anti-Nazi League from an anti-racist perspective can be found in Paul Gilroy's book, *There Ain't No Black in the
Union Jack*. Gilroy maintains that the ANL was a retreat from the earlier
politics of Rock Against Racism. For Gilroy, RAR was a transgressive
space, which took the radical ideas of reggae and taught them to white
punks, who responded by mocking the Union Jack and royalty. The ANL,
by contrast, capitulated to traditions of English nationalism. In labelling
the National Front as 'Nazis', it effectively portrayed them as foreigners,
suggesting that racism could be removed by a return to the wartime traditions of British conservatism. 'The ANL deliberately sought to summon
and manipulate a form of nationalism and patriotism as part of its broad
anti-fascist drive . . . This may have led to the electoral defeat of the NF,
British Movement and their allies', but the League's victory 'was
achieved ironically by reviving the very elements of nationalism and xe-
nophobia which had seen Britannia through the darkest hours of the
Second World War.'[20]

Few anti-racists from the time agree. John from south London insists
that the very purpose of the Anti-Nazi League was to oppose racism. 'I
don't think that it did give in to nationalism. Fascism was regarded as
British fascism. The National Front had the Union Jack; we didn't try to
appropriate it. That wasn't part of it at all.' Another activist, Ian, concurs:
'I'm sure if you go through the files carefully enough, you may find bits
of Anti-Nazi League propaganda that do use a nationalistic rhetoric that I
wouldn't be wildly happy with, but in general that isn't the case. By focusing on the Nazis, the ANL showed people the logic of racism, and
raised the general question of racism.'

Indeed, it is hard to find *any* evidence to back up some of Paul Gilroy's
claims. His distinction between Rock Against Racism and the Anti-Nazi
League makes no sense to Roger Huddle or Red Saunders, prominent
members of RAR, who also worked closely with the League. According to
Roger Huddle, 'The argument wasn't about the war; it was about what fascism was. We had to show that the NF stood for the camps, the swastika,
the death camps for the Jews and the Roma.' Gilroy's argument 'doesn't
touch any chord with me', Saunders argues. 'From the midst of Lewisham I
could see that the nationalism was the police and the NF. They were all
white. They looked like the underbelly of a dead fish. Lewisham was about
black and white together. On the day, I saw every youth gang in London;
they knew that the nationalism was all on the other side.'

Gilroy's assertion is that the Anti-Nazi League relied on a mythology
of the Second World War, 'Britain's darkest hour', but such language is

almost entirely absent from any of the ANL's publications. The references in League material to the heroes of the Second World War, the positive descriptions of 'Britannia', simply are not there. There were other groups that sometimes used this imagery – including sometimes the Communist Party – but not the ANL. The League did use Nazi Germany as a negative example of why fascism should be fought (invoking the memory of the Holocaust as an example of what might happen if fascism were ignored), but these anti-fascists never claimed that the best alternative to the National Front was a return to Britain's wartime spirit.

How successful was the Anti-Nazi League in fighting institutional racism? Paul Gilroy is surely correct to argue that racism was about more than the bonehead followers of the National Front. What is more questionable is his suggestion that anti-fascists ignored the broader issues. For many young black and Asian people living in Britain, the ANL stood as a key part of a bigger movement against racism. It is no coincidence that this period also witnessed the formation of a number of black and Asian organizations, including the Southall Youth Movement, the Anti-Racist Committee of Asians in East London, the Action Committee Against Racial Attacks, and the Bradford-based United Black Youth League. Nor is it accidental that one of the high points of black (and white) struggle against the police came in 1981, after the ANL had pushed the most important carrier of open white racism into retreat.

Avtar Jouhl, general secretary of one of the three national Indian Workers' Associations, was asked whether his members should join the Anti-Nazi League. 'Yes, certainly!' he replied. 'We are living in the UK, and the Nazis are here. Therefore we should be shoulder to shoulder with the white people. Indeed, in my opinion we should be in the forefront . . . The ANL has made a tremendous contribution by highlighting the influence of the Nazis and effectively checking their advance on the streets and in the elections.'[21]

The Anti-Nazi League sponsored the Campaign Against Racist Laws. Part of the energy of the campaign came from anti-deportation campaigns in Bradford and west Yorkshire. For ANL activists it was a chance to raise the question of Britain's immigration laws. Several leading members of the League joined CARL's executive committee, and there were attempts to build a different sort of anti-racist movement, opposed not just to fascism, but to institutional racism as well. Jerry Fitzpatrick of the ANL was the treasurer of the Campaign Against Racist Laws and Dave Cook from the Communist Party was national secretary (Pete Alexander took over from Fitzpatrick in summer 1980). There were joint chairs, one from each of the big Indian Workers' Associations: Avtar Jouhl and Prem Singh. 'The success of the ANL', insists Alexander, 'enabled us to be more effective in mobilizing against state racism.'

Following the New Cross murders, when 14 party-goers were burned to death in a fire, with the police taking almost no action to catch the culprits, the ANL and CARL supported a black People's Day of Action, called for 2 March 1981. In Linton Kwesi Johnson's words, 'di whole a black Britn did rack wid rage', and 20,000 people joined the protests. It was one of the largest, blackest marches Britain had seen.[22]

John was a young Asian teenager, then living with his family in a predominantly white area in Eltham. Through the 1970s, John recalls, he was routinely attacked at school, called names and beaten. The growth of the National Front encouraged an atmosphere of hatred. 'The day after one of their broadcasts, I decided to bicycle to school. Even then I could hear them calling me names.' Other forces also contributed to the climate of fear. 'I remember the day of the Jubilee, with all the flags. The more flags I saw, the more my heart sank.' John remembers hearing about Lewisham on the news: 'It was the first time we heard of people fighting back.' He later became an active supporter of the Anti-Nazi League, and attended concerts on Rock Against Racism's Militant Entertainment tour. 'I didn't understand it all at the time, but we needed something and something happened.' For this teenage activist, the ANL was a success because it demoralized the hard core of active racists. 'Things were still nasty in Eltham in the 1980s, but my family and other Asian people, we felt more confident.'

Robin Denselow suggests that the anti-National Front campaign legitimized black culture in the eyes of the white audience. He cites Red Saunders, the man who founded RAR: 'Black music, black style, began to influence whites. The massive influence of black music culture on the last two generations has yet to be placed in history.' Aswad's Drummie Zeb concurs: 'RAR was the starting point. The sound and rhythm of reggae and dub is taken for granted now.'[23]

Balwinder Rana argues that anti-fascists raised the confidence of black and Asian people in Britain. The campaign was 'the first time I could remember when Asians came out in large numbers to fight racism and fascism. There was a perception people had of Asians as very quiet, peaceful people. But the ANL sent a message to white racists that we weren't a pushover. It changed people's perceptions.' Dub poet Linton Kwesi Johnson is more guarded: 'the mix of punk and reggae would have happened anyway because the kids grew up together. Black kids would have found an affinity with punk because it's anti-establishment.'[24]

Michael Riley of Steel Pulse complained that whites didn't always understand the differences. 'Many punks don't really know what we're on about, although they come along and claim that they're oppressed like us. With punk bands it's often Mum who bought the equipment, but that can't happen with black bands because Mum is broke too.'[25] Yet other musicians were more favourable. Brinsley Forder of Aswad remembers that 'Before RAR, a lot of white people would be terrified to go to a reggae show. And it was a platform for saying things that wouldn't have been said. It was the start of more bands being politically aware.'[26] Most black people knew they needed allies. Most black musicians and activists welcomed the support. Indeed, as late as 1982 Red Saunders of Rock

Against Racism was able to get a sense of how wide the ripples had gone. Having travelled to Bob Marley's old studio in Kingston, Jamaica, Saunders was shown around by Marley's backing singers, the I-Threes. A copy of RAR's launch statement was mounted on the wall.[27]

From December 1976, Don Letts was the disk jockey at London's Roxy Club. He recalls a healthy dub–punk alliance.

We became closer by revelling in our differences, not by trying to be the same. They dug the bass lines, beats and attitudes of the tunes I played, not to mention the ready rolled spliffs you could buy at the bar (the punks couldn't roll their own). I remember a punk asking the dread behind the bar for two beers and one spliff, but after a moment's thought changed his order to two spliffs and one beer. We're talking serious cultural exchange.[28]

Meanwhile Jake Burns of Stiff Little Fingers also has an upbeat memory of the campaign.

I think that the fact that a number of fairly high-profile bands took the time to stand up and say 'this is wrong' at least made people stop to ask themselves whether they thought it was or not, rather than simply accepting it as a fact of life. I think it highlighted a concern that a large number of people in the country had, that institutionalized racism of the kind portrayed as entertainment in TV programmes such as *Love Thy Neighbour* was simply not acceptable. In short, I think it gave the 'silent majority' a voice.

It's also important not to treat white people as if they were all the same. Mike from the ANL office recalls an incident at one protest.

There was one guy Johnny. He and his brother Jimmy came from a family of dockworkers and were active in anti-fascist circles. They were tough: Jimmy was a lightweight boxer. One day, there was an anti-fascist march through Hackney. Johnny came on the demo. The NF had some counter-demo. There was a skinhead watching him, all the time, and the skinhead had his face half covered in bandages. Finally the skinhead shouts, 'It's you!' 'You race traitor!' Johnny didn't shout back the obvious retort 'class traitor', which wouldn't have bothered the skinhead. Instead, he starts pulling his arms out and back, as if he was wearing braces. What he meant was 'Me? A race traitor? No. I'm Irish.' That was important. The Nazi could only think in terms of race, and Jimmy turned it on its head. By then it felt like we had the measure of the fascists, politically and on the streets.

While the absence of black or Asian faces would have been a valid criticism of the League, some caution is required. Fighting racism meant challenging the ideas in white heads. Racism was a white disease, and needed to be fought there. The longer the campaign continued, meanwhile, the blacker it became. The 1978 Manchester carnival and the 1981 Leeds carnival were the most diverse events either city had seen.

Nazi funk

One of the clearest signs of the success of the anti-fascist campaign was the increasing publicity given to it in the National Front's press. The verbal attacks on anti-fascists began at around the same time as Lewisham, swelling in aggression. The September 1977 issue of *Spearhead*, the NF's 'theoretical' publication, claimed that the Socialist Workers Party was an entirely 'alien' (meaning Jewish) organization, set up as a giant conspiracy against the whole British people. Featuring prominent photographs of Tony Cliff and his wife, as well as Steve Jeffreys of the SWP Central Committee and Paul Holborow, *Spearhead* continued, 'The reader will immediately notice not only the psychopathic stare of the eyes which characterises warped personalities in rebellion against society, but their distinctly alien features'. The same issue also contained much bluffing on events at Lewisham. 'It was hoped that the threats of violence from the ultra-Left groups connected with ALCARAF, such as the SWP and the IMG, would either intimidate the NF into calling off its march, or intimidate the Police into exercising their powers under the Public Order Act into banning the NF march in the interests of avoiding a riot.' *Spearhead* claimed that the mere holding of an NF demonstration was a victory, no matter the breaking up of the march on the day.[29]

In May 1978, *Bulldog*, the National Front's youth paper, explained to its readers that 'the reason why the communists hate anyone who loves Britain, including the National Front, is simply because they are essentially NOT British'. In November 1978, the paper reported that 'a mere 500 degenerates' attended a carnival in Harwich. The organizers of the event claimed four times as many. Whichever figure was right, it was still the biggest political event the town had ever seen! In the same month, a *Spearhead* article reported one NF member's attempts to infiltrate the local Anti-Nazi League. In winter 1978, the NF also published its fullest statement of contempt, a full pamphlet dedicated to *Lifting the Lid off the 'Anti-Nazi League'*.[30]

At about the same time, *National Front News* was also forced to report a series of bombings against left-wing targets, including an SWP bus driver and a milkman in High Wycombe, the Communist Party headquarters in King Street, the offices of the local government trade union NUPE and Housman's bookshop. *National Front News* claimed that the victims had planted the bombs themselves, in order to secure a ban on the NF before the pending election.[31] 'Labour created the Anti-Nazi League', the NF claimed, 'for the sole purpose of destroying the National Front'. But the League had failed. As proof, *National Front News* cited the fact that the general election had been delayed from autumn 1978 to spring 1979. The paper used this 'fact' to claim that both the ANL and Labour were running scared of the NF.[32] On the ground, however, the mood was rather different.

Carnival Two

'The decision to run the first carnival', recalls Paul Holborow,

> really took us to entirely different heights. The size, the imagination, the audacity, we got people to march five miles! RAR had booked a 2-foot-high platform through the GLC. It was only four days before the event that we realized this would be completely inadequate. The contrast between our little office in Newport Street, and the 80 coaches from Manchester: once the carnival had delivered, that was it. We had to have new phone lines put in. It became a completely all-absorbing campaign. I would think nothing of starting a day at the office at 9 a.m., working till lunchtime, taking a train up to Glasgow for a major speech, sleeping on the night train back, and then being in the office by 9 in the morning again the next day.

This first carnival was followed by local carnivals in many areas. Thirty-five thousand came to a Manchester Carnival, 5,000 attended the next in Cardiff, 8,000 came to Edinburgh, 2,000 to Harwich and 5,000 to the carnival in Southampton. It was also in the aftermath of the first carnival that the Communist Party finally gave its official support to the Anti-Nazi League, hushing in retrospect its earlier criticism of the Socialist Workers Party's tactics at Lewisham.[33]

The May local elections were a considerable setback for the National Front, which secured disappointing votes in areas of previous strength, including Bradford and east London. The NF lashed out. A Bangladeshi garment worker, Altab Ali, was murdered on his way home. On 14 May 1978, following the murder, around 6,000 young Bengalis took part in a protest against racism in Brick Lane. It was the biggest Asian demonstration in British history. Older men brought macs and umbrellas; the younger activists created makeshift headgear from the round ANL lollipops to cover them from the rain. Placards asked, 'How many more racial attacks? Why are the police covering up?' Askan, one of the march organizers, was interviewed by Rock Against Racism's Dave Widgery: 'These racial attacks, they are getting worse all the time. Worse since National Front on the scene. Worse still since Mrs Thatcher. We're not getting co-operation with the police. Mr Callaghan and his colleagues, do they realise what is happening all the time to our people?'

Working as a doctor in the area, Widgery observed countless examples of petty racism – an elderly Asian porter sacked for looking ill, a Bangladeshi woman sectioned in the seventh month of pregnancy, a white trade unionist driven to insomnia by window bashing, after he defended his Asian neighbour. For Widgery, the death of Altab Ali threw 'into harsh relief the general level of racial violence in the East End, the indifference of the police and the prejudices of the non-Asians'.[34]

On 11 June, following a series of tabloid stories announcing that the

GLC planned to move Bengalis to housing 'ghettos' in east London, some 200 National Front supporters went on the rampage, attacking people and shops along Brick Lane. The following Sunday, 4,000 anti-racists marched again through the East End. John S was then a college lecturer in south London. They were the first demonstrations on which he had seen so many Sikhs: 'It was so different from the meek image of law-abiding Asians.' Tassaduq Ahmed, an educational worker in the East End, also commented on the growing self-organization among young Bengalis living around Brick Lane:

> The bare facts of assaults and killing of Asians in the East End by the National Front's bully boys are known; what is not being sufficiently stressed is the strong multi-racial response that these acts have evoked, in particular among the Bengali youth, who have joined enthusiastically with their white friends in combating a menace which in its ultimate form will spell the death knell of a democratic Britain.[35]

On 7 July, David Lane, chair of the Commission for Racial Equality, paid his first visit to Brick Lane, receiving considerable publicity. A series of demonstrations in August culminated in a 5,000-strong march to remove the National Front presence permanently from the area. White and Asian activists worked together to occupy the street each Saturday and guard it from the NF. Jerry Fizpatrick's memories of this time are vivid:

> Brick Lane was a serious example of how the Front were providing their supporters with a public focus, to organize racist attacks, and as a rallying point for their members. We tried to respond. I remember waking up every Sunday morning, getting ready to go down to Brick Lane. It was skirmishing on skirmishing. But the fact that we were protesting against the Nazis, I know that gave confidence to the Bangladeshi youth. They became more cohesive, you could see it.

The Manchester carnival took place on 15 July 1978. The following day saw a giant protest of black, white and Asian people, demonstrating against the Nazi Front, who had previously been able to sell their newspaper on London's Brick Lane. *Socialist Worker* spoke of 'a barrier of men and women against the Nazis who peddle their poison in the street market every week'. The same weekend saw the ANL carnival in Cardiff, and a large Anti-Nazi contingent at the Durham Miners' Gala.[36]

A second national Rock Against Racism carnival took place in Brockwell Park on 24 September 1978, with Sham 69 headlining. 'The second carnival', Paul Holborow explains, 'was booked for when we thought would be slap bang in the middle of the election.' Alongside Sham 69, other bands, including Crisis, Charge, Eclipse, Inganda, RAS, the Derelicts, the Enchanters, the Members, the Ruts and the Straights, played from floats along the course of the march. It was a huge event, even larger than the first carnival, with 100,000 involved. Joe Garman, chair of NORMANCAR, the North Manchester Campaign Against Racism, described the day in vivid terms:

> The music blared, slogans were shouted, some old some new. I liked 'One, two, three and a bit, the National Front is a load of shit.' The 'Queen' waved to us, all dressed up as she sat on the throne perched on the top of a bay window. There were lots of kids, some in pushchairs, some perched on dad's shoulders. There was a Notts collier in pit clothes, his enemy was the National Front even tho' his 'blackness' washed off.

At the end of the march from Hyde Park to Brockwell Park, Garman described his aching feet – 'yet another reason for hating the Nazis'.[37]

For many of those who took part, this carnival was every bit as exciting and jubilant as the first. But the success of events in Brockwell Park was partly clouded by news of a National Front mobilization in east London. This was the story that captured the interest of the press.

Called only after the carnival had been publicly announced, the National Front march was simply intended to embarrass the organizers of the anti-fascist event. Within the Socialist Workers Party, people were warning Paul Holborow and others to make sure that the NF was prevented from marching. 'For weeks before,' Andy recalls, 'lots of us were trying to make sure that Brick Lane was covered. The ANL wanted to keep an eye on just one thing, the carnival. They didn't think we could spare people, but we could.' Jerry Fitzpatrick disagrees:

> I felt that the success of the march depended on us going through Brixton. That was more important than any stunt the NF pulled. Even if we had sent more numbers to Brick Lane, it couldn't have been enough. The police always had it covered. The Front were contained. We were always going to be contained, which is in fact what happened. We had to keep our eyes on the prize, on the carnival.

Some on the left insisted that the entire carnival should be called off, and that the vast numbers of people present should be sent instead to chase the 250 fascists marching through the East End. Members of the Spartacist League told carnival-goers that they were 'SCABBING on the struggle'. Although there would not have been any point in sending the whole crowd against a small National Front march, certain numbers did need to be sent. The leadership of the Anti-Nazi League were caught in a dilemma. How would they know that enough people had been sent? And what could be done if the numbers were too low? On the day, confusion grew, and Paul Holborow, the national organiser of the ANL, admits that the leadership simply failed to send enough people to stop the NF demo. 'We collectively bungled it.'[38]

Two hundred and fifty National Front marchers assembled in the East End. According to Steve Tilzley, 'The National Front marched practically unopposed through the East End and held a rally in Curtain Road, off Great Eastern Street. There had been a small, token anti-racist presence in the area to protest against their presence but they were heavily outnumbered by the Nazis and the police.'[39]

Tilzley's memories were written up more than 20 years later, as part of a longer critique of the Anti-Nazi League, and so should be read with a certain caution. A counter-demonstration did in fact take place and involved several hundred people, but it arrived late and failed to disperse the National Front group. Mike from Preston was at Brick Lane and remembers 'the sectarian left' criticizing the League, while themselves 'refusing to actually organize physically against the very young NF kids'. David L's memories are Pythonesque:

> There had been demos before along Brick Lane, and lots of people came out when the NF were leafleting there. But this time it was much smaller. What I remember . . . was bizarre. The RCP [Revolutionary Communist Party] were out in force. But in all, the left was outnumbered roughly two to one. What I remember is the RCP starting a chant of 'Police protect the Nazis'. Generally, that's my analysis. But this time, the police were protecting us!

Dick was sent from Brixton to support the anti-racists isolated in east London. It took him hours to reach Brick Lane, and by then it was too late. 'Yes we did mess up. I remember quite a lot of bitterness being addressed to people who had been at the carnival.'

The organizers of the carnival did not have enough forces in the East End; nor had they established good enough communication links to keep fully abreast of a changing situation. There were no mobile phones to enable people to exchange news quickly. According to Dave Widgery, 'The transport logistics were not worked out and the anti-fascists who did attempt to block off the Front in Brick Lane were demoralised and easily pushed about by the belligerent police pressure. The Front were harassed but not stopped and by the time reinforcements had arrived by Victoria line from Brixton, the National Front had dispersed.'[40]

According to Mike from the Anti-Nazi League office, 'The main people we were relating to were people who were willing to put themselves on the line, to defend meetings, to defend marches. The carnival showed that we could relate to much wider groups of young people, ones who wouldn't show themselves in the same way.' While it might have been possible to divert some of the organizers to Brick Lane, he argues, the ANL's mass audience was not malleable in the same way. Tony Cliff took a full page of *Socialist Worker* to apologize for his party's handling of events at Brick Lane.

> Under the threat of mobilising thousands of anti-fascists into Brick Lane, Commander Hunt of Scotland Yard announced on Friday that the NF would not be allowed East of Shoreditch High Street into the Brick Lane area. This statement led to a complacency among the mass of ANL supporters. There was too a terrible failure of communication. Three thousand ANL supporters did come from Brockwell Park to Brick Lane

. . . they arrived far too late. At 6 o'clock or so. But the 2000 anti-racists who held Brick Lane throughout the day – an extremely arduous and frustrating task – all anti-fascists owe a tremendous debt. Thanks to them a mass anti-fascist movement has been kept intact. Thanks to them the Carnival was able to go on.[41]

Back in Victoria Park, the music continued. Red Saunders was the compère again. He had swapped his cape from Carnival One for a 'much more thought out' uniform: 'Yellow boiler suit covered in RAR stencilled slogans with a huge stove pipe hat with the Love Music, Hate Racism slogan all over it. Plus shades, of course.' Sham 69 had been rattled by a series of death threats, and Jimmy Pursey took the stage to explain that his band could not play. Instead Stiff Little Fingers opened the set. We can quote Dave Widgery again:

> When Jake Burns took off his specs and donned his leathers he transmogrified himself into one of the most stinging vocalists and fiery guitarists punk ever possessed. The Stiffs' incendiary songs brought in the Irish dimension so important to any movement against racism in Britain, even though Burns denounced troops out. But better, they did punk homage to Bob Marley's classic *Johnny Was*.[42]

Bernie was standing by a Rock Against Racism stall when he found a backstage pass that had been left unattended. He sneaked backstage and watched Elvis Costello playing Nick Lowe's song 'What's So Funny about Peace, Love and Understanding?' 'Lowe had tears in his eyes.' Aswad played into the night.

Labour MP Tony Benn walked with the crowd from Park Lane to Piccadilly: 'the youngsters were rushing along and pushing ahead – it made me feel like an animal in a herd! By the time we got to Brixton there must have been a hundred thousand people gathered.'[43]

Mark Steel attended the carnival with his friend Jim, who came from Swanley. It was their first march: 'neither of us had any idea what would happen when we got there. What is a march, we pondered? Do you actually march, in step, with someone yelling at you to get in line?' For these young punks, the carnival was no disappointment.

> 100,000 ambled joyfully from Hyde Park to Brockwell Park in Brixton. All the scenes which would become so laboriously familiar, the hordes of leaflets thrust at you from all angles, the flamboyant but awful drumming costumes, the chanter screaming into a megaphone and becoming increasingly, thankfully hoarse, it all seemed so thrilling. And there was Aswad and Tom Robinson and Elvis Costello, and instead of feeling angry I felt jubilant because now I was *doing* something.[44]

Geoff from Manchester felt a similar sense of elation. At the time of the first carnival, he recalls, it was not clear whether the National Front would be defeated, but 'the second was a victory march'.

8

Southall

The first peak of the anti-fascist campaign came with the events at Lewisham in August 1977, which led to the formation of the Anti-Nazi League and from there to the two Rock Against Racism carnivals. The events at Southall were different. Sustained fighting between anti-fascist demonstrators and the police ended this time with the defeat of the anti-fascists and the killing of one demonstrator, Blair Peach. Peach's murder resulted in a series of further events: an inquest, a verdict of unlawful killing and the eventual disbanding of the Met's Special Patrol Group. Within days of Southall, Margaret Thatcher had also been elected prime minister. The Front suffered a humiliating setback. But so did Labour. Both the left and the far right suffered.

The fighting at Southall needs to be set against a background of clashes between the National Front and the left or young Asians. There were places of conflict in west, north, east and south-east London. Anna recalls weekly fighting at Chapel Market in Islington. 'It got very bad in the winter of 1978 and 1979. You'd see seven or eight Union Jacks on a great spike flag, a hundred fascists at a time.' So how did anti-fascists respond? 'We produced leaflets every week, on a Gestetner machine. We were getting support from the local unions. We leafleted every estate. We knocked on every door. The clashes at the market were just at the end of that work.'

Demonstrations now routinely ended in fighting. Early in 1978, the NF attempted to stage its first Young National Front Rally in the centre of Birmingham. Five thousand people protested against them, clashing with police wielding batons and riot shields.[1] In Leicester, on 21 April 1979, an estimated 2,000 anti-fascists mobilized to oppose some 1,000 NF supporters. The police re-routed the shaken NF march out of Leicester, and then attacked the remaining anti-fascists. The news showed police dogs chasing anti-fascists on to the Leicester University campus. Eighty-two people were arrested, including Balwinder Rana from Southall in west London, who was stopped by four plain-clothes officers and bundled into an unmarked car while on his way home. For Mike from Preston, Leicester was a victory 'even more clearly than Lewisham'. David from Leeds was less upbeat: 'The police were completely out of control and I remember discussing that someone was going to be killed soon.'[2]

Whose police?

Many anti-fascists also remembered the role of the police at Wood Green or at Lewisham, when anti-racists had hoped to block marches called by the National Front, but had instead come face to face with the Metropolitan Police, and had been on the receiving end of considerable violence. After Lewisham, *National Front News* publicly thanked the police for their successful 'organization' of the day's events, which had allowed the march to continue for as long as it did.[3] The following month, Arthur Bailey, secretary of the Lancashire Police Federation, gave a public speech criticizing the Trades Union Congress for its public endorsement of anti-fascism, suggesting that the trade union campaign against the far right marked 'the beginning of the end of free speech'.[4]

According to David R from Leeds, 'the police response [to anti-racism] was at best sneering and abusive, and at worst brutal'. For Kim Gordon of the black socialist group Flame, the crucial issue was stop and search – 'police harassment' that rose with the soaring black unemployment of these years. The black paper *Samaj* suggested that young blacks were victims of a police desire for reprisal, following the riots at the Notting Hill Carnival in 1976. 'Because there is nothing that the police can find against them, they are being charged for "Sus" ("being suspected persons loitering with intent to steal") or for "conspiracy with persons unknown to rob persons unknown".'[5]

In Preston, according to local Anti-Nazi League activists, the National Front openly boasted of having a 'sympathetic friend' within the force. Such claims might be dismissed as bluster, were it not for the signs of co-operation between the state and the far right.

In Manchester a defence campaign was created to support Nazir and Munir Ahmed. On 2 July 1978, strangers attacked the Ahmeds' shop in Longsight. There was racist graffiti up all over the area, and the Ahmeds assumed that the attackers were linked to the National Front. But when the brothers attempted to call the police, they learned that their assailants were in fact plain-clothes officers. Nazir and Munir Ahmed were eventually charged on several counts, including assault on a policeman, wounding with intent and carrying offensive weapons. They could count themselves doubly unfortunate. For most victims of racist attacks, the police merely contributed to the problem; they were not the problem itself.[6] Steve, the defence lawyer for Nazir and Munir Ahmed, suggests that the Longsight police were operating lynch law. 'The police were just out of control. That was beyond anything that would have been sanctioned by the top cops.'

After Lewisham, the use of truncheons and riot shields became standard. More resources were given to the Special Patrol Group, more use made of the Public Order Act. Police from as far away as Birmingham marshalled Martin Webster's one-man march through Hyde. A young doctor, Annie, recalls watching the pictures of this march on television in Brazil, where she was on holiday. Walking at the head of several hundred police, NF leader Webster's demonstration looked as much to her like a police as much as a fascist exercise. 'A Labour government was prepared to use whatever it took to ensure that a fascist could march.'

Manchester chief constable James Anderton was a passionate authoritarian, who believed that God sanctioned his interventions. Anderton attempted to ban gynaecologists from the city (or at least those who allowed abortions), and enforced the harassment of gay men. His officers introduced a 'preference' system for journalists, and also prosecuted more obscenity cases than every other force in the country combined. Activists were not pleased to learn in March 1978 that Manchester police had received a special delivery of Armalite rifles and Sterling sub-machine guns. They were later tested in exercises in Collyhurst, a working-class district. The Manchester police were said to possess more powerful guns in greater numbers than even the Royal Ulster Constabulary in Belfast.[7]

Throughout the late 1970s, many anti-racists continued to believe that the police were neutral or even on their side. Bev from Nottingham 'didn't get involved in any confrontation during demos' and generally found the police 'quite tolerant and unprovocative'. If the police stopped anti-fascists, others argued, then this was only because the fascists were the ones holding the meetings, and the anti-fascists were the ones on the attack. The initiative belonged to the far left. If the situation were reversed, surely the police would protect anti-fascists? Colin Barnett of the Northwest TUC argued this line through the protests in Hyde. He suggested that, once the first fascist march had been banned, opponents would do better to ignore subsequent provocations and leave the handling of the National Front to the police.[8] Generally, it was members of the Labour Party who argued this line, but even some socialists attempted at times to avoid permanent confrontation. If the fighting was always between police and anti-racists, as it had been at Lewisham, then the lines dividing left and right might be obscured.

While some anti-racists argued that police hostility was purely a tactic, and that in the last resort the police would come to their aid, others remembered the protest in support of the Lewisham 21 in July 1977, a month before the more famous Lewisham anti-fascist protest. There, it was fascists who had charged and attacked anti-racists. The police still found 23 anti-fascists to arrest. Others remembered the brutal scenes at Grunwick in July and August 1977, when the police had determined to remove the pickets supporting around 100 Asian strikers. Police officers were observed smashing press cameras, hitting one teenager's head repeatedly against the bonnet of a car, dragging strike leader Jayaben Desai by her hair through the crowd, and kicking one black worker repeatedly in the face.[9]

The argument between anti-fascists over whether police racism was accidental or institutional came again to the fore at Southall, on 23 April 1979. It was a full police riot against the left and the Asian community.

Southall kids are innocent

Southall had a largely Asian population. According to the 1976 census, 46 per cent of the local population had parents born in the Common-wealth or Pakistan, or were born there themselves. The National Front had few supporters in Southall or anywhere in the borough of Ealing. Their intervention was all about muscling into an area from the outside. The protests began when the Conservative council agreed to let the town hall to the NF, to hold an election meeting. In June 1976, an NF-inspired gang had stabbed Gurdip Singh Chaggar in Southall. Local people had re-sponded by turning out in large numbers to remember the dead youth, before marching on the town's police station. The following weekend, some 7,000 people marched through Southall carrying placards, 'Powell is a murderer' and 'We are here to stay'.[10] They also joined a great dem-onstration against racist attacks through central London. The memory of the state's failure to take action against the killers helped to give later events their edge. Prominent Anti-Nazi League activist Balwinder Rana remembers reading about the NF meeting in the *Ealing Gazette*: 'The news spread like wildfire. People felt very angry and insulted.'[11]

Pete Alexander was a former student and anti-apartheid activist. By spring 1979, he was the Socialist Workers Party west London organizer. Alexander recalls the strength of local organization. Forces included a large Anti-Nazi League group and the Southall Youth Movement (SYM), established in 1976 after the murder of Gurdip Singh Chaggar. There were also branches of the SWP and a black socialist organization, Peoples Unite, with its headquarters at 6 Park View. Each group worked with the local branches of the left-wing Indian Workers' Association, led by Vishnu Sharma, who was close to the Communist Party, and his deputy, Labour councillor Piara Khabra.[12] The International Marxist Group also had members in Southall, and the IMG's leading speaker, Tariq Ali, was a Socialist Unity candidate for Southall in the April 1979 election. The Indian Workers' Association, based in Coventry, had a branch in Southall, known as the IWA(GB). Better here than elsewhere, Alexander argues, there were organizations that could mobilize popular anger.

We should not exaggerate, however, the warmth of the relationships between different left-wing and community groups. Balraj Purewal was one of the founders of the Southall Youth Movement. He remembers having contact with left-wing parties, and takes pride in the independence that his young comrades kept from a majority 'white' left. 'Even now I don't know what left and right in Southall means. Every time we tried to protest and give our own identity the left tried to take it over . . . they gave us their own slogans and placards.'[13]

Balwinder Rana, recalls this period differently. He had emigrated from India back in 1964. In 1969, he had been the founding president of the Indian Youth Federation, one of the first political Asian youth organizations in Britain. He joined the International Socialists in 1974 and worked as a full-time organizer. He had also led anti-National Front campaigns at Gravesend in Kent. Today, he remains sceptical of the community movements:

> Before 1979, I felt that people in Southall were not interested. I used to organize coaches to protest marches against the NF everywhere. But it all used to be white people; never more than twenty Asians came. The Southall Youth Movement, when it started, was very good. Locally, they often fought against the fascists and they gave us a hope that we had reached a turning point in our struggles against fascism. But they did not develop politically and became very parochial. They hardly ever went outside Southall to confront the fascists and would often say that the NF would never come to Southall. It was a big shock for people when the NF came into Southall.

If the left succeeded in mobilizing people, this took hard work and a practical desire for unity.

Following the news that the council had agreed to let the hall, local activists decided to call a mass meeting to organize protests. Rana contacted Vishnu Sharma of the Indian Workers' Association. Why didn't they just organize a small activists' meeting under the auspices of the Socialist Workers Party, or the Anti-Nazi League? 'If the left had called it, the press would have been hostile.' The plan was to hold a delegate meeting, with no more than two people present from any one organization. 'We didn't want the churches or the community relations council taking it over.' Local socialists toured around the unions, women's and community groups in Hounslow, Southall, Ealing and Hayes to build support for the meeting. When it gathered, the entire local movement was represented – not just community groups, but engineers, teachers and hospital workers.

The meeting itself was divided. Two police officers showed up. A vote was taken to exclude them. Piara Khabra from the Indian Workers' Association argued that the best tactic would be to call a stay-away. The focus should be on a demonstration before the National Front's meeting. Yet the Anti-Nazi League and their allies in the unions were determined to confront the NF head-on. Socialists addressed the IWA meeting. Vishnu Sharma was also sympathetic to their ideas. Pete Alexander remembers, 'We moved a resolution that workers should go on strike and walk out, to stop the meeting taking place. The top table didn't know how to respond. They went into closed session, and then came back. They agreed.' A programme was also agreed:

> To petition the Ealing Borough Council to request the cancellation of the booking of the hall for the National Front;

The petition to be put to the Council on the day before the demonstration, on Sunday 22 April, after a march from Southall to Ealing Town Hall;

That all businesses, restaurants, shops, etc. should shut down on 23 April from 1 p.m. onwards.[14]

It was decided that on the day of the NF meeting there should be a peaceful sit-in on roads around the town hall, and that those arrested should comply peacefully. Rana was elected chief steward. The meeting also set up a co-ordinating committee, which distributed some 25,000 leaflets and 1,000 window posters around the borough, stressing that the protest was to be peaceful. As well as these materials, the ANL produced a number of leaflets in English and Punjabi, while *Socialist Worker* ran a front-page headline, 'Shut Down Southall'.

On 18 April, representatives from the co-ordinating committee met with Merlyn Rees, the Home Secretary, visiting Ealing as part of Labour's election campaign. Rees insisted that he possessed no powers to ban an election meeting. The Chief Superintendent of Southall Police requested a meeting with 'community leaders', including some protest organizers, such as Vishnu Sharma. Balwinder Rana was also there. 'When I came in, they were sat there with their hands clasped; it looked like they were praying. The Superintendent made a speech warning that left-wingers wanted to destroy the town: "Next week evil is coming."' Rana responded that he only knew one kind of evil, the racism of the National Front. 'Then Vishnu Sharma jumped up, and supported what I said. Then all the others began to nod their heads in agreement!'

On Sunday, 22 April, the day before the election meeting, 5,000 marched to Ealing town hall to protest, handing in a petition signed by 10,000 people. This was a huge demonstration, with all sections of the population represented, including older women in long white dresses and Sikh men in turbans and beards. But even this march was attacked, with the police picking fights all along the way. Rana recalls his attempts to negotiate with the senior officer in the car park before the demonstration set off. 'I asked him why there were so many police, and horses. He said that they were for our protection. He had information that the National Front might attack us. I said there's five thousand of us here, there's no way the NF are going to try anything. But he wouldn't take them away.' In an atmosphere of mistrust, trouble was always likely to break out:

> One young demonstrator was playing around. He flipped a copper's hat off as a joke. But rather than taking it as a joke, they arrested him and dragged him away. I stopped the march, we all sat down in the middle of Southall, outside the police station, and I went in to talk to the chief superintendent. They wouldn't let him go. So I said, 'If you don't let him go, I can't be responsible for what happens.' They threatened to arrest me, and I said, 'Go on then', and within five minutes, they'd let him go.

At this point, there were 5,000 people in the middle of Southall, with more watching. The police were not going to try anything there. But as the marchers left central Southall, snatch squads grabbed another 20.

Despite such provocations, Pete Alexander recalls that protesters remained optimistic about preventing the National Front meeting from taking place. 'We had wind that the strikes were going to happen. It was clear that the protests were going to be big.' Black and Asian workers, including staff at Heathrow airport, were at the front of the protests. Activists, including members of the Socialist Workers Party, were also able to pull off a strike at Ford Langley. A number of other local workplaces with a predominantly white workforce also backed the strike call, including workers at Sunblest bakery, Walls' pie factory and Quaker Oats.[15] These were large-scale strikes, uniting black and white workers, to protest against the NF presence in Southall. Maybe more than anything else, they reveal the success of several years' active campaigning by left and black activists. The Anti-Nazi League provided the opportunity to make unity work.

A very British coup

Monday, 23 April was St George's Day. To celebrate, the borough council chose this day to fly the Union Jack from Southall town hall. To most passers-by, this decision seemed crass. Why did the council choose this day of all days to proclaim their British nationalism? On closer reflection, the decision seems even odder. If they wanted to celebrate *England*, the council could have chosen the red and white cross of St George. But the Union Jack was the *British* flag. To the young anti-racist protesters, such 'accidents' felt sinister. As far as they were concerned, just about the only people in 1970s Britain under the age of 50 who spontaneously identified with flag-waving nationalism were the supporters of the Front. It seemed the council had decided that the most appropriate response to the presence of an Asian minority among their own people was to support the violent racists of the NF.

The police began to arrive in Southall early in the morning. Coaches were parked all over the town centre, and officers on horses were seen patrolling the streets. People felt that the presence of such large numbers of policemen, so early in the day, was a provocation. The mood was tense. Local shops, factories and transport closed at 1 p.m., and people began to gather at the town centre from lunchtime. One problem for the organizers was that the National Front were not even due to start their meeting until 7.30 in the evening. If workers were going to strike against the NF, as many did, then it should be at least a half-day strike. According to Balwinder Rana, 'the shops closed at 1 p.m. We asked people to assemble outside the town hall at 5 p.m.' Before the left and the striking workers, young Asians arrived on the scene first.

Rumours had spread that the police were already trying to smuggle National Front members into the town hall. Thus members of the Southall Youth Movement (SYM) began to assemble outside the town hall from around 12.30 p.m., while others were waiting for the official 5 p.m. starting time. Balraj Purewal led a march of some 30 to 40 members of SYM, along South Road, to the town centre. People joined along the way, so that on reaching the town hall, the SYM contingent had swelled to around 100, and eventually 200 people. They attempted to form a picket outside the town hall and were forcibly dispersed by the police. Soon, up to 40 arrests had been made. Members of the SYM attempted to meet with senior police officers, but were turned away.[16]

The people around the Southall Youth Movement had fallen victim to rumours and were determined to confront both the National Front and the police. According to one activist interviewed by the BBC in Southall, 'This is our future, right? Our leaders will do nothing . . . our leaders wanted a peaceful sit down, but what can you do with a peaceful sit down here? We had to do something, the young people. We don't want a situation like the East End where our brothers and sisters are being attacked every day.'[17] Pete Alexander contrasts the mass tactics of groups such as the Indian Workers' Association with those of the SYM:

> The IWA mobilised their forces through the afternoon and did march at about 5 p.m. in the afternoon, i.e. on time. The Southall Youth Movement lacked discipline. Responding to the provocation of the police, and in an attempt to show how militant they were, they marched a few hundred youths towards the town hall in the early afternoon. Given their relatively small numbers, it was easy for the cops to deal with. This not only took some of them out of the fray before things had really started; it also gave the cops some justification for occupying the centre of Southall.

The left set up headquarters initially at the offices of the National Association for Asian Youth, at 46 High Street, close to the centre of town, but far enough to prevent the building from coming under attack. Stewards were provided with red armbands. First aid centres were set up, and there was a legal advice unit and even an unofficial ambulance. The organizers of the protests feared that the police would turn violent. Paul Holborow recalls that 'There was a threatening police presence throughout the day. Their only purpose was to intimidate people.' Pete Alexander goes further: 'It was a military occupation.' A Catholic priest, Father Thomas Lloyd, described seeing a police coach with the ace of spades held against the window, and 'NF' written by officers on the steamed-up glass.[18] Huge numbers of police, some 2,756 officers in all, were used to break up the anti-fascist protests.

By 2 or 3 p.m., the police were in control of the town hall. The members of the Southall Youth Movement were dispersed across the surrounding area, and as new contingents of demonstrators arrived, they too were moved on – frequently by force. One of the most frightening aspects that Balwinder Rana remembers was the noise that the police made by drumming their sticks against their riot shields. The purpose of the police operation was not to arrest any wrongdoers, but to intimidate and ultimately hurt as many of the protesters as possible. By 3.30, the entire town centre was closed, and the police declared it a 'sterile' area, meaning that it was now free of anti-fascists. Meanwhile, rain had begun to fall by the bucket-load, further dampening the mood.

In order to keep the town centre secure, the police established a series of roadblocks that nobody was allowed to pass – not even the people who actually lived on the streets that were being closed. At one stage the police observed that several dozen anti-fascists had boarded a number 207 bus in an attempt to escape through the police lines. The police then boarded the bus and removed demonstrators by force. Several windows were smashed in the fighting.

According to Pete Alexander, 'Our original headquarters, where we had planned to have medical and legal support, was in the offices of the National Association for Asian Youth, but because of the police occupation we could not operate from there. As a consequence we moved further out, into the Peoples Unite building.' This community centre was associated with the band Misty and the Roots. It was just outside the main roadblock. By late afternoon, four separate protests had been established at each of the main blocks, with thousands of people at each one. Balwinder Rana tried to keep people's morale up, speaking on platforms, working to ensure that as much of the protest as possible could be held together. There should be no repeat of the situation in mid-afternoon, when one group had been cut off from the rest. The situation was desperately unclear. Protesters were still anxious to block the town hall. Police officers meanwhile were refusing to negotiate even with the organizers of the protest. Their orders were that there should be no compromise with the crowd. Rana also noticed that the diversity of Sunday's protest had not been reflected in Monday's scene. The older men had not appeared. There were fewer of the women who had marched. Rumours of a fight were keeping many people at home.

Pete Alexander recalls the geography of the police riot:

> At the centre of Southall there's a crossroads: one road going to the west (Broadway), one to the north (Lady Margaret Road, one to the east (Uxbridge Road) and one to the south (South Road). The town hall, where the meeting took place, is on the corner between the north and east streets. The police station is about 80 metres along Uxbridge Road, on the same side of the road as the town hall. After the Southall Youth Movement's abortive march, the cops took control of the crossroads and the whole area between it and eastwards beyond the police station. When I say 'took control' I mean armoured cars, cavalry, the ordinary riot cops in large numbers and helicopters. The Indian Workers' Association and others blocked the South Road; we – the Anti-Nazi League and others –

blocked the Uxbridge Road. Blair Peach and others worked their way around to the Broadway, but we had too few people to the north and the police were able get the National Front in that way.

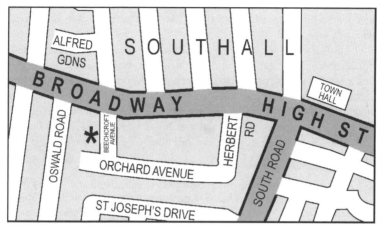

The area of the Southall protests: the asterisk marks the place where Blair Peach's body was found

The real trouble started as the day turned to dusk. There was still a large group of demonstrators, sitting peacefully on the Broadway, blocking the western route into Southall. One demonstrator, Peter B, was part of this group. In his memory,

> At about 7.30 p.m. the good humour of the crowd was shattered . . . a roar went through the crowd, emanating from the rear. People turned and looked westwards down the street. I saw, to my amazement, a coach being driven fast straight into the back of the crowd. It was a private coach, an ordinary 30–40 seat char-a-banc. At a cautious estimate, I would put the speed of it at 15 m.p.h., which is murderous when it is being driven into a crowd.[19]

The coach was carrying police officers and some 20 members of the National Front, whose objective was the town hall.

From this point onwards, the situation was one of a general mêlée. The crowds were dispersed, the coach broke through. The crowds gathered again. Other police vehicles followed, and demonstrators attempted to block them. They were beaten back. One anti-fascist later reported, 'Every time people tried to push through the police lines, mounted police on horse-back laid into the demonstrators, beating them to the ground and arresting some of them.'[20]

Jerry Fitzpatrick contrasts Southall with previous protests. 'After Lewisham, it was much more disparate. The ANL was trying to work with the IWA and with the local community. There was no centralized decision-making. The police were more determined, and willing to use violence. We were broken up too quickly. The police had more control.'

According to Rana, 'People started to throw bricks. The police used horses. They drove vans into the crowd, and fast, to push us back. They used snatch squads. People rushed back with whatever they could pick up.' Individuals ran into the park, or sheltered in homes, or in the Peoples Unite building where medical facilities were stretched beyond breaking.

The police could see how Peoples Unite on Park View was being used, and determined to clear the building. Officers entered the building, occupied it, and gave instructions to the people sheltering there to leave. They formed a gauntlet along the hall and the stairs, and beat people as they tried to escape. Tariq Ali was in the building, bleeding from his head. Clarence Baker, the pacifist manager of Misty and the Roots, was hurt so badly that he went into a coma. The solicitor John Witzenfeld was inside when the police attacked:

> They kicked in the panel on the door to the medical unit and waving their truncheons told us to get out. I was pushed into the hall with the others behind me. Suddenly I felt a blow to the back of my head and I managed to half-turn and saw a hand holding a truncheon disappearing downwards . . . Whilst we were waiting for the ambulance, two police stood in the doorway with their backs to us whilst people were brought down from upstairs and I saw truncheons rise and fall and I heard shouts and screams from the women.[21]

The building itself was so badly damaged by the police action that afterwards it had to be demolished. Officers with batons smashed medical equipment, a sound system, printing and other items. Jack Dromey, a senior official of the Transport and General Workers' Union, told an inquiry called by the National Council of Civil Liberties, 'I have never seen such unrestrained violence against demonstrators . . . The Special Patrol Group were just running wild.'[22] His view was echoed by Mrs Dialo Sandu, a Southall resident who was spat at by one police officer as she watched the riot unfold from the security of her front garden 'They treated us like animals. It's the first time I would ever speak against the police. But I saw what happened with my own eyes.'[23]

Between 7.30 and 9 p.m., Southall witnessed a full-scale police riot. Dozens of anti-Nazis were beaten. At least three suffered fractured skulls. Others were kicked until they lost consciousness. There is no doubt that the police sought to inflict as much pain, physical and psychological, as they could. Caroline, then an active member of the Anti-Nazi League in Ealing, spent the night driving between Southall and Heathrow. 'Many of the Asian kids that the police arrested, they beat them up for a bit, and then they took them out of London. They dropped them in the middle of nowhere, on the side of motorways, nowhere near telephones or anything. These young kids were confused, crying. The police just wanted to humiliate them.' So why were the police so violent? According to Caroline, 'They wanted revenge for Lewisham.'

After the storming of Peoples Unite, Balwinder Rana was forced to escape by jumping over a garage, and hid from a street full of police horses. The organizers had the numbers of all the phone boxes in central Southall, and had thought that they would be able to keep in contact. But the police occupied the town centre, including the boxes. Angered, disorientated, the protesters attempted to regroup.

Perminder Dhillon described her memories of the day's events in an article for the socialist feminist magazine *Spare Rib*.

> Around ten, many of us gathered to watch the news at a restaurant where Rock Against Racism and Indian music had been blaring out all evening, drowning out the National Front speakers inside the town hall. Their wounds still bleeding, people saw the Commissioner of Police, the Home Secretary, and other 'experts' on the black community condemning the people of Southall for their unprovoked attack on the police! As usual, only pictures of injured policemen were shown – nothing of the pregnant women being attacked and the countless other police assaults.[24]

One historian, Nigel Copsey, has described how the police 'contributed to disorder' as the day went on, 'first by making peaceful protest impossible, and then by attempting to disperse the crowd using aggressive tactics, such as "snatch squads", charging with riot shields, truncheons and horses, and even driving vans into the crowd'.[25] By the end of the day, according to police records, over 700 had been arrested, and some 342 people charged. This number actually underestimated the number of police detentions. These were the largest arrests in Britain on a single day for decades.

Blair Peach was part of the crowds blocking the western approach, as Uxbridge Road joined the Broadway. Along with his friends, Peach saw the police break a route through for the National Front to hold their meeting. Frightened by the intensity of the police violence, Peach and friends headed south. Beechcroft Avenue was not cordoned off, and it must have seemed a way to escape from the fighting. But Beechcroft Road was no haven: at its far end, the road led straight back on to Uxbridge Road – back to the police lines. According to one later report:

> The police formed up across Northcote Avenue, moved across the Broadway and charged into Beechcroft Avenue, carrying riot shields and truncheons. They were moving at a fast walk, but according to some witnesses broke into a run. Once into Beechcroft Avenue, they made way for two Special Patrol Group vans which drove into a street beside them, went round the junction with Orchard Avenue and stopped inside Orchard Avenue. The police officers moved after them. The vans opened, and now more police officers got out. It was at this time, at the junction of Beechcroft and Orchard Avenues that Blair Peach was attacked and fatally injured.[26]

Peach's body was found towards the end of the road, on a corner that faced back towards the town hall. The family opposite tried to shelter him, not realizing that he was already dying. Peach had sustained a head injury and was taken to Ealing Hospital by ambulance, arriving at about 8 p.m. Death was pronounced shortly after midnight.

By about 10 p.m., the organizers of the anti-fascist protest had succeeded in opening a second headquarters. Most of the protesters had gone, and the police began to scale down their operations. The mood was downbeat. Balwinder Rana heard the news of his fellow demonstrator's death. 'I knew Blair Peach. We used to gather every Sunday at Brick Lane. The NF tried to speak there, and we tried to stop them. The police said whoever comes first can have the spot. So we would camp out there Saturday night, even Friday night, to stop the fascists. It was there I met Blair Peach.' It is one thing to lose a stranger, another to lose a comrade whom you have known in struggle.

Blair Peach

In the aftermath of 23 April, anti-fascists were riven by competing feelings of guilt, anger and remorse. The very next morning, at 11 a.m., Commander Cass, who was in charge of investigating the previous day's events, began by interviewing Amanda Leon, who had been with Blair Peach when he was killed. Leon quickly took the initiative. She told Commander Cass, 'I saw a police officer strike Blair Peach with an overarm blow with a truncheon . . . I only saw one blow struck. The truncheon made contact on Blair Peach's head. I don't know what part of the head the blow fell on. My impression was that it was the back of his head because he was running away.' She described Peach's killing as an assault. She said that she herself had been hit on the head with a baton by a police officer and that she had seen a man lying on the ground with a policeman bending over him and hitting him in the testicles. Leon tried to use her interview with Cass to begin a complaint against the police. He, of course, refused to investigate it. Later, the police attempted for seven years to keep the text of their interview secret. It was only released following a High Court injunction.[27]

Blair Peach was a teacher and a member of the SWP. He was 33, a trade unionist and a veteran of campaigns for the participation of the local community in education, in solidarity with struggles in Ireland and South Africa. According to Roger Huddle, 'He was a very gentle, quiet man. He was absolutely incensed about racism.' Chris Searle describes Peach in the following terms: 'there was a particular electricity about Blair's spoken interventions. He had a stammer that sometimes interfered with his delivery. Yet his personal courage was such that his words and arguments always emerged, forged through a determination that you could feel was willing his voice forward.'[28]

Annie was the doctor in the first aid room. Even today, she holds that Blair's killing had been given the highest authorization.

What was remarkable on 23 April is that only one person died, given the number of overarm truncheon blows to the head. Those of us in 6 Park View were made to go through a gauntlet of police doing this to each and every one of us as we left the house, and then we were told to go back into the house. Most police would have or should have been trained in the possible effects of blows to the head, and in fact police in general are told to try to avoid hitting on the head, as any blow to the head is potentially fatal. The reason is not only the blow itself, but the after-effects of it, which include bleeding into or around the brain, which may not be detected until it is too late. On 23 April, not only were heavier than normal truncheons used, but police throughout the demo used these heavy truncheons to hit people on the head. Someone somewhere must have said this was OK. Someone somewhere was prepared to see people killed on a demo in Britain. It was perhaps the first time in the twentieth century that this was considered an acceptable result of policing a demo in Britain.

After the storm

On 23 April, the Metropolitan Police 'won'. The police succeeded in attacking and hurting as many ordinary people as possible, and also kept Ealing town hall open for the National Front meeting to take place. The Special Patrol Group was fêted for its proud role in having defended democracy from the people of Southall. In the days afterwards, the partisans of British justice took a vindictive approach towards their enemies. Some of the mood that followed can be seen in the account of one of the trials of the anti-racist protesters:

> A 14-year-old Sikh boy appeared before a magistrate at Ealing juvenile court. He had been charged with 'threatening behaviour' and being in possession of 'offensive weapons' at 6.20 p.m. on 23 April 1979. The sum total of the prosecution case was the evidence of one policeman who stated that he had seen the accused with an offensive weapon . . . The defence produced several witnesses. These included a white doctor, a white solicitor and a white ambulance man. They all testified that the boy, at the time, was being treated for a hand wound and had suffered a severe loss of blood. They knew because they were all in the legal aid room at 6 Park View. I was with them, when the police raided this address and arrested the boy in question and numerous others. But defence witnesses, even respectable ones, are not permitted to obstruct 'the due process of law'. The boy was found guilty and fined £100. The defence argued that he had no job and no source of income. The Magistrate replied, 'Let him find a job.' The defence retorted that it was a criminal act for a 14-year-old to gain employment. But the Magistrate had meant a 'paper round' or something like that. The boy in question will be paying 75p a week for the next two years.[29]

This was not an article from the revolutionary press, but from the liberal *Guardian*. In the days following Blair Peach's killing, the police and the courts were arrogant in their defence of power. To be black or Asian, to be young or to oppose racism was enough to constitute a crime. Mark Steel was a young activist caught up in events at Southall. Back home afterwards, he experienced a complex of emotions, ranging from shock at the news of Blair Peach's death to remorse that he had been excited by the clashes with the police, and guilt that he had escaped when someone else had died. What angered him most was the press coverage afterwards. 'Every paper, news bulletin, politician, police officer and respectable member of society was yelping at how this demonstrating mob must be stopped . . . From the way it was reported, there must have been people who thought, "What on earth made those violent Anti-Nazi people want to kill that poor teacher?"'[30]

The papers swung overwhelmingly behind the police. The *Guardian* was almost alone in the mainstream press in challenging the police riot.[31]

The *Daily Express*, *Daily Mail*, *Daily Mirror* and *Daily Telegraph* all covered the story as their front-page lead. The headlines were: 'BATTLE OF HATE. Election Riot: Police Hurt, 300 arrested', 'RACE RIOTERS BATTLE WITH POLICE ARMY', '300 HELD IN RIOT AT NF DEMO' and '300 ARRESTED AT POLL RIOT'. One edition of the *Daily Mail* went furthest in deliberately confusing the racists and the anti-racists, proclaiming, 'RACE RIOTERS BATTLE WITH POLICE ARMY'. What was so offensive about this story, and indeed about the general press coverage, was the way in which it depicted a mixed-race group of young anti-racists as violent, aggressive thugs, as much a threat to society as the National Front.

Regional papers were even worse. The *Hereford Evening News* was critical of Southall residents for responding to the National Front. 'However understandable the resentment of the large Asian community in the west London suburb where the National Front chose to stage a deliberately provocative election meting, there can be neither excuse nor forgiveness of their violent attacks on the police.' Yet in some ways this article was untypical. The Hereford paper was almost alone in recognizing that the trouble had not been stirred up entirely by the Anti-Nazi League. The *Oxford Mail* was yet another paper to speak up for the police: 'Because this is a free country, where even detestable organisations have to be allowed to hold election meetings to support their candidates, a big force of police was present. The organisers of the demonstration caricatured this as police repression.' The *Swindon Evening Advertiser* claimed that 'The Anti-Nazi League, which was originally sponsored, in part, by a number of respectable people who did not stop to think twice, has now degenerated into an umbrella for extreme left malcontents.' The *Nottingham Evening Post* bemoaned the fact that 'If the extreme political nut-cases want to behave as they have done, in this country of free-speech, there is little we can do to stop them, short of banning them completely.'[32]

A number of papers called for bans against the far left. According to the *Oldham Evening Chronicle*, 'the real consensus in Britain is to get the rabble of both Right and Left off the streets'. The *Bradford Telegraph and Argus* asked, 'What price the Anti-Nazi League when the people it persuades to demonstrate use Nazi methods?' The *Oxford Mail* termed anti-Nazi protesters 'enemies of democracy'. Finally, the *Lancashire Evening Post* developed this phrase, suggesting that while the political right were irresponsible, the left were more dangerous. The ANL were an urgent and pressing threat to democracy. 'In the short term they are more dangerous than the National Front because they hide their revolutionary and totalitarian aims behind a noble cause.'[33]

Yet, in the days that followed, it slowly became clear that the police and their allies had gone too far. It became clear that the vast majority of local people felt an extraordinary sympathy for Blair Peach, the man who had died for them. The Metropolitan Police's 'military' victory crumbled. The murder of Blair Peach became a symbol of the unjustified use of police violence, and even re-legitimized the Anti-Nazi League within the wider Labour movement. Fifteen thousand people marched the following Saturday, 28 April, in honour of the dead man, with 13 national trade union banners taken on the demonstration, and Ken Gill speaking on behalf of the General Council of the Trades Union Congress. Workers at the Sunblest bakery raised £800 for Peach's widow.[34] Balwinder Rana remembers that for the next week, protesters were everywhere, flyposting, speaking, organizing, discussing the lessons of the police riot. The police were around, in very large numbers, but they did not dare to stop people from organizing. It was almost as if the police were shamed by the enormity of what they had done.

One activist Kathy had been unable to attend the Southall demonstrations, but her husband Harry took part, and was badly beaten the police. She knew Blair Peach, and tried to make sense of his death in a poem, 'We cannot offer words / to express our grief and our anger / we throw red flowers / in silent explosions of pain . . . the red arrow of the anti-nazis / fuelled to rocket power with our collective anger.'

Rock Against Racism brought out a special leaflet, *Southall Kids are Innocent*: 'Southall is special. There have been police killings before . . . But on April 23rd the police behaved like never before . . . The police were trying to kill our people. They were trying to get even with our culture . . . What free speech needs martial law? What public meeting requires 5,000 people to keep the public out?' Questions were asked in the Indian and New Zealand parliaments. Even the *Daily Telegraph*'s reporter described how the police cornered one contingent: 'Several dozen crying, screaming demonstrators were dragged to the police station and waiting coaches . . . Nearly every demonstrator we saw had blood flowing from some injury.'[35]

For eight weeks, Blair Peach's body remained unburied. The day

RAR leaflet: the picture is of Clarence Baker in hospital

before the funeral, he was accorded a 'lying in state' at the Dominion Theatre in Southall. Mike from the Anti-Nazi League office had the job of protecting Peach's body overnight.

> I remember at dawn, we were supposed to open up the building. There was already a queue of people. Later, two police showed up, an officer and a sergeant. They were asking to see Paul. Given what had happened, I was rather unhappy, but I didn't have the gumption to stop them. After five minutes, the sergeant came out, walking quite quickly. There was the officer, after him, looking straight ahead. Then Paul's head poked out, 'And don't you ever come back!' In the circumstance of a large community and attacks on a white demonstrator who had been killed, the police quite clearly felt out of their depth.

People remembered Blair Peach as a fighter. To them, Peach represented the best instincts of the anti-racist left. According to one commentator, Peach's death had 'particular reverence for the predominantly Sikh Punjabi community, both as a white man who chose to assist them and thereby defend their right to reside in the country, and as an enemy of tyrannous oppressors whose struggles with the Sikhs are still talked of and remembered in popular *bazaar* calendar art.'[36] Finally, on 13 June 1979, Peach was buried. Ten thousand joined the procession.

Following this powerful show of support, another 10,000 people marched through Southall again in memory of Blair Peach the following year.[37] A middle school was named after him and further memorials have been organized on anniversaries since.

Bringing the police to justice?

Faced with such anger, the officials of the state did their best to close ranks. Despite 147 MPs signing a motion calling for a public inquiry, the Labour government refused this request. Labour Home Secretary Merlyn Rees told Sir David McNee, the Commissioner of the Metropolitan Police, that the government gave its full support to his actions. A number of documents were compiled but not published, including an internal Metropolitan Police report by Commander Cass into Blair Peach's death, a report by Sir David McNee to the Home Secretary, the Linnet Report on complaints against the police, and a report by Deputy Commissioner Pat Kavanagh on the work of the Special Patrol Group. Following the general election, the new Conservative Home Secretary Willie Whitelaw also refused to take action. Justice Griffiths later opposed an appeal, saying that 'on its worst construction, this is one isolated occasion of a policeman possibly using a weapon he should not have used, and hitting too hard'.

The Home Office dragged its heels in opening the inquest into Peach's death. Writing in the *New Statesman*, Paul Foot complained of the delays.

> I wonder what the reaction would have been if a policeman, not a demonstrator, had been killed at Southall. Would the inquest have been postponed until the middle of the summer holidays? Would there have been almost total silence in the press about the murder hunt? Would the suspects have been left to carry on their jobs without being charged or even cautioned?'[38]

When it opened, the inquest limited itself to the sole question of how Peach had died. Pathologist Professor Mant explained that the damage done to the dead man's skull involved an instrument that had not pierced his skin. He concluded that the weapon was a cosh or a blackjack, perhaps a police radio. Sitting without a jury, the coroner refused to accept Professor Mant's findings.

In December 1979, Blair's brother Roy appealed the coroner's findings, taking the case as far as the Court of Appeal. Represented by the barrister and novelist John Mortimer, the family was successful in obtaining a ruling that the inquest should be carried out in front of a jury. Lord Denning, the Master of the Rolls, heard the case. 'When allegations of brutality or misconduct are made against the police', Denning found,

> and a fatality does occur, then, if the circumstances are such that something may have gone wrong, and there is a danger of it happening again, a jury should be summoned . . . We have to decide it on the hypothetical circumstances that Mr Blair Peach was struck by a policeman with something heavier than a truncheon . . . On those hypothetical circumstances, Mr Blair Peach's brother is entitled to say that there must be a jury, however difficult it may be for the coroner to conduct the inquest in those circumstances.[39]

At the inquest, the police solicitor tried to use Professor Mant's evidence in support of his employers. If it was true that a baton had not caused Blair Peach's death, then it followed that Peach could not have been killed by any police officer. The coroner instructed the jurors to release the police from scrutiny. Not surprisingly, then, the verdict passed was not the condemnatory one of unlawful killing but simply 'death by misadventure'. Yet in addition to their main verdict, the jury added three riders. First, senior officers should supervise the Special Patrol Group more closely. Second, police officers should be issued with maps before major demonstrations. Third, police lockers should be regularly searched. The effect of these three riders was to restore blame on to the police for the Southall riot. In the words of the Anti-Nazi League's Paul Holborow, 'We regard the verdict as establishing beyond any doubt that police killed Blair Peach.'[40]

The *Sunday Times* published reports based on leaks from the Cass Report. Attention focused on the officers of Special Patrol Group unit 1/1. At least six members of this unit were known to have travelled in the van that held Blair Peach's killer: they were police constables Murray, White, Lake, Freestone, Scottow and Richardson. When the lockers of unit 1/1 were searched in June 1979, one officer, Greville Bint, was discovered to have in his lockers Nazi regalia, bayonets and leather-covered sticks. Another constable, Raymond 'Chalkie' White, attempted to hide a cosh in his anorak pocket. Either of these instruments would have been consistent with the weapon identified by Professor Mant. A brass handle was also found, a metal truncheon encased in leather about 8 inches long, a lead weight and a wooden pickaxe handle.[41]

The National Council of Civil Liberties (NCCL) organized an unofficial committee to investigate events at Southall. The members of the committee included Roger Butler of the engineering workers' union; the lecturer Stuart Hall; Patricia Hewitt of the NCCL;[42] Bill Keys, a member of the General Council of the Trades Union Congress; Joan Lestor, the Labour MP; Dick North from the executive of the National Union of Teachers; Paul O'Higgins, a law lecturer from Cambridge University; Ranjit Sondhi from the Asian Resources Centre in Birmingham; Hewlett Thompson, the Bishop of Willesden; and Pauline Webb from the Methodist Church. The Oxford philosopher Michael Dummett chaired the committee. The Metropolitan Police boycotted the committee, giving the excuse that their time would be better spent seeking an improvement in race relations in Southall.[43] The final report attempted to remain even-handed, and at several points its authors explicitly criticized the organizers of the Southall protests. The idea of the committee was to draw lessons from the entire situation on the day. But the final paragraph should be quoted in full:

> The outcome of the police operation on 23 April could hardly have been worse. Many police officers and members of the public suffered serious

injury. One person died, apparently at the hands of the police. And the confidence of many people in Southall in the police, and the institutions of the law, was shattered. Those protesters who, deliberately or in the heat of the moment, used violence against the police must carry their share of the responsibility for what happened. But we do not accept that the responsibility was wholly or even mainly theirs. We regard the decision to prevent the demonstration to cordon off Southall as entirely misconceived, and the failure to communicate the decision to the community organisations as disastrous. Those who regard our proposed alternatives as unsatisfactory should seriously consider whether such unacceptable consequences would have flowed from a police operation which respected the community's right to protest; which kept them informed of the police plans; and which enabled stewards and community leaders to exercise authority over the protesters in order to ensure that, as far as was humanly possible, the demonstration remained the peaceful protest which had always been intended.[44]

The horror of Southall closely linked to events outside. Five days before Southall, 200 police were deployed to prevent anti-fascist protests in Battersea. Three days before, 5,000 police were used at Leicester. Two days afterwards, over 4,000 officers, including Special Branch, SPG and mounted police, were used against ant-fascists at Newham. Over 1,000 police were employed in West Bromwich on 28 April, and similar numbers at Bradford two days later. One further National Front meeting, held in Caxton Hall on 1 May, required 5,000 police to ensure that it could go ahead.[45] The surrounding area was sealed off all day. With this many police officers used, so often, and with such determination, it was in fact remarkable that only one person was killed.

Just as importantly, the National Front public meeting at Southall was held as part of that year's general election. As Blair Peach lay dying, a new Conservative government was waiting to emerge. Margaret Thatcher had already staked her claim to the loyalties of former NF voters. Speaking out against immigration, Thatcher had taken up the cause dearest to them. The situation appeared all the more alarming for those young, politically conscious people who led the Anti-Nazi League. Many activists were in their mid- or late twenties. They had been schooled by the events of May 1968 and the victories of the working-class movement in the years between 1972 and 1974. They had seen local cuts and closures. But it was still possible for them to think that this brief downtime might shortly be reversed. Only slowly was the realization dawning that the worse years of the 1980s were ahead. In retrospect, we can see, the conjuncture of Blair Peach's death and Margaret Thatcher's victory symbolized the end of an age.

9

The Anti-Nazi League: Mark Two

The 1979 election was a catastrophic defeat for the National Front. For months beforehand, NF propaganda had fixed on the election, arguing that Labour's entire political agenda was determined above all by its nervousness at the prospect of electoral defeat at the hands of the NF.[1] The National Front stood over 300 candidates, exhausting its networks of support in an attempt to win new voters, and bankrupting the party. Where they stood, the NF's candidates averaged barely more than 1 per cent of the vote.

Paul Holborow counted the NF's results: 'It was clear that something catastrophic had happened to the Nazi vote. In east London, the Nazi vote fell by more than a fifth compared to what it had been; in Leicester, it fell by a half. It fell – not just compared to their high point in 1976, but even compared to the lower results of 1974.' 'It was extraordinary how fast the Front declined after the election,' recalls Steve Jeffreys. 'Where they had been active, you hardly saw them at all.' Paul Holborow agrees: 'We were receiving countless reports of Nazi demoralization. They didn't dare march any more. They were no longer willing to have their leaders shown up as Nazis.'

This setback was not accidental. The National Front was defeated rather by a combination of factors, of which the two most important were the revival of the Conservatives under Thatcher, and the anti-fascist campaign. Their significance is assessed in the next chapter.

The late 1970s witnessed a proliferation of anti-racist groups. Some co-operated closely with the Anti-Nazi League, while others were imitators or even rivals. Nigel Copsey emphasizes the role played by *Searchlight* magazine. '*Searchlight* supplied photographs of NF leaders Tyndall and Webster in Nazi regalia and provided revealing quotations from both Tyndall and Webster who had been members of the National Socialist Movement in their youth.'[2] In this period, the National Front experienced an extraordinary turnover in its membership, with up to 14,000 people joining and then immediately leaving the party between 1977 and 1979. These people did not like to consider themselves fascists, and shuddered when the leaders of their party were photographed in full neo-Nazi regalia. The tactic of anti-fascist exposure undoubtedly helped to drive a wedge between the fascist ideology of the NF's leaders and the more conservative racism of its rank-and-file members.

Local papers increasingly sided with the anti-Nazis. One of the first to do so was the *Hornsey Journal*, which responded to the fascist march through Wood Green with the headline, 'Forty years on, the evil march of fascism fouls our streets.' The *East Ender*, having adopted a 'neutral' stance at the Greater London Council elections in May, published a racy exposé of the National Front in August 1977, with the sensational front-page headline, 'Exposed, The Nazi Menace in the East End' above a photograph of two Nazi-saluting NF followers. This article was based on revelations by a National Front defector, John Considine, who declared that the NF was 'something very evil masquerading as a party'. Even the *Leicester Mercury*, which had previously been criticized for running stories with racist sentiments, finally answered its critics and came out against the NF: 'To give the National Front the chance of power to implement its cruel policies would be a rejection of humanity.'[3]

The National Front was also increasingly refused the hire of halls outside election periods. Labour-controlled local authorities such as Newham refused on the basis that halls should not be made available to racists.[4] Labour's National Executive Committee endorsed this policy in September 1978, and in the same document instructed its candidates not to appear on platforms or radio or TV broadcasts with members of the NF. In spring 1979, Tory-controlled Great Yarmouth council agreed to hold the NF's conference on council property. Shortly afterwards, there were local elections and this contract was a major issue. Labour won control of the council and refused to allow the NF to use its halls.[5]

The effect of all this anti-racist campaigning was to force the National Front on to the defensive. Its activists were unable to put their message across, their graffiti were painted out and they could not march. One minor event, from small, affluent Winchester, gives a sense of the scale of the movement. In early 1979, the Anti-Nazi League was able to mobilize 3,000 people to stop the NF from marching. The National Front's Robert Relf was in jail and it called a demonstration in his support. Pete Alexander takes up the story.

> Our only real contact with the place was my family connections, and I was sent to organize the march. My sister was a student at the arts college and leading members of the Labour Party lived near my parents – these were the keys to mobilizing. Our counter demonstration was the largest in the city's history for 100 years, and most of it – perhaps two-thirds – was mobilized locally. The police allowed us to march to the gates of the prison – the National Front's main objective – where of course we stayed put until it was clear that the police had kept their promise and confined the fascists to a small part of the city centre. Meanwhile, Balwinder Rana and others went into the centre and laid into the relatively small band of fascists who had assembled. Somewhere there is a good photograph of a

heavy municipal rubbish bin being hurled across the road at them. Once again, we had ensured that they 'will not pass', demoralizing them and providing a boost to our side. This was in Winchester, and was mainly a consequence of local mobilization, showing the extent to which anti-fascism had become a popular cause.

Peter Hain recalls this period as one of success:

> There was virtually no press coverage at the beginning. The thing took off despite the media, and despite the political parties – Labour included. Then people realized that something was happening. By 1978, we were really pushing the National Front off the streets. The strategy of confrontation was difficult. It was controversial with the press, the Labour Party and the public, but it simply drove the NF off the streets. We also started to win the arguments about elections. We pushed them back, politically. We had quotes from Tyndall and Webster, we could show that they were overt Nazis. Rock Against Racism also helped. It became unfashionable to be a Nazi. All these things pushed the National Front back.

In the general election of April 1979, Margaret Thatcher's Tories won a 40-seat majority. Meanwhile, the National Front received a mere 1.3 per cent of the vote. Demoralized, the Front split into three rival factions and its support crumbled. Failure in the 1979 elections led to the resignation of John Tyndall as NF chairman in January 1980.

Over the following decade, all sections of the British far right turned away from electoralism, arguing that the tactic was inevitably flawed. The main figure in the National Front for the next four years was Martin Webster. For much of the next decade, the NF was led in most towns by 'Strasserites', a generation of younger football hooligans who claimed to draw inspiration from Hitler's Nazi opponents. As the Strasserites turned to violence, so did the British National Party (BNP) and British Movement (BM). All three were shaped by the election defeat.

Nazi rock

By summer 1979, the National Front was clearly in retreat. Its electoral strategy had failed, while the British Movement was seen as the more radical home for violent ultra-Nazis. Briefly, the NF attempted to respond to the Anti-Nazi League by copying the success of Rock Against Racism's Militant Entertainment tours. Joe Pearce, a leading NF supporter since his early teens, was dragged in to launch Rock Against Communism (RAC).[6] Pearce boasted that the NF possessed its own record label, recording studios, and ten bands to dedicate their services, including the Dentists, Damaged, White Boss, Phase One, Beyond the Implod, and the Raw Boys. RAC had its first public outing in August 1979, at London's Conway Hall. Around 150 boneheads turned up, to face an anti-fascist protest. White Boss and the Dentists played. Skrewdriver were still afraid to declare openly for the NF and cried off. Their distributors, Rough Trade, smashed every Skrewdriver disk they possessed and dumped the pieces in bags outside Conway Hall.[7]

Over the past 20 years, the physical-force wing of far-right politics has sustained itself on the funds generated by a series of Nazi bands. Almost every act has taken its origins from the late 1970s, including Skrewdriver, Combat '84, No Remorse and Sudden Impact. In the early 1980s, however, Rock Against Communism initially failed to catch on. The gigs were not organized, the bands failed to materialize. Rock Against Communism remained little more than a weekly column in the National Front's press, a top-ten of the songs that young fascist skinheads liked to listen to. Ironically, the organizers found it impossible to sustain the list without naming such acts as the Clash and Sham 69, even though they knew these bands were their mortal enemies.

Rather than establishing a successful neo-Nazi music culture, the efforts of the young supporters of the National Front and British Movement were quickly dedicated instead to attacking Rock Against Racism gigs. Bands targeted included Sham 69, Crass, Scritti Politti and the Angelic Upstarts. Attila the Stockbroker recalls being 'attacked on stage by Nazis at Skunx, a punk/skin club in London. We fought back. Someone (who shall be nameless) from the Redskins was there. "Under the table you must go".'[8] According to David Brazil of the *Leveller*, 'The BM way of messing up a rock gig has revolved around hard core of 20 to 30, at the most, getting through the doors, with or without their spoof blue and white ANL badges or their mod-smart Union Jack enamel badges, and coming heavy with the other kids they run into, especially those with RAR or ANL insignia.'

Rock Against Racism responded by circulating journalists, music papers, pub landlords and promoters, suggesting such precautions as banning National Front or British Movement badges and refusing bookings for fascist-supporting acts.[9] But the argument was not going to be won by persuading landlords and bouncers, as both sides knew. It was in the hearts and minds of the young that the real battle was being fought. For the time being, the omens were good.

Rock Against the Tories?

Left-wing activists attempted to make sense of the new political period after April 1979. 'People had really underestimated how right-wing Thatcher would be,' recalls Steve Jeffreys, 'how close her policies were to those of the Front.' As early as the winter of 1978–9, Colin Sparks of the Socialist Workers Party had argued that the National Front would not be the source of reactionary developments for British capitalism.[10] If it was not going to be the NF, then there were other options on offer, including what he perceived could be a 'statist' right-wing Conservatism. One anti-racist paper, *CARF*, produced a poster 'ConservaFront', showing National Front and Tory politics merging together.[11]

Martin Barker of Bristol Socialist Workers Party condemned 'the new racism'. Unlike the National Front, the Tories condemned black culture, and not black blood. But they were racists all the same.[12] Following the 'Winter of Discontent' and then the Conservative victory at the 1979 election, Dave Widgery wrote, 'We face a new Toryism, frankly elitist, not just making racialism respectable but Reaction itself fashionable.'[13] According to Paul Holborow, meanwhile,

> I was very focused on the Anti-Nazi League, but also on Thatcher. That had as much impact on me as the decline of the National Front vote. I was completely committed to defeating the Nazis, of course. But I could also see things in a wider context. There was a growing dissatisfaction in the trade unions among the left of the Communist Party. I was always interested in the realignment of the left. The Communist Party dominated the first ten years of my political life, but by 1979 the CP was rent with divisions. The SWP were hoping to realign the left in Britain. But this didn't happen; we were caught up by Thatcherism, the industrial downturn, and the rise of Bennism. Meanwhile people like Hain had a very clear sense of how the Labour left was going to benefit from the Anti-Nazi League. We had a different conception. Events as it happened worked to support his view.

The problem was not just that the Tory Party had moved right. What worried more people were the signs that Thatcherism had widespread support. In spring 1980 Peter Hain, radicalized by his experiences in the Anti-Nazi League, agreed to chair 'the debate of the decade', a 2,000-strong debate held in Central Hall between the Labour Party and the revolutionary left. Hain's introduction to the published form of the discussion began by contrasting the mood of the late 1960s, when such militant unions as the engineers' AUEW had seemed capable of transforming society, and of the early 1980s, when the left of all descriptions lacked popular appeal. In his words,

> The trade union movement as a whole is in political disarray, unsure of its grass roots base, uncertain about its national direction; the left outside the Labour Party is weaker in terms of its political base; the student movement is passive and middle-of-the-road in its politics; and the Labour Party, whilst moving significantly leftwards, still has not shaken off a dominant right-wing leadership. Above all, socialism patently lacks the appeal and allegiance in the working class which it once had.[14]

Meanwhile, Stuart Hall told the Communist Party's magazine *Marxism Today* that Thatcher represented 'authoritarian populism', 'a weakening of democratic forms and initiatives, but not their suspension'. Hall sought to explain Thatcher's success as a cultural project, using family values and Conservative morality to place its imprint on political, economic and ideological life.[15] If Thatcherism was primarily a form of cultural politics, then it followed that the Tories could best be resisted in the cultural sphere. Hall praised Rock Against Racism in particular as 'one of the timeliest and best constructed of cultural interventions, repaying serious and extended analysis'. So was the alternative to Conservatism a revised Rock Against Racism/Anti-Nazi League alliance, perhaps with the name 'Rock Against the Tories', or some other such title? The idea was tried: by the Campaign for Nuclear Disarmament, by Artists Against Apartheid, and by Billy Bragg and others in Red Wedge.[16]

With the perfect, twenty-twenty vision of hindsight, we can see now that Margaret Thatcher had history on her side. In terms of high politics, 1979 marked something like a counter-revolution. Free-marketers captured Parliament and have held office for the next 18 years and more. The welfare state was attacked, and nationalized industries were privatized. The young activists whose energy had sustained the Anti-Nazi League did not realize just how aggressive the Tories would be. Defeat after defeat sapped the energy of all the protest movements.

John O'Farrell was then a young Labour activist in Exeter. His book *Things Can Only Get Better* captures the feeling that Labour had lost the support of the majority.[17] Labour suffered further catastrophic defeats in the 1983, 1987 and 1992 general elections. If even parliamentary Labour could be smeared as 'loony', the prospects for revolutionaries were still worse. People entered the 1980s full of hope, but watched valuable campaigners go down to defeat, including the coal miners, the hospital workers and those who fought against Section 28. Rock Against the Tories sounds easy to organize, but what happens when every campaign has its own 'Rock Against' and still loses?

The dilemmas of the left are expressed in the title of Dave Widgery's history of Rock Against Racism, *Beating Time*. Written in the dark night of Thatcherism, one purpose of his book was to defend his political moment against the limits of the gloomier present. He was writing in the spirit of rock against the downturn, as the generation that became adults in May 1968 came to face the tougher 1980s.

Yet if all this sounds depressing, we should also remember some of the contradiction of the 1980s. The right won in the sphere of politics and economics, but the left (buoyed up in part by its success with the Anti-Nazi League) prospered in the cultural sphere. While the state became more racist, popular racism actually declined. The first losers were the far right – in the 1979 election.

The Anti-Nazi League saw a brief upturn in activity, as the NF crumbled and its mantle was taken up by the more violent British Movement and John Tyndall's New National Front, which split from the National Front in early 1980[18] and was eventually renamed the British National Party. In retrospect, the radicalization of these fascist parties was actually a sign of their isolation. They moved towards violence precisely because their popular audience had been lost.

More than just a campaign

After the election, both left and right attempted to evaluate the new situation. 'For the rest of 1979', recalls Pete Alexander,

> there was actually very little Nazi activity to be 'anti', though also the big focus for them – and us – of the general election had come and gone. The ANL centre still functioned for a while, mainly I suppose because of the Blair Peach campaign. Sometime in 1979, Paul Holborow, Jerry Fitzpatrick, Mike and Joan, the four ANL full-timers, all moved on. I think we thought of it as a campaign that had come to an end, rather than as something in hibernation.

Jerry Fitzpatrick recalls the period around the election in similar terms:

> The Anti-Nazi League had won. We'd made a major impact. We'd mobilized way beyond anything the left had done in years. The National Front was neutered, demoralized, in retreat. You've also got to understand that the key organizers were in a state of physical exhaustion, it had been the most intense period of our lives, and we were tired. Also with Thatcher coming in, she was a more sophisticated and determined threat. The issues were different now. The plates had moved.

The period after April 1979 saw new challenges for the generation who had established the Anti-Nazi League. The decline of fascism also made it harder to organize the mass confrontations on which the ANL's early vigour had been built. Ronnie remembers the movement slowing down. 'I moved to Runcorn at the end of 1979 and the Anti-Nazi League was winding down then. We had one disco in Netherley which got around 30 people where the previous one that summer had sold 400 tickets. I know this because I wrote them out by hand on pre-cut cardboard.' The anti-racist movement was larger, but also less active. The ANL was compelled to evolve.

Some of the people who had been attracted to anti-fascism began to question whether a different anti-racist strategy would bring more reward. They were not hostile to the Anti-Nazi League; these activists just wanted to broaden out the anti-fascist campaign. In Manchester, Greg 'came to the conclusion that those who saw the fight against fascism as the conclusion were mistaken. I tried to read about the rise of Hitler . . . My conclusion was that we weren't in a parallel situation.' What distinguished 1970s Britain from Weimar Germany?

> The organization of the National Front was not as far advanced as the NSDAP of 1930. The situation of British business (although shaky) was far more secure than the situation of pre-Hitler German industry. The British ruling class had plenty of more obvious strategies still open to it. They could work through the complicity of the trade union leaderships with the Labour government, or there was Thatcher for them to call on. You could have a strong state without fascism.

Greg argued with the Longsight CARF group that they key priority was to fight institutional racism. The group reoriented away from anti-fascism towards anti-deportation campaigns.

This is not to argue that the National Front had entirely gone away. On 29 June 1979, supporters of the NF attacked black and white dancers at a rave at Acklam Hall, Ladbroke Grove, in west London. The young black street-poet Benjamin Zephaniah dedicated his poem, 'Call it What Yu Like', to the young, mainly white members of the Anti-Nazi League who fought off the National Front that day,

> Outside is a shout / De Punks are about
> A shout / Nazis out, Nazis out.
> O Punk, O Punk, de fight nu long
> Yu battle well / Everybody start scatter
> Me an me people jus / Exit.
> De place was as mad as de world / Not good
> We hav fe leave dat scene / Not one police number came.
> O Punk, O Punk, de fight nu long / Yu battle well.

One line from the poem recalls the argument of the last chapter. The fascists attacked and 'Not one police number came'.[19]

December 1979 saw the arrest of anti-fascists at Chapel Market. According to Anna, 'The chief superintendent wanted to put an end to all our protests.' Anti-fascists responded by setting up a Chapel Market 11 defence campaign. Not all officers were as opposed to the anti-fascists. Anna recalls one man, Inspector Barker, watching her sell papers. A small group of fascists set upon them, kicking with steel-capped boots. 'Suddenly Barker leapt out of his car, and chased this fascist down Upper Street. I remember him saying to his colleagues, "We've got a chap in there and he's just attacked that lovely lady from the Anti-Nazi League."' Barker was soon moved on. The second time that there were arrests, the police tried to detain just Anna. 'You could tell they were the Special Patrol Group, they didn't have numbers, just initials on their epaulettes. "You'll have to move," one said, "you're obstructing the highway. Move on, or I'll arrest you." They weren't interested in anyone else.' The scene quickly degenerated from high drama to domestic farce. Anna's daughter and her friend tried to grab hold of her mother's arm, and stop her being arrested. Meanwhile, the contents of Anna's bag were strewn all over the ground. 'I was shouting at him, "Unmesh, whatever you do, pick up my make-up!"'

An anti-National Front protest was also held in Lewisham in April 1980. Christine from Lewisham, by now a member of ALCARAF, wrote up the protest for West Lewisham Labour Party.

> Notice was taken that the Anti-Nazi League was assembling at Lewisham Town Hall at 1 p.m. and it was decided to maximise support by calling ALCARAF supporters to rally in the same area . . . Permission to

use the car park having been refused, the rally was held outside Eros house. Anti-Nazi League demonstrators joined the rally and there were speakers form Lewisham Council and the Trades Council. Hundreds of local men and women, black and white, turned out to demonstrate against the National Front.[20]

An article from the Communist Party newspaper, the *Morning Star*, was gently critical of the way the Anti-Nazi League had developed. Dave Cook complained that 'Despite the significance of its past role, the ANL has tended to become submerged in [the Campaign Against Racist Laws] and the Blair Peach Committee. It [has] only come to life in response to a fascist mobilisation.' What was the alternative? Cook sought 'a perspective to redevelop the ANL, enabling it to play a more general propaganda role, with carnivals and propaganda aimed at particular sections, in addition to its important role as a mobiliser.'[21]

March against the National Front, 1980: Pete Alexander is in the front in dark glasses

Dave Cook was not the only activist thinking along these lines. Sometime in early summer 1980, the Socialist Workers Party's Pete Alexander wrote a letter to his party's central committee criticizing the handling of an anti-racist demonstration in Newham. He argued that some form of anti-fascist organization was still required. Alexander was invited to work full time as an organizer for the Anti-Nazi League.

Soon afterwards, the League was relaunched on a new basis. The focus of opposition was no longer the mass support behind the National Front, but now the more violent ultra-Nazis of the British Movement. This required some change of emphasis.[22] When the NF or the BM attempted to march, there was still a need for mass opposition, and local demonstrations could be built quickly thanks to the large passive support that the ANL enjoyed. However, more of the emphasis had to be placed on smaller numbers of anti-fascists, keeping a permanent watch on the also small numbers of fascists. The hope was now to prevent racist attacks, and this required a new style of organization.

'The British Movement did not have the soft, respectable support,' recalls Pete Alexander, which the National Front had cultivated.

> We were dealing with people who openly acknowledged and were proud of the fact that they were Nazis. It was clear that many of the youth – and actually some of them were just young teenagers – who supported the BM did so on an anti-establishment basis. In this situation we still needed to mobilize against BM marches – it would have been a mistake to give them the space to grow – but we also needed some anti-establishment movement on the left that could appeal to these youth. One thing we did was hold a conference in London, I think it was called Youth against the Nazis,[23] where we tried to provide space to various left organizations.

Socialist Worker editor Chris Bambery records some of the activities that the Anti-Nazi League organized in this period:

> In April 1980 it mobilised against the Nazis on the terraces of West Ham football club. It mobilised two thousand in July against the Nazis in Oxford, and organised a campaign in Harrogate to remove an NF leader, Andrew Brons, from his lecturing post. In August the ANL distributed fifty thousand leaflets in one day after a racist murder in Coventry and finally that same month organised the forty-thousand strong Northern Carnival Against Racism in Leeds. [It was] the 'youngest and most working class' [of all the carnivals] according to *Socialist Worker*.[24]

Not all these events were organized by the Anti-Nazi League office. In Oxford, for example, other networks, including the International Marxist Group and the Workers Socialist League also played a part. Gerry Gable of *Searchlight* describes some of those who took part. 'Students at Ruskin in those days included dockers, miners and steel workers as well as white-collar trades. The Trades Council was full of workers from Cowley . . . they could take on anything and win. The cops did not want the BM in town and gave the anti-fascists a free run at them. They never came back.'

In addition to the demonstrations listed above, the Anti-Nazi League was also active in Brighton and Hove. There were three National Front rallies there at the Level, a piece of ground in the town centre where the left and trade unions had traditionally met, as Tony describes:

> At the first demo, large numbers of people met at the Level while the fascists mobilized and marched from Hove towards Brighton. Those of us

who went up to confront them were outnumbered and there were large numbers of arrests, including myself, as groups of us took them on. On the second march we occupied their meeting place (Norfolk Square) and fooled both the police and the fascists who had an initial pre-meeting on the beach. We gradually drained people from Norfolk Square down to the beach where we confronted them . . . By the time of their third demonstration they had lost all credibility among their own followers and they could only hold a meeting at the Level because the police surrounded it in a ring. When the police lost their bottle, the fascists quickly disbanded.

The strategy behind the relaunch of the Anti-Nazi League was to maintain the large protests (when required), but in the meantime to reduce the permanent organization, which indeed had already been winding down. Key activists were encouraged to turn their organizing energies against Thatcherism instead – as, indeed, many already had. 'After Southall in 1979 and 1980', Jerry Fitzpatrick recalls, 'I was organizing with John Dennis and John Ellis a RAR tour to Belfast and Derry in support of the H Block prisoners who subsequently went on hunger strike for political status. There were priorities for me other than ANL.' Again, in summer 1981, the Anti-Nazi League's Peter Hain was nominated as Labour candidate for Putney.[25] Others from the ANL generation threw themselves headfirst into the campaigns for the steelworkers and then the miners.

One Anti-Nazi League leaflet from this period suggested that the movement should have three immediate goals: first, to bring out anti-racist propaganda; secondly, to expose the links between British and continental fascists; and thirdly, to combat the active ultra-racists of the British Movement, who were winning new recruits among young people. In 1980 and 1981, the ANL continued. The idea was to balance the different needs of the movement. It was a tough hand to play.

In August 1980, the Anti-Nazi League called a demonstration after the National Front attempted to march through Birmingham. The police forced the NF through Nuneaton instead, where they were whistled and jeered.[26]

An international event was organized at the Friends' Meeting House in central London, with speakers including an Italian mayor and a former inmate of a German concentration camp. Another national conference was held in March 1981. Members of the League joined anti-racist marches in Paris. There was a young people's conference, designed to win young working-class kids away from the British Movement, which had some success, mainly in Sheffield. There the ANL organized regular discos in the Bow Centre, a drop-in centre for young unemployed workers. The music played was uncompromising skinhead music, ska and reggae; bands like the Specials and the Beat. Badges were launched, 'Skins hate the NF', and in Luton, Manchester and Cardiff, ANL groups also tried to base themselves on unemployed school leavers.[27]

The Anti-Nazi League's Peter Hain gave an interview to the *New Musical Express* on the reasons for the League's relaunch:

Our success was so great from 1977 to 1979 that it allowed people to feel that the problem had been solved. But none of us had any illusions in the leadership that the problem could be solved on anything but an emergency, short-term basis, and that it would come back in a different form.[28]

The League continued to exist, but the movement had changed. It no longer felt like a huge, vibrant, national network. Instead the movement was experienced as a series of local 'fire-fighting' operations, one-off initiatives responding to specific fascist threats. The Anti-Nazi League responded to a series of racist murders in Coventry by handing out over 50,000 leaflets in the town, over just one weekend in July 1981. The ANL worked with local groups including the West Indian Youth Council, the Indian Workers' Association and local unions. After this massive show of anti-racist feeling, the killings stopped.[29]

A carnival in Leeds was organized with Rock Against Racism. Misty in Roots played and the Specials, Aswad and the Au Pairs.[30] Just 42 people joined a National Front counter-protest.[31] Pete Alexander was the chief steward:

The march was really wonderful, much bigger than the police or I expected. The Nazis were totally outnumbered. It was a long march and as it wound its way through working-class areas it got bigger and bigger. The cops tried to have us moving down one side of the road, but I was able to insist on us taking up the whole road, making it much more powerful. To begin with, when we went past shops, kids would peel off and steal things, so I stopped the march and held a short meeting with the main local stewards to discuss the problem. We agreed that this was our march and we weren't having it spoiled by crime, so after that we sent our stewards, local youth, out to every shop we passed, and there were quite a few of them, and we stopped the pilfering. When I organized this I think I had had Orwell and Barcelona somewhere in my mind. At another point, one of the top cops tried giving an instruction to one of the stewards, so I stopped the march again. This time I explained to the Chief Super, their top guy, that any instructions had to go through me. He could see that, unless he agreed, the march wasn't going anywhere, so he gave in. In the end, this chief cop told me that ours was the biggest march in the history of Leeds, and even thanked us for being so well organised.

The carnival was 'fantastic'. 'The Specials were the main band, and really superb. My last memory of the day was having to jump on the back of a mini-bus containing the band, trying to fend off their many young fans. Later people wanted to touch the hand that had touched the hand of, I suppose, Jerry Dammers.'

In autumn 1981, *Temporary Hoarding* published what was to be its final issue. The reports from local groups insisted that the movement continued, but there were signs in them that the energy was dissipating, or being used elsewhere. Sheffield Rock Against Racism confessed to having 'packed up around the beginning of 1980, partly through exhaustion, partly through the temporary trailing off of activities after Thatcher got in. But also because we were fed up of grovelling to musicians in bands who were only interested in RAR as a way of getting gigs.' Recently, RAR had provided the music float for a Sheffield Skinheads march against police harassment. 'With six to seven hundred kids on the march there were a number of Nazis who would dearly have loved to move in. But with black and white and male and female all marching, and reggae and ska booming over their heads, they had to keep their traps shut.' In Brighton, RAR had joined together with No Nukes Music to set up a group, Revolutions per Minute, raising money for Rock Against Racism, the Campaign for Nuclear Disarmament, the Anti-Nazi League, the Child Poverty Action Group, the Gay Switchboard and the New Cross Defence Fund. Bradford RAR was now one of the older groups, boasting of continuous existence since early 1979. 'Fortunately we have always managed to get a lot of support from the student unions at the university . . . At the moment we're supporting CND's No Nukes Music Tour with the Thompson Twins and a benefit for CND's Easter Trans Pennine March with Crass and Poison Girls.'[32]

The Leeds carnival was Rock Against Racism's farewell party, as Red Saunders recalls. 'There were splits on the committee. There were arguments about money, bidding for grants.' Part of the problem was RAR's very success. 'When we had first started, our first editorial said we wanted crisis music, rebel music. Well, try listening to the Specials' "Ghost Town". There hadn't been music like that, when we started. Black and white musicians simply didn't play together.' The nature of music had changed. The threat of fascism had also receded. 'We were a broad group of people, with a single aim – to stop fascism. When the NF collapsed, we lost the focus of what we were about. RAR was about fighting the NF, and also raising the issue of racism. When we started, there had been no such thing as Two Tone.'

Black anger against police racism, which had risen steadily through the 1970s, finally exploded later in 1981 with the inner-city uprisings, in Brixton, Toxteth and elsewhere. Not that these were only race riots: large numbers of white youth also took part. Socialists, trade unionists and even lesbians and gays gave their solidarity to the rioters.[33] The police were once again on the other side of the barricades. The fighting appealed to exactly the same layer of angry white youngsters that the British Movement was courting. 'In a very practical way,' suggests Pete Alexander, 'the riots showed that if you want to be seriously anti-establishment, you have to be prepared to link up with black kids against the cops, and hence also break with the British Movement.'

The riots in Liverpool broke out on the very same weekend as the Leeds Rock Against Racism carnival, and the mass Anti-Nazi League leafleting in Coventry. The same weekend also saw fighting in Southall, as a group calling itself the 'White Nationalist Crusade' attempted to hold a meeting at the Hamborough Tavern. By the end of the evening, the racists had been forced out of Southall, and the pub set ablaze.[34] The press tried hard to link these events, but for most who took part, the striking fact was the absence of rioting in Leeds, when there was fighting in London, Birmingham, Manchester and Liverpool. It is almost as if the carnival released the tension that might otherwise have been expressed.

Steve from the Manchester Campaign Against Racism and Fascism found himself caught up by accident in the middle of the Liverpool protests. He had been invited by the Isaac Wooton Centre to address a meeting there on the politics of immigration controls. To his consternation, the meeting hall was right in the middle of the protests, and he found himself speaking even as the rioting began. Yet this mixed crowd of black and white leftists seemed keener to wait and hear Steve speak to the end of his talk, than to get involved in the real struggle going on outside the hall.

> At some point in the meeting, there was a large noise outside and various lights. As it continued, there was more and more noise. Something very major was clearly happening outside. I assumed that the meeting was over and we would all go outside. So I started to get up and leave. Someone asked, 'Where are you going?' Before we could join the protests, there had to be a formal vote. Some people actually voted to stay in, most to go outside. I ended up in Toxteth all night – there was no way I could get home.

Steve also recalls the participation of local whites in the fighting. 'I remember middle-aged ladies handing out wet towels for their kids to deal with the smoke. This was a community that hated cops.'

The 1981 riots were rainbow protests, involving both black and white. They carried the legacy of the Anti-Nazi League, expressed in the slogan of the carnivals, 'Black and White, Unite and Fight'.

Squaddism

'By late 1981', Pete Alexander insists, 'it had become pretty clear that the BM threat had passed.' Among most activists there was a strategic consensus that the Anti-Nazi League should be wound down.

> The riots were important, but so too was the fact that everywhere they demonstrated we mobilized in greater numbers. Sometimes you could see kids hovering around deciding whether to join them or us, with the decision having nothing to do with politics and everything to do with who was going to win. Another factor was that a lot of the BM were really lumpen, and I think quite a few were arrested. The reality is that we could respond to BM activities through local or regional mobilizations. The national structure was a conference, occasional meetings of the steering committee, a membership, mailings to the members and secretaries of local ANL branches (this included a free copy of *Searchlight*), the occasional pamphlet, myself and one other person in the office, and

mobilizations that I would push from the centre. I just gradually let things slide. There was no big announcement about the office closing, or the staff declining to just me, or us no longer sending out mailings, and so on. In fact, nominally, the ANL continued to exist and nominally I continued to be its organizer. Letting things run down like this meant the BM couldn't take advantage, and, indeed, if they or some other Nazi group did revive, so could we. It also made it more difficult for those individuals for whom anti-fascist activity had become a way of life, a reason for existence in some cases, to develop an effective campaign against us.

In 1978 and 1979, the Anti-Nazi League had been a mass movement, with widespread support. By 1980, it had become something different, a sort of residual brand around which different people grouped locally, in response to events on the ground. As the membership of the ANL fell, so the character of local activists changed. Whereas, once, they might have been Labour or Liberal voters, young and new to politics, by 1980 or early 1981 these new faces had drifted off, and the gap was most often filled – at a local level – by members of the Socialist Workers Party.

Debates about the how to organize anti-racist work expressed themselves within the Socialist Workers Party. There was a brief, sharp, internal argument. At the end of it, about a dozen people were expelled from the party and similar numbers left with them. The numbers involved were small, but expulsions are a relatively rare event in any left-wing party, and so were widely discussed elsewhere. The issue at stake was the question of how anti-fascist tactics should evolve.

With fascism in retreat, there was some confusion within the anti-racist campaign. A minority of activists seem to have become 'permanent' anti-fascist activists. In Hackney, Manchester, Brighton, Oxford and elsewhere, there were arguments within the anti-Nazi camp as to what tactics were required to protect people from fascist attacks.

The problem was complex. Although the number of active fascists had fallen sharply, the remaining minority were resorting to violence and in certain places were more of a nuisance than ever. The previous National Front goal of building a mass party had been shelved. Local fascists could make up for their political isolation by attacking black people or the left. Even negative publicity ensured that they remained in the press. Through 1981, the fights continued between fascists and anti-fascists around Chapel Market in Islington.[35] In February of that year, Peter Hain's house was firebombed. Week after week, the names and addresses of prominent supporters of the Anti-Nazi League were published in NF papers. It was a clear incitement to violence.[36]

In December 1981, eight anti-fascists from Manchester were jailed for between six and fifteen months, for possession of offensive weapons.[37] By their account, they had gone out to defend left-wing students from a fascist attack. But they took the students' union van without permission. Their actual activities amounted to kidnap, and when they were caught, the sheer stupidity of their plans must have been obvious even to them.

Their supporters within the local SWP district argued that socialists should establish defence units to protect anti-racists from National Front or British Movement thugs. According to Martin, an Anti-Nazi League (but not SWP) activist from Manchester, the so-called 'squaddists' even found some support among groups that had not been involved in earlier campaigns.

What was the League's leadership supposed to do? In the 1970s, the League had grown through mass activity. Its strength was its popular support. The permanent anti-fascist campaigners would not be satisfied as long as one fascist remained alive. The tactics they envisaged were violent and elitist, and threatened to diminish the mass support for anti-fascism that the movement had so far enjoyed.

In the early 1980s, Alan worked as a full-time organizer for the Socialist Workers Party in Manchester and then Liverpool. On one occasion, he was sent as part of a group to attack a National Front organizers' meeting in Blackburn. This was not a positive experience for him. 'There was no discussion. It was not a mass activity. We were a group of about 12 men, beating people up. I didn't like the feel of it. It felt sad and squalid.' Alan believes that the origin of the squad tactic can be traced back to the early 1970s, to the period before the Anti-Nazi League was formed. He argues that, alongside the tactic of mass action, there was also a different tradition within the movement. The physical confrontation of the late 1970s was a collective action. It was very different from the targeted violence of the squaddists: 'The people who come on anti-racism demonstrations are working, they've got families. We can't train people for violence in the way fascists can. Their thugs will always be better than our thugs. By contrast, open organization will always work better.' Alan argues now that the squad culture that took root after 1979 thrived in an atmosphere of drink and sexism, and was incompatible with the socialist and anti-racist goals of the League. 'Horrible things were said by comrades, which I was ashamed of.'

Mark Steel describes going home on the coach after one demo, to find the organizers being condemned for failing to lead the masses into a final physical confrontation with the Front.

> All this was to miss the point of the ANL. The exuberant school kids who distributed the badges, the tenants who formed groups to wash off the graffiti . . . were the real army that defeated fascism in 1979. It should be *celebrated* that most people who attended the counter-demonstrations weren't hardened brawlers and were probably secretly frightened. For it proves that thugs can be beaten by ideas.[38]

Danny from ALARAFCC is another who thinks that a generation of anti-fascists were fighting on the wrong ground: 'These people were of a particular kind – the emphasis was on action not propaganda. But you had to fight on both fronts.'

In north London, Anna felt like a mother to the young lads who wanted to carry on fighting fascism. She couldn't understand the complaints against them from within the movement. 'If you are involved in a movement that engages in conflict with violent opposition, then unfortunately as well as all the good comrades, you will attract people with the excitement of the conflict. For me, it was an ideological battle, but it became a physical conflict for survival.'

Gerry Gable insists that even the squad tactic needs to be placed in context. 'The violence of these anti-fascists was for the most part a punch in the nose or a kick in the balls, whereas the Nazis were into killing or attempted murders.' In Islington, he observes, National Front supporters attacked a left-wing bookshop. 'The manager had two compressed fractures to her skull.' In Birmingham, a man influenced by NF propaganda decided to attack a left-wing bookshop. He stole a car and drove into the shop. In the boot was a woman he had kidnapped earlier. 'The police could not determine if she was dead before the fire or not.'

Another activist, Ronnie from Liverpool, was a member of this unevenly politicized milieu. For his part, he is willing to accept the claim that the priorities of the movement had become distorted.

> The Socialist Workers Party was the first taste of revolutionary politics most of us had experienced and when I joined I was not the finished article. I met people who had lived all their lives in the north end who admitted they had been racist in the past because no black people lived by them, so they grew up not knowing any. As far as being homophobic is concerned, well I was. I had a gay uncle and I used to go for a pint with him and his mates, but I was embarrassed about him until I joined the SWP and saw that, even though I couldn't get my head around it, he and his friends were as good as anyone else and better than most.

John from Manchester recalls that some time around 1979 a squad of people had emerged – not deliberately, but simply because they were the comrades who took the greatest interest in anti-fascist defence. Through 1979–80, these comrades played a useful role, protecting paper sales and other events from fascist attack. Over time and without anyone intending it, though, the squaddists separated themselves from the rest of the party. 'The SWP in South Manchester had lost the plot. I remember one district committee meeting – I turned up and we had the meeting with just two of us, instead of twelve.' Why were the numbers down? 'Because the meeting wasn't about fighting the Nazis.'

'In its essence', argues Pete Alexander, 'squaddism was about squads of anti-fascists – almost always young men – covertly attacking fascists. The main centre of this was in Manchester – from where most of the expellees came – but there was some support in Hatfield and elsewhere.' Why, then, did the tactic emerge? Pete Alexander puts this episode in context:

> The SWP's success in fighting fascism was based on recognizing the importance of two interrelated components: mass mobilization and physical force. The French in general and the Labour and Communist parties in Britain only did the first, whilst the squaddists just did the

second. The lesson that some liberals took from the ANL was that it succeeded because of rock concerts and razzmatazz. Actually, had there not also been Lewisham and many smaller battles, the Anti-Nazi League would not have worked. The problem with the squaddists is that they drew the opposite lesson, not appreciating that fascism is a political as well as a physical force.

Some showdown was inevitable. In many people's minds, the Socialist Workers Party had become the 'beating-up-fascists party'. It continued to have this image, two years after British fascism had gone into sharp decline. The episode needed to be brought to an end. The Anti-Nazi League had moved people in ways that no political movement had in Britain since CND. The people who identified with it, did so with a vengeance. They believed in the League. They wanted the moment of 1977 or 1978 to continue for ever. The squaddists would have continued to argue for militant anti-fascism, even if fascism had been in terminal decline.

NF = No Future

Meanwhile, most anti-racists and anti-fascists were thinking in the opposite direction to the squaddists. Rather than seeking a revived anti-fascism, by 1981 or 1982 most of the activists thought that there was less need for an anti-fascist movement than there had been in 1976 or 1977. Activists from Rock Against Racism and the Anti-Nazi League took up different radical causes, including the Right to Work marches, the Campaign Against Racist Laws, anti-deportation campaigns and the Campaign for Nuclear Disarmament. Steelworkers went on strike, and then there were other battles including print workers and eventually the miners. There was the rise of Tony Benn, which excited many people, and later there was also Livingstone in London and the Militant Tendency in Liverpool. The League's office was never formally closed, although in practice the movement was run down between summer 1981 and the end of the year. The ANL badges were packed away or traded, and the movement entered into people's memory. Many of the best-known RAR bands moved into the more glamorous and rewarding world of chart music. Meanwhile, the more politically active bands tended to remain at the margins. The Conservatives' election victory in 1983 also had its effect, further demoralizing many activists who could see that the moment of the ANL had now passed.

From her vantage point of Chapel Market, Anna could see that the battle had now been won. 'Even the fascists were being exhausted, and turning public opinion against them . . . Committed passionate resistance wore them down. They couldn't best that.'[39] With the National Front dying on its feet and the British Movement also in retreat, there was less need for the Anti-Nazi League. Some time in late 1981,[40] the League went dormant. According to Pete Alexander, 'Very few people wanted to keep the ANL going. Our activity was commensurate with the level of events. We kept up local activities as necessary, and there was no date when the ANL office was officially closed.'

'It's actually much more difficult', Alexander continues, 'to carry this kind of operation than to mobilize for demonstrations etc., which becomes like second nature.' The Anti-Nazi League in its second incarnation may have been less well known than the first, but its work was still valuable. The campaign took seriously the need for a continued organization. The organizers took seriously the need to develop their tactics in opposition to a changing opponent. The National Front was in tatters, but other parties were still there. Indeed, had the ANL not been revived, it is perfectly possible that groups such as the British Movement might have grown.

In December 1982, Peter Hain brought Martin Webster of the National Front to court, alleging libel. 'It's a difficult thing to bring a case like that, as a politician.' Hain was protesting against an NF pamphlet that accused him of advocating violence, when his entire activist career had revolved around the advocacy of non-violent direct action. 'A family friend had been executed in South Africa. Webster was libelling me, as if I had been involved, as if when I was a young schoolboy I had planted bombs. I also wanted to tie him up in time, effort and expense.' After a two-day hearing, Martin Webster was found to have committed libel, and Hain was awarded damages plus £20,000 costs.

Sheffield historian Richard Thurlow has surveyed the membership of the National Front through these years: 'At the time of the 1979 general election membership was around 10,000. With the poor performance in the 1979 general election and the split between Tyndall and Webster, the numbers collapsed . . . After the removal of Webster, membership slumped to reach 3,148 on 1 October 1984 and fell precipitously to just under 1,000 in January 1985.'[41]

An organization that shed nine-tenths of its membership in a little over five years was evidently far less of a threat than it had been. As the National Front's membership continued to decline, so did its vote. Other right-wing parties began to supplant it, yet their growth remained more potential than real. For ten years and more, the NF's enemies – the people of the left, and black Britain – were able to live with that fear removed. The activists of the anti-fascist movement could look back with pleasure on a job well done.

Conclusion

The anti-fascist campaign was the largest mass movement in Britain since the Campaign for Nuclear Disarmament in the 1960s. Between 1977 and 1979, around 9 million Anti-Nazi League leaflets were distributed and 750,000 badges sold. Around 250 ANL branches mobilized some 40,000–50,000 members. On the strength of individual donations, the League raised £600,000 between 1977 and 1980. The ANL conference in June 1978 attracted over 800 delegates. The steering committee raised £70,000 to cover fines and legal expenses for the Southall Defence Fund. Meanwhile, the work of the League was complemented by the activity of Rock Against Racism. In 1978 alone, RAR organized 300 gigs and five carnivals. The following year's Militant Entertainment Tour featured 40 bands at 23 concerts, and covered some 2,000 miles on the road.[1] Probably around half a million people were involved in anti-racist activity, joining demonstrations, handing out leaflets or painting out graffiti.

An extraordinary range of local initiatives took place under a single banner. In Sheffield, one member of the Anti-Nazi League infiltrated the local National Front branch, then left, publishing a pamphlet that revealed the openly Nazi pedigree of local fascists. Meanwhile, 50 Labour parties affiliated to the ANL, along with 30 AUEW branches, 25 trades councils, 13 shop stewards' committees, 11 NUM lodges, and similar numbers of branches from the TGWU, CPSA, TASS, NUJ, NUT and NUPE. By the end of the campaign, even Len Murray, General Secretary of the Trades Union Congress, could be seen addressing anti-fascist rallies in London's Brick Lane.[2]

At the end of this book, it is only right to consider the lessons of this time. Clearly anti-fascism succeeded in mobilizing very many people, but did it *work*? In the years since the Anti-Nazi League existed, different writers have generated very different accounts. Christopher Husbands believes the League spread the 'NF = Nazis' message 'more widely and successfully than almost any other medium could have done'. Dilip Hiro also comments positively on the League: 'the role played by the anti-racist whites, belonging either to the mainstream trade unions or to fringe leftist groups, was crucial'. More critically, another historian, Richard Thurlow, has argued that the Anti-Nazi League was only of secondary importance, and that it was Mrs Thatcher's racism that played the decisive role in the failure of the National Front, bringing lost right-wing voters back to the Tory fold. Roger Griffin likewise argues that fascism has no place in modern society: 'what marginalises fascism . . . is the irreducible pluralism of modern society, and not the strength of liberalism as such, let alone the concerted opposition of anti-fascists.'[3]

There may be a grain truth in the argument that Margaret Thatcher undermined the National Front. In the words of Pete Alexander, 'The Nazis could complain about immigration, but she could stop people coming into the country. They could talk about patriotism, but she could sink the *Belgrano*. They could complain about Communism, but she could break its base in the unions.' The problem comes when people treat this one factor as decisive, placing all emphasis on it, and ignore as a consequence the impact of popular anti-fascism on the NF.

Those who place all emphasis on the Tories' right turn cannot address the evidence that the National Front had grown fastest in earlier periods just as the leaders of the Conservative Party pushed themselves furthest to the right. It was Enoch Powell's infamous 'Rivers of Blood' speech that first dragged the NF into prominence, and it was Conservative and press attacks on the Kenyan and Ugandan Asians that helped the NF to build a mass following in 1968 and 1972. If Thatcherism did hurt the National Front, then it did so only because the far right was already in retreat. It was because NF voters and other supporters already saw their own organization in tatters that they defected to the Conservative in droves.

John from south London describes the process: 'The ANL ended up achieving a split between street fighters and the more respectable racists. It proved that fascism could be confronted on the streets.'[4] It follows that without the League, the National Front's organization would have continued and prospered. The NF would have been larger, and although it might still have gone into some gentler decline in the early 1980s, it would then have found it far easier to revive when circumstances were more favourable. Given a context in which broader economic and political processes helped, the Anti-Nazi League was a major factor in preventing the further growth of fascism.

According to Ian, another active member of the Anti-Nazi League,

> I think the real achievement was that by confronting the National Front we ensured that only their hard-core thugs came out on the demos. The vast mass of their electoral support was quite different – a lot of pensioners, I think. So we prevented them from turning their electoral support into street support, and they began to decline and collapse.

Mark Steel rejects as ludicrous the idea that Thatcher stopped the National Front. 'The argument', he writes, 'is classically British, in that it imagines no political action has an impact outside of parliament':

> Are they saying the millions of leaflets, badges, stickers and placards, the gigs, the carnivals and demonstrations had no effect at all? That disillusioned people considering a vote for the someone appearing to offer something new weren't influenced by the constant reminders that these

people were brutal, violent and fascist? But one speech from Margaret Thatcher and they all changed their mind? What a depressing thought then, if fascist parties return. Because the only way to stop them will be to persuade the leader of the Conservative Party to make a racist speech. Maybe he should chuck a brick through a curry house window. Then the fascists wouldn't stand a chance.[5]

It is possible to investigate the argument that without the Anti-Nazi League, fascism would have grown. One way to test this claim is by comparing late 1970s Britain to early 1980s France. In general terms, the conditions in both countries were similar and broadly advantageous to the far right. In both countries there was an indigenous racist tradition, going back at least to the British Brothers' League in early twentieth-century England, and the Dreyfus Affair in 1890s France. By the period in question, both countries were governed by parties of the left, Callaghan's Labour in Britain, Mitterrand's Socialists in France. Each left government was judged to have failed its supporters, leading to a right-wing backlash. In both cases, parties of the right were willing to flirt with the small fascist groups, both the Conservatives and the Gaullists believing that this process would work in their favour.

Margaret Thatcher's lurch to the right did have the effect of persuading former members of the National Front to side with the Conservatives, either rejoining the her party or at least voting for it in 1979. In France, by contrast, similar calculations had the reverse effect. A right-wing pact in local elections in Drieux was followed by the first Front National breakthrough in the 1984 European elections. Unlike the NF, Le Pen's Front National became a successful and entrenched electoral party with a national profile. What made this breakthrough possible?[6]

The difference between France and Britain cannot be explained in terms of a different national history, or a different conjuncture of favourable circumstances, as these were more similar than opposed. It follows that the explanation can only be found in the different tactics of anti-fascist organizations in France and Britain. This is a point made by two historians of the French far right, Peter Fysh and Jim Wolfreys, who describe the failures of SOS Racisme, the French equivalent of the Anti-Nazi League. Although SOS was at least as successful as anti-fascists in Britain in using music and other media, the organization was far more closely linked to the French Socialist Party. Its organizers, people such as Harlem Desir, spoke of the need to confront fascism on the grounds of French public opinion, precluding physical confrontation:

> The issue of fighting racism is not a left-wing or right-wing issue ... I think the electors of the right-wing democratic and traditional parties cannot accept any kind of alliance between their party and the extremist neo-Nazi ideology. So we are organising a big campaign all over the country. We show that a majority of the French people, left-wing or right-wing, refuse the idea of racist violence, of segregation.[7]

The gap between this formulation and the equivalent pronouncements of Paul Holborow or Peter Hain was small, but telling. The ANL combined a political and a physical strategy; SOS Racisme had only the former. Thus it tended to dissipate rather than strengthen grass-roots anti-racist organization.

What began as a radical movement against fascism became instead a lobbying organization to raise money for local communities. As 'SOS-Racisme . . . evolved into a decentralised lobbying organisation sucked into a role of conflict management', so it turned away from the important task of mobilizing young people against racism, on the streets. At the moment of its breakthrough, the Front National was relieved of the pressure of militant anti-fascism, a pressure that only revived in the mid-1990s.[8] It is striking that the revival of militant anti-fascism in France, following the public sector strikes of 1995, was closely followed by splits in the Front National, from late 1998 onwards. That event would seem to support the argument that mass anti-fascism can work.

The success of Rock Against Racism and the Anti-Nazi League led to the creation of a number of similar alliances, which were explicitly modelled on British anti-fascism and were unlike the later French campaign. In the United States, this movement took the form of a new Rock Against Racism, involving such bands as the Dead Kennedys. The US Rock Against Racism lasted from 1979 to 1987.[9] In Germany, the 1970s witnessed various counterparts of both the ANL and RAR, including 'Rock gegen Rechts'.[10]

Those people who took part in the UK campaign generally remember it as a remarkably successful movement. At a time when politics was moving to the right, when racist ideas were becoming more acceptable, the Anti-Nazi League succeeded in isolating the National Front, the most visible carrier of organized racism in Britain. According to Mike from Preston, the campaign 'played a great part in reducing people's fear of the NF, the ANL made them look very small and insignificant. It also had a big role to play in making racism indefensible, especially to the young.'

Another former activist who speaks fondly of this time is Owen. Having arrived at Salford University in 1976, he describes himself as having been then 'politically right-wing'. But the Anti-Nazi League 'had an impact on me. I was from a white, working-class background, and had never thought about this stuff before.' Owen attended the Manchester carnivals, and having heard Neil Kinnock address the Cardiff carnival ('A young firebrand speaker . . . I wonder what happened to him?'), he moved towards the left. The police attacked him during a demonstration in Longsight. His involvement was 'all pretty low-key stuff', but speaking to him, there is a sense of someone who helped to challenge racism, and helped to advance the values of democracy and equality. He is proud of his contribution to the campaign.

Thinking about the campaign 25 years on, most anti-racists from the time are of the opinion that the League worked. According to Einde,

The ANL and RAR helped to make racism unacceptable in a way that had not been the case. At last an activist campaign said simply racism is unacceptable and fascism of any form is beyond the pale. It was a good feeling for an anti-racist to see all the ANL stickers everywhere. And the badges – this was the great era of badge wearing – gave a sense of identity and strength, because you saw people wearing them all the time.

Ian's account is typical of those who took part:

In the 35 years I've been in the SWP, the ANL period was the one where I am reasonably certain that the party's intervention did have some impact on the course of mainstream politics in this country, by preventing the far right from taking off in a situation that was favourable to them. There have been other times when I have had the sense of being part of a movement that was affecting the course of events – Pentonville Five, Poll Tax – but then the party was merely participating in a broader movement. In the case of the ANL I think our intervention as a party was crucial.

Jerry Fitzpatrick is similarly proud:

The events of 1977 and 1978, Lewisham and the two carnivals, they were a unique coming together of music, rock, culture, a spontaneous burst of energy. It was a political action with passion and vision of its time and place. It was an insurrectionary and revolutionary moment post-1968 if you combine the mass carnivals and the determined resistance to Nazi NF marches. OK, the turbulence was sometimes visceral as well as intellectual and political, but for that moment it demonstrated that the left could organize mass action with the potential to change the world. Of course, I'd say all that, I was one of the organizers. But it wasn't just me or Paul [Holborow]. There was Peter Hain working in ways that are never acknowledged, winning us allies, breaking it away from the usual people. There were the local activists across the country, and people like Mike [working for the ANL]: how many leaflets did he send out, how many hours did he spend stuffing envelopes? There were plenty of individuals who did a huge amount, and it really was one of the most successful moments in the history of the left.

Graeme is positive about the past, but perhaps more pessimistic about the future, given the decline of trade unionism in the 1980s. 'If you were to look today and there was a similar recurrence, we would not be able to mobilize the same forces today. That tradition has been lost.' Mike imagines what Britain could have been like without the anti-fascist movement:

We forget now that in the late 1970s, the National Front was the strongest fascist organization in Europe. The fascists came here from all over Europe to share in that. Everyone who participated in its defeat can feel that they contributed to something. If the movement had not existed, there could have been a right-wing formation playing a central role in British politics, like the Front National in France, or the Freedom Party in Austria. Who knows what it would have been?

Even those who did not support the Anti-Nazi League regard it as an important part of their history. Danny remembers that the ANL won young people away from the politics of the right. 'They made it fashionable to be Anti-Nazi.' David L was then a young Jewish anti-fascist, primarily active in the Campaign Against Racism and Fascism. He thinks that the anti-racism of the League was too narrowly conceived. Yet faced with the argument that Thatcher beat the National Front, David springs to the League's defence. 'I don't buy the argument that Margaret Thatcher pulled the plug on the National Front. People have said that, and belittled the role of the movement. That seems unfair to me.'

A number of the people who now lead Britain's trade unions first cut their teeth as local activists with the Anti-Nazi League. They include Mick Rix, the former General Secretary of ASLEF, who in the late 1970s was a supporter of Rock Against Racism in Leeds. Billy Hayes of the postal workers' union joined the Anti-Nazi League on Merseyside. The first political step taken by Andy Gilchrist, the leader of the Fire Brigades' Union, was going to watch the Clash play at Victoria Park. Geoff Martin of London UNISON was another to follow this route, as was Billy Bragg, the left-wing songwriter: 'The first political thing I ever did was to go the Rock Against Racism concert in Victoria Park.'[11]

One of the most important statements was made at a memorial meeting celebrating the life of Dave Widgery, the East End doctor and Rock Against Racism activist, who died prematurely in 1992. Darcus Howe, the journalist and activist, gave one of the valedictory speeches. 'Howe said that he had fathered five children in Britain. The first four had grown up angry, fighting forever against the racism all around them. The fifth child, he said, had grown up "black and at ease". Darcus attributed her "space" to the Anti-Nazi League in general and to Dave Widgery in particular.'[12]

Another important statement came from an unlikely source. In 1982, as we have seen, Peter Hain brought a libel case against Martin Webster of the National Front. Hain described Webster's court defence:

> He was still extremely bitter and remarkably candid. The picture he gave, and he clearly believed it, was that prior to 1977, the NF were unstoppable and he was well on the way to becoming Prime Minister. Then suddenly the Anti-Nazi League was everywhere and knocking the sheer hell out of them. He said that the sheer presence of the ANL had made it impossible to get NF members on to the streets, had dashed recruitment and cut away at their vote. It wasn't just the physical opposition to the marches, they had lost the propaganda war too.[13]

Understanding the alliances

Why did the campaign work? Several writers have argued that the cultural politics of Rock Against Racism was crucial to the League's success. One clear effect of the Anti-Nazi League was that it established a tradition that anti-fascist work should be exciting, popular, bold and political. Pete Alexander, then an organizer for the League, argues that it was the combination of defensive confrontation with an alternative politics of hope that proved decisive. 'The ANL succeeded because it combined mass propaganda against racism, especially the carnivals organized in conjunction with Rock Against Racism, with militant action on the streets.'

Dave Widgery's *Beating Time* suggests that it was the cultural politics of Rock Against Racism that enabled the Anti-Nazi League to succeed. At different points, his account offers a changed formulation of the balance between music and politics, but at every stage he insists that the cultural was critical to the success of the operation.

> It was a piece of double time, with the musical and the political confrontations on simultaneous but separate tracks and difficult to mix. The music came first and was more exciting. It provided the creative energy and the focus in what became a battle for the soul of young working-class England. But the direct confrontations and the hard-headed political organization which underpinned them were decisive.

According to Widgery, the success of the Anti-Nazi League revealed the potential power of any future radical alliance that could combine music and politics:

> Politics is not just about alliances, but the terms on which they are made. Without the post-electronic, youth-oriented input of RAR, the ANL alliance would have had a lesser impact . . . The lessons lie in the connections and political timing. The ideas, the culture, the ingredients, the potential had all been there but they could only be utilised in a genuine crisis . . . The struggle on the streets could set the tempo and the politicians and celebrities support and generalise but not dictate to it. It demonstrated that an unrespectable but effective unity between groups with wide political differences (the SWP, the organizations of the black communities and the Labour Party) can reach and touch an audience of millions, not by compromise but by an assertive campaign of modern propaganda.

By placing his emphasis on the music as a key to the success of first Rock Against Racism and then the Anti-Nazi League, Widgery raises a number of incidental questions. Could anti-fascism have flourished without punk, or indeed without reggae? Are particular kinds of music particularly relevant for particular social movements? In general, the answer must be no. The meaning of any musical style is set in dialogue with its audience; it is contextual and changes over time. Beethoven's music must have seemed revolutionary in its epoch; it takes context and sympathy – in short, *effort* – to find the same characteristics in it today. Member of the British folk music milieu may have judged Bob Dylan's adoption of the electric guitar a betrayal; few generations since have agreed. The 'anarchism' of the Sex Pistols meant something more in 1977 than it did in 1981 – after Malcolm McLaren and the militant cynicism of *The Great Rock and Roll Swindle.*

Chapter 3 of this book argued that part of the musical success of bands such as the Clash derived from their ability to import the historical crisis around them into their music, through the adoption of more complex musical motifs, including a partial fusion with reggae. There was an intimate relationship between the music of Rock Against Racism and the politics of the Anti-Nazi League. This is a more modest statement than Dave Widgery's suggestion that some such musical synthesis was necessary to make the mass movement possible.

The fact that punk and reggae combined to make Rock Against Racism possible does not mean that either was a necessary component, or that any other popular style was inherently incapable of fulfilling a similar role. Most RAR staples never made it into the top ten, and some of the most important, such as Carol Grimes, barely charted. The New Wave of the 1980s was frequently less strident than punk, but it produced a series of left-wing bands with best-selling singles, and a consistent audience in at least the hundreds of thousands. The most we can say is not that RAR or the Anti-Nazi League needed punk, but that they needed *something* – a culture that was new and dynamic, rather than the repetition of settled styles and established bands.

Beating time, beating on

Does any of this matter? Did the campaign add anything to the experience of the people who lived through it, and after? For most of the 20 years after 1981, fascism was irrelevant to British life. By and large, activists concerned themselves with other tasks – challenging Thatcher, Major and the neo-liberal tendencies of New Labour. In September 1993, the British National Party did win a council seat at Tower Hamlets, but it lost the seat less than 12 months later (admittedly on a higher vote, which rose from 1,480 to 2,041). Only in the present decade, however, has the BNP been able to establish any sort of consistent success. Three fascist councillors were elected in Burnley in May 2002. The number of BNP councillors reached five that winter, 16 following elections in 2003, and 21 by May 2004.

The successful anti-fascist campaign of the late 1970s has lessons evidently for anti-fascists alarmed by the electoral success of the British National Party. But it has lessons also for activists involved in other present-day campaigns. The need for new visual imagery, new organizational forms, is common. So are the demands for practical unity among people of different backgrounds, divided by race or politics. So also is the question of how to organize campaigns when the government is Labour, with all the political contradictions that implies.

When I was finishing this book, one friend suggested to me that the black and white unity of the 1970s had been a necessary precondition for the recent alliances between Muslims and non-Muslims in the movement against the Iraq war. At its best, the Stop the War Coalition has indeed enjoyed a similar organizational breadth to the Anti-Nazi League, and its moments of real cultural innovation, such the toppling of George Bush's statue at the time of his visit in autumn 2003, have had something of the anti-fascist campaign's style, its commitment to street theatre: a common characteristic of both the RAR *and* the ANL leaderships. We might also say that both alliances were conditional, bringing together people with little previous history of alliance (reformist and revolutionary, black and white, Muslims and secular radicals) and threw up all sorts of potential obstacles as well as many potential gains. In that sense, the 1970s provide a stock of experiences on which present-day activists have drawn.

Ultimately, the best test of the anti-fascist movement is the one that it set itself. Rock Against Racism and the Anti-Nazi League both intended to turn back the growth of the National Front. In this, they were remarkably successful. As a by-product of their success, RAR also generated musical styles that had not existed before, while the ANL showed what a mass radical politics could look like. It is their anti-fascist success that should be remembered. In the mid-1970s, British fascism was powerful and growing. The ANL gave the NF a defeat from which its successors have not yet recovered. The rest of us have been left freer to concentrate on the many tasks at hand if the world is ever going to be free of the values of fascism, as well as fascism itself.

Notes

Preface

1. See the Ben Watson, Esther Leslie joint paper at www.militantaesthetix.co.uk/ Punkcomb.html.

2. J. Ashley, 'Give the BNP a platform – and kick it from under them', *Guardian*, 1 May 2002.

3. D. Widgery, *Beating Time: Riot 'n' Race 'n' Rock and Roll* (London: Chatto and Windus, 1986); P. Gilroy, *There Ain't No Black in the Union Jack: The Cultural Politics of Race and Nation* (London: Routledge, 1987), pp. 114–62, 117–18; J. Savage, *England's Dreaming: Sex Pistols and Punk Rock* (London: Faber and Faber, 1991); P. Alexander, *Racism, Resistance and Revolution* (London: Bookmarks, 1987); N. Copsey, *A History of Anti-Fascism in Twentieth Century Britain* (London: Macmillan, 2000); R. Messina, *Race and Party Competition in Britain* (Oxford: Clarendon Press, 1989), pp. 109–25; Revolutionary Communist Group, *The Anti-Nazi League and the Struggle against Racism* (London: Revolutionary Communist Group, 1978); M. Farrar, 'Social movements and the struggle over "race"', in M. J. Todd and G. Taylor (eds), *Democracy and Participation: Popular Protest and New Social Movements* (London: Merlin Press, 2004).

4. Savage, *England's Dreaming*, p. 451.

5. Gilroy, *There Ain't No Black*, pp. 131–4.

6. J. R. Howe, 'Fascism, anti-fascism and Britain in the 1940s', *The Lecturer*, February 2001; also see the reply published, D. Smyth, 'Letters', *The Lecturer*, May 2001.

7. D. Renton, K. Flett and I. Birchall, *The Battle of Wood Green* (London: Haringey Trades Council, 2002); D. Renton, 'Anti-fascism in the northwest 1976–1982', *North West Labour History*, vol. 27 (2002).

Chapter 1   In 1977, I Hope I Go to Heaven

1. For the National Front in the 1970s, see M. Walker, *The National Front* (Glasgow: Fontana, 1977); R. Thurlow, *Fascism in Britain: From Oswald Mosley's Blackshirts to the National Front* (London: I. B. Tauris, 1998), pp. 245–67; M. Billig, *Fascists: A Social Psychological View of the National Front* (London and New York: Harcourt Brace Jovanovich, 1978); D. Edgar, *Racism, Fascism and the Politics of the National Front* (London: Race and Class, 1977).

2. P. Alexander, *Racism, Resistance and Revolution* (London: Bookmarks, 1987).

3. T. Bogues and K. Gordon (eds), *Black Nationalism and Socialism* (London: Flame and Socialist Workers Party, 1979), p. 63.

4. C. L. R. James, *The Black Jacobins: Toussaint l'Ouverture and the San Domingo Revolution* (London: Allison and Busby, 1980).

5. I. Birchall, 'Striking against Suez', *Socialist Review*, November 1986, p. 28.

6. I. Goodyer, 'The cultural politics of Rock Against Racism', MA thesis, Sheffield Hallam (2002), p. 4.

7. Billig, *Fascists*, pp. 268, 272, 277.

8. M. Haynes, 'The long boom and the advance world 1945–1973' in D. Renton and K. Flett (eds), *The Twentieth Century: A Century of Wars and Revolutions* (London: Rivers Oram, 2000), pp. 183-203, 185.

9. See R. Darlington and D. Lyddon, *Glorious Summer: Class Struggle in Britain 1972* (London: Bookmarks, 2000), p. 5.

10. Haynes, 'The long boom', p. 186.

11. See the minutes of the cabinet discussion of 12 July 1966, recorded in the cabinet files in the Public Records Office, CAB 128/41.

12. C. Harman, *The Fire Last Time: 1968 and After* (London: Bookmarks, 1998 edn), p. 263.

13. T. Bunyan, *The Political Police in Britain* (London: Quartet, 1977), p. 267.

14. E. P. Thompson, 'The secret state within the state', *New Statesman*, 10 November 1978.

15. K. Laybourn and D. Murphy, *Under the Red Flag: A History of Communism in Britain* (Sutton: Stroud, 1999), p. 138.

16. N. Harris and J. Palmer (eds), *World Crisis: Essays in Revolutionary Socialism* (London: Hutchinson and Co., 1971), pp. 27, 34.

17. J. Eaden and D. Renton, *The Communist Party of Great Britain since 1920* (London: Palgrave, 2002).

18. F. Lindop, 'Racism and the working class: strikes in support of Enoch Powell in 1968', *Labour History Review*, vol. 66, no. 1 (2001), pp. 79–100.

19. R. Eatwell, 'The extreme right in Britain: the long road to "modernization"'; in R. Eatwell and C. Mudde (eds), *Western Democracies and the New Extreme Right Challenge* (London: Routledge, 2004); D. Cook, 'Exposing the fascists', *Samaj in Babylon*, October–November 1976, p. 8.

20. D. Widgery, *Beating Time: Riot 'n' Race 'n' Rock and Roll* (London: Chatto and Windus, 1986), p. 17; K. Leech, *Struggle in Babylon: Racism in the Cities and Churches of Britain* (London: Sheldon Press, 1988), pp. 84–5; Bethnal Green and Stepney Trades Council, *Blood on the Streets* (London: Bethnal Green and Stepney Trades Council, 1978).

21. J. Fenton, 'An evening with Robert Relf', *New Statesman*, 9 July 1976.

Chapter 2   Race and Racism

1. P. Fryer, *Staying Power: The History of Black People in Britain* (London: Pluto Press, 1984), p. 1.

2. T. Bogues and K. Gordon (eds), *Black Nationalism and Socialism* (London: Flame and Socialist Workers Party, 1979), p. 64; the point has been made again, more recently, in P. Linebaugh and M. Rediker, *The Many Headed Hydra: Sailors, Slaves, Commoners and the Hidden History of the Atlantic* (Boston: Beacon Press, 2000).

3. The classic account is M. Davis, *Late Victorian Holocausts: El Niño Famines and the Making of the Third World* (London: Verso, 2001).

4. R. Brown, 'Racism and immigration controls', *International Socialism*, vol. 68 (1995), pp. 3–36, 11.

5. Fryer, *Staying Power*, pp. 372–3. For black and Asian migration to Britain, see A. Sivanandan, *From Resistance to Rebellion: Asian and Afro-Caribbean Struggles in Britain* (London: Institute of Race Relations, 1986); Campaign

Against Racism and Fascism, *Southall: The Birth of a Black Community* (London: Institute of Race Relations, 1981); J. Solomos, *Race and Racism in Contemporary Britain* (London: Macmillan, 1989); R. Ramdin, *Arising from Bondage: A History of the Indo-Caribbean People* (London: I. B. Tauris, 2000); D. Widgery, *Some Lives! A GP's East End* (London: Sinclair-Stevenson, 1991), pp. 191–201.

6. P. Foot, *Immigration and Race in British Politics* (London: Penguin, 1965), p. 255.

7. N. Todd, 'Black-on-Tyne: the black presence on Tyneside in the 1860s', *North East Labour History Bulletin*, vol. 21 (1987), pp. 17–35, 19.

8. *The Times*, 5 April 1971.

9. P. Gilroy, *There Ain't No Black in the Union Jack: The Cultural Politics of Race and Nation* (London: Routledge, 1987), pp. 114–162, 117–18; the history of these campaigns is recorded in Sivanandan, *From Resistance to Rebellion* and Fryer, *Staying Power*.

10. P. Alexander and A. Jouhl, 'Organising Asian workers', *Socialist Worker Review*, April–May 1981.

11. T. Mehmood, *Hand on the Sun* (Harmondsworth: Penguin, 1983); also T. Mehmood, *Where There is Light* (London: Carcanet, 2003).

12. Race Today, *The Road Make to Walk on Carnival Day* (London: Race Today, 1977), pp. 5–11.

13. 'Sus and Conspiracy', *CARF*, vol. 3, winter 1977–8, pp. 9–10.

14. D. Widgery, *Beating Time: Riot 'n' Race 'n' Rock and Roll* (London: Chatto and Windus, 1986), pp. 30, 36.

15. W. James, 'Reflections on radical history, *Radical History Review*, vol. 79 (2001), pp. 99–102.

16. 'A wave of my own', *New Musical Express*, 21 January 1978.

17. 'Local press and the Labour Party broadcast', *Searchlight*, February 1978.

18. I. Ahmed, 'Racialism and their media', *Samaj in Babylon*, September 1976.

19. *Daily Express*, May 1976; Bethnal Green and Stepney Trades Council, *Blood on the Streets* (London: Bethnal Green and Stepney Trades Council, 1978), pp. 51–2.

20. F. Wheen, 'When self-defence is an offence', *New Statesman*, 20 October 1978.

21. Bethnal Green and Stepney Trades Council, *Blood on the Streets*, p. 8; Fryer, *Staying Power*, p. 396; Institute of Race Relations, *Police Against Black People* (London: IRR, 1979).

22. R. Witte, *Racist Violence and the State* (London: Longman, 1996), p. 53.

23. (Anti-fascist Research Group), *Anti-fascist Bulletin*, no. 4, December 1970–January 1971.

24. Circle for Democratic Studies, *Guide to Extremism in Britain 1973: Extreme Right* (Croydon: Circle for Democratic Studies, 1973), pp. 3–4, 7.

25. C. Sparks, 'Fascism in Britain', 'Fascism and the Working Class, part two: the National Front today', *International Socialism Journal*, no. 3 (1978), pp. 17–38; R. Messina, *Race and Party Competition in Britain* (Oxford: Clarendon Press, 1989), p. 110; M. Harrop, J. England and C. T. Husbands, 'The bases of National Front support', *Political Studies* (1980), vol. 28, no. 2, pp. 272–83, 282; also C. T. Husbands, 'The National Front: a response to crisis?', *New Society*, 15 May 1975; S. Taylor, 'The National Front: backlash or boot boys?', *New Society*, 11 August 1977.

26. R. Thurlow, 'Fascism and Nazism: no Siamese Twins (I)', *Patterns of Prejudice*, vol. 14, no. 1 (1980), pp. 5–15; also R. Thurlow, 'Fascism and Nazism: no Siamese twins (II)', *Patterns of Prejudice*, vol. 14, no. 2 (1980), pp. 15–23.

27. Thurlow, 'No Siamese twins (I)', pp. 5–15, 9.

28. I should say that Richard Thurlow has since revised his views of this time.

29. D. Renton, *Fascism: Theory and Practice* (London: Pluto, 1999), pp. 18–29.

30. *Sunday Telegraph*, 2 October 1977.

31. This encouraged one rank-and-file docker, Brian Nicholson, to write his own critique of the Front: B. Nicholson, *Racialism, Fascism and the Trade Unions* (London: Brian Nicholson, 1974).

32. For Imperial Typewriters, 'The National Front and the trade unions', *Searchlight*, April 1975; and 'Back to work at Imperial', *Race Today*, September 1974. The social origins of the Union Movement, Oswald Mosley's fascist party set up in 1948, are discussed in D. Renton, 'The attempted revival of British fascism: fascism and anti-fascism 1945–51', PhD thesis, Sheffield University (1998), pp. 64–90.

33. *'A Well-Oiled Nazi Machine': An Analysis of the Growth of the Extreme Right in Britain* (Birmingham: A. F. and R. Publications, 1974), p. 15.

34. 'Why I was a racist', in Big Flame, *A Close Look at Fascism and Racism* (Liverpool: Big Flame, 1978), p. 8.

35. R. Tomlinson, *Ricky* (London: Time Warner Books, 2003), pp. 83, 85, 87.

36. This had been an anti-NF slogan in the early 1970s.

37. Rev. T. Holden, *So What Are You Going to Do about the National Front?* (Birmingham: Sidelines, 1978), p. 4.

38. Z. Layton Henry, *The Politics of Race in Britain* (London: George Unwin, 1984), p. 93; Searchlight, *From Ballots to Bombs: The Inside Story of the National Front's Political Soldiers* (London: Searchlight Publishing, 1984), p. 4; S. Taylor, *The National Front in English Politics* (London: Macmillan, 1982), p. 102.

39. For Red Lion Square, see T. Gilbert, *Only One Died* (London: Kay Beauchamp, 1975); also National Union of Students, *The Myth of Red Lion Square* (London: NUS, 1975).

40. C. Rosenberg, 'Labour and the fight against fascism', *International Socialism Journal*, no. 39 (1988), pp. 55–95, 71.

41. 'What their papers say', *Searchlight*, February 1977, September 1977, June 1978.

42. There is a good history of the International Socialists and Socialist Workers Party in I. H. Birchall, *'The Smallest Mass Party in the World': Building the Socialist Workers Party, 1951–1979* (London: Socialist Workers Party, 1981). This history is out of print but a copy can be read on the website of *Revolutionary History*, http://www.revolutionary-history.co.uk.

43. Widgery, *Beating Time*, p. 12.

44. Ibid., p. 27.

45. *Race Today*, November/December 1977.

46. *Race Today*, April/May 1977.

47. *Samaj in Babylon*, September 1976, p. 9.

48. C. Hitchens, 'White socialism', *New Statesman*, 31 May 1974.

49. The history of the 43 Group is discussed in M. Beckman, *The Forty Three Group* (London: Centreprise, 1993 edn); and D. Renton, *Fascism, Anti-Fascism and Britain in the 1940s* (London: Macmillan, 1999).

50. 'Ban on "provocative" marches first aim in anti-racial drive', *The Times*, 8 September 1976; Messina, *Race and Party Competition*, p. 111; News Release, Labour Party Information Department, 14 September 1976.

51. Labour Party, *Statement by the National Executive Council: Response to the National Front* (London: Labour Party, 1978).

52. The history of the Communist Party between 1945 and 1951 is discussed in D. Renton, 'Past its peak', *International Socialism Journal*, no. 77 (1997), pp. 127–39; for the Communist Party at Lewisham, see C. Rosenberg, 'Labour and the fight against fascism', *International Socialism Journal*, no. 39 (1988), pp. 55–92, 75–6; for the party in the 1970s, see D. Renton and J. Eaden, *The Communist Party of Great Britain since 1920* (London: Palgrave, 2002), pp. 143–83.

53. *Samaj in Babylon*, April–May 1977, p. 8.

54. R. Clutterbuck, *Britain in Agony: The Growth of Political Violence* (London: Penguin, 1980), pp. 201–16.

55. 'Police attack anti-racists', *Socialist Worker*, 7 October 1972; *Socialist Worker*, 22 May 1976; M. Cottram, 'Keeping in front of the Front: a few ideas on tactics', *IS Bulletin*, September 1976.

56. 'They shall not pass!', *Socialist Worker*, 24 July 1976.

57. For the anti-racist politics of the IMG, see International Marxist Group, *Fascism: How to Smash it* (London: International Marxist Group, 1974).

Chapter 3   Reggae, Soul, Rock and Roll

1. Clapton is quoted in *Samaj in Babylon*, March 1977, p. 4. For Phillips, see R. Denselow, *When the Music's Over* (London: Faber, 1989), p. 139. I am grateful to Brian Davies for this reference.

2. 'Rock Against Racism', *Socialist Worker*, 2 October 1976.

3. *Temporary Hoarding*, no. 1; D. Widgery, *Beating Time* (London: Chatto and Windus, 1986), pp. 40–53, 40, 43.

4. I. Goodyer, 'The cultural politics of Rock Against Racism', MA thesis, Sheffield Hallam (2002), p. 3. Goodyer reports that Roger Huddle and Red Saunders had already been planning a one-off concert, to be called Rock Against Racism, when the news of Clapton's outburst came through.

5. Goodyer, 'Cultural politics', p. 17.

6. C. Coon, 'Rebels against the system', *Melody Maker*, 7 August 1976.

7. Cited in B. Watson, *Art, Class and Cleavage: Quantumlumcunque Concerning Materialist Esthetix* (London: Quartet Books, 1998), p. 256.

8. G. Marshall, *Spirit of '69: A Skinhead Bible* (Dunoon: S. T. Publishing, 1994 edn), p. 68; J. Burchill and T. Parsons, *'The Boy Looked at Johnny': The Obituary of Rock and Roll* (London: Pluto, 1978).

9. See, for example, Denselow, *When the Music's Over*, p. 145.

10. J. Savage, *England's Dreaming: Sex Pistols and Punk Rock* (London: Faber and Faber, 1991), p. 398; *New Musical Express*, 18 February 1978.

11. Goodyer, 'Cultural politics', p. 18.

12. M. Smith, 'No future in England's dream', *Socialist Review*, June 2002.

13. Marshall, *Spirit of '69*, pp. 73–9; 'High tension', *Socialist Worker*, 11 March 1978.

14. Marshall, *Spirit of '69*, p. 73.

15. J. Hoyland and M. Flood Page, 'You can lead a horse to water', *Socialist Review*, June 1978.

16. M. Steel, *Reasons to be Cheerful* (London: Scribner, 2001), pp. 12–13.

17. J. Cope, *Head-On* (London: HarperCollins, 1999), pp. 28–30.

18. J. Rose, 'Rocking Against Racism', *Socialist Review*, June 1978; A. Xerox (D. Widgery), 'Long time see them a come', *Temporary Hoarding*, no. 9.

19. L. Bradley, *Bass Culture: When Reggae was King* (London: Viking, 2000), p. 472.

20. I. Julien, 'Introduction', in I. Julien and C. McCabe, *Diary of a Young Soul Rebel* (London: British Film Institute), pp. 1–7, 2.

21. C. May, 'Rocking Against Racism', *Black Music*, February 1978.

22. Bradley, *Bass Culture*, p. 452.

23. R. Eddington, *Sent from Coventry: The Chequered Past of Two Tone* (London: Independent Music Press, 2004).

24. For a potted history, see M. Hoover, 'Pop music and the limits of cultural critique: Gang of Four shrinkwraps entertainment', *Popular Music and Society*, autumn 1998.

25. D. Goldstone, *Elvis Costello: A Man out of Time* (London: Sidgwick and Jackson, 1989), p. 19; Savage, *England's Dreaming*, pp. 487–8.

26. Savage, *England's Dreaming*, p. 482.

27. *New Musical Express*, 25 February 1978, 11 March 1978, 8 April 1978.

28. D. Haslam, *Manchester, England: The Story of the Pop Cult City* (London: Fourth Estate, 1999), p. 160.

29. R. Huddle, 'Hard rain', *Socialist Review*, July–August 1978.

30. For some friendly criticism of what you might call folk-song socialism, see I. Birchall, 'Culture', *Young Guard*, September 1963, p. 6; I. Birchall, 'Pop music dialectics', *Young Guard*, April 1965, p. 5; I. Birchall, 'The rhymes they are a-changing', *International Socialism*, vol. 23 (1965), pp. 16–17; also D. Harker, *One for the Money: Politics and Popular Song* (London: Hutchinson, 1980); and D. Harker, *Fakesong: The Manufacture of British 'Folksong', 1700 to the Present Day* (Milton Keynes: Open University Press, 1985).

31. Haslam, *Manchester, England*, p. 105; also see C. P. Lee, 'Ewan MacColl: the people's friend?', in *Northwest Labour History*, vol. 26 (2001), pp. 33–8.

32. For the Communist Party's view, S. Aaronovitch, 'The American threat to British culture', *Arena*, vol. 2, no. 8 (1951), pp. 3–22.

33. The article is quoted in full in the SWP's *International Discussion Bulletin*, no. 5, November 1977.

34. See the comparison between political music of the 1970s and 1980s in S. Frith and J. Street, 'Rock Against Racism and Red Wedge: from music to politics, from politics to music', in R. Garofalo (ed.), *Rockin' the Boat: Mass Music and Mass Movements* (Boston: South End Press), pp. 67–81, 68.

35. Savage, pp. 482–3.

36. Goodyer, 'Cultural politics', p. 8.

37. R. Thurlow, *Fascism in Britain: From Oswald Mosley's Blackshirts to the National Front* (London: I. B. Tauris, 1998), p. 256.

38. Goodyer, 'Cultural politics', p. 15.

39. G. Weightman, 'Flogging anti-racism', *New Society*, 11 May 1978.

40. This section is loosely based on 'Dave Widgery: the poetics of propaganda', in D. Renton, *Dissident Marxism: Past Voices for Present Times* (London: Zed, 2004), pp. 205–34.

41. D. Widgery, *The National Health: A Radical Perspective* (London: Hogarth Press, 1988), pp. xiv, xv, 56.

42. R. Neville, *Hippie Hippie Shake: The Dreams, the Trips, the Trials, the Love-ins, the Screw-ups . . . the Sixties* (London: Bloomsbury, 1996), pp. 173, 271; N. Fountain, *Underground: The London Alternative Press* (London and New York, Comedia, 1988), p. 43; J. Green (ed.), *Days in the Life: Voices from the English Underground 1961–1971* (London: Minerva, 1988), p. 65. For the memories of John Gillatt, a contemporary of Widgery's in Windsor, http://www.gaijin.demon.co.uk/mylife.html.

43. P. Foot, 'Dave Widgery', *New Left Review*, no. 196 (1992), pp. 120–4, 123; B. Light, 'The human face of revolution', *Socialist Review*, November 1992.

Widgery's books include *The Left in Britain* (Harmondsworth: Penguin, 1976); *Health in Danger* (London and Basingstoke: Macmillan, 1979); *Beating Time* (London: Chatto and Windus, 1986); *The National Health: A Radical Perspective* (London: Hogarth Press, 1988); *Preserving Disorder* (London: Pluto, 1989); (with M. Rosen) *The Chatto Book of Dissent* (London: Chatto and Windus, 1991); and *Some Lives* (London: Sinclair-Stevenson, 1991).

44. Frith and Street, 'Rock Against Racism and Red Wedge', p. 76.

45. Widgery, *Beating Time*, p. 43.

46. Goodyer, 'Cultural politics', p. 7.

47. Widgery, *Beating Time*, p. 56.

48. *Rentamob*, issue 1. Another participant in this movement, Sherrl, recalls that 'The Universal Button Co. laughed when I ordered 2,000 Stuff the Jubilee badges in March 1977. They'd just won the order for 250,000 official Jubilee items. By June 1977 they'd stopped laughing. I'd helped organise a mass campaign of badges, posters, Stuff the Jubilee parties and Agit prop events and distributed 40,000 badges from the Outer Hebrides to Kenya!' See http://www.artbites.co.uk/profiles/sherrl.htm.

49. Widgery, 'Rocking Against Racism', in *Preserving Disorder*, pp. 115–21, 116. A similar argument appears in J. Evans (ed.), *The Camerawork Essays: Context and Meaning in Photography* (London: Rivers Oram, 2000).

50. D. Widgery, 'How did Biko die?', *Temporary Hoarding*, 1977, in *Preserving Disorder*, pp. 159–61, 161.

Chapter 4   Lewisham

1. D. Widgery, *Beating Time* (London: Chatto and Windus, 1986), p. 45.

2. These two accounts are taken from D. Renton, K. Flett and I. Birchall, *The Battle of Wood Green* (London: Haringey Trades Council, 2002), pp. 15–17.

3. A. Deason, 'Socialists march where blackshirts ruled', *Socialist Worker*, 7 May 1977.

4. P. Foot, 'Police on racist rampage', *Socialist Worker*, 11 June 1977.

5. 'A mugging – but the police look the other way', *Socialist Worker*, 25 June 1977.

6. J. Adams, 'Behind the "Lewisham 21"', *New Statesman*, 9 September 1977.

7. J. Dromey and G. Taylor, *Grunwick: The Workers' Story* (London: Lawrence and Wishart, 1978).

8. 'An appeal for united left action', *Socialist Worker*, 18 June 1977.

9. *South London Press*, 7 October 1977.

10. D. Peers, 'Poison!', *Socialist Worker*, 9 July 1977.

11. 'Nazis off the streets!', *Socialist Worker*, 13 August 1977.

12. W. Ellsworth-Jones, J. Ball and M. Bilton, '214 seized, 110 hurt in clashes at Front march', *Sunday Times*, 14 August 1977.

13. Widgery, *Beating Time*, pp. 45–7, 45.

14. C. Rosenberg, 'Labour and the fight against fascism', *International Socialism Journal*, no. 39 (1988), pp. 55–94.

15. J. Savage, *England's Dreaming: Sex Pistols and Punk Rock* (London: Faber and Faber, 1991), p. 393; Widgery, *Beating Time*, pp. 45–7.

16. 'The day we stopped the Nazis . . . and the police ran amok', *Socialist Worker*, 20 August 1977.

17. Ellsworth-Jones, Ball and Bilton, '214 seized', 14 August 1977.

18. The story is perhaps apocryphal. The size of the WARF contingent is

certainly exaggerated. The story is accurate, however, in conveying the confidence and the unruliness of the crowd.

19. 'John Tyndall's vision', Camerawork, *Lewisham: What Are You Taking Pictures For?* (London: Half Moon Photography Workshop, 1977), p. 6.

20. Ellsworth-Jones, Ball and Bilton, '214 seized', *Sunday Times*, 14 August 1977.

21. Widgery, *Beating Time*, pp. 45–7, 45; Rosenberg, 'Labour and the fight', pp. 55–92, 75–9.

22. Ellsworth-Jones, Ball and Bilton, '214 seized', *Sunday Times*, 14 August 1977.

23. *Sunday People*, 14 August 1977; *Daily Mail*, 15 August 1977; *Daily Express*, 15 August 1977; *New Statesman and Nation*, 29 September 1978.

24. L. Mackie, 'The real losers in Saturday's battle of Lewisham', *Guardian*, 15 August 1977.

25. C. Bambery, *Killing the Nazi Menace: How to Stop the Fascists* (London: Bookmarks, 1992); p. 33; 'Liberals call for ban on Front marches', *The Times*, 15 August 1977; Rosenberg, 'Labour and the fight' p. 77.

26. D. Thomas, *Johnny Rotten in his Own Words* (London: Omnibus, 1988), p. 22; 'What the Nazis did to our HQ', *Socialist Worker*, 10 September 1977.

27. T. Picton, 'What the papers said', Camerawork, *Lewisham*, p. 7; T. Ali, 'The lessons of Lewisham', *Socialist Challenge*, 1 September 1977.

28. *The Times*, 15 August 1977; A. Callinicos and A. Hatchett, 'In defence of violence', *International Socialism* (1977), pp. 24–8.

29. Savage, *England's Dreaming*, p. 395.

30. 'The Battle of Lewisham', *Socialist Worker*, 20 August 1977.

31. *Morning Star*, 26 August 1977; Rosenberg, 'Labour and the fight', p. 77.

32. *Women's Voice*, September 1978; *CARF*, no. 3, October–November 1977, p. 11.

33. 'Labour hysterical as "Smash the NF" campaign flops', *National Front News*, no. 11, winter 1978; M. Webster, 'Establishment conspirators and Red mobs fail to stop National Front advance', *Spearhead*, September 1977.

34. Widgery, *Beating Time*, p. 49.

35. *CARF*, no. 3, October–November 1977, p. 10.

Chapter 5   Even God has Joined the Anti-Nazi League

1. *CARF*, no. 1, May 1977, p. 4.

2. *CARF*, no. 2, August–September 1977, p. 11, describes members of Haringey SWP selling the paper.

3. D. Widgery, *Beating Time* (London: Chatto and Windus, 1986), p. 50.

4. Ibid., p. 50.

5. In late 2004, Peter Hain was the leader of the House of Commons and a member of Tony Blair's cabinet.

6. *New Society*, 11 May 1978, p. 294; Widgery, *Beating Time*, p. 49.

7. ANL, 'Campaign conference – declaration', press release, 8 July 1978.

8. In 1977, the offer was declined, although Bill Dunn, the London District Industrial Organizer for the Communist Party, did join the ANL steering committee in spring 1978, following the first RAR carnival.

9. Harris may be taken to mean that Kinnock was more interested in securing his own personal association with the ANL, than in doing much to build the campaign. Neil Kinnock became leader of the Labour Party in 1983. Although he had

192 When We Touched the Sky

been associated with the Labour left, in part as a result of involvement in campaigns such as the ANL, Kinnock took Labour to the right, preparing the ground for New Labour in the 1990s.

10. *Guardian*, 11 November 1977.

11. 'Anti-Nazi League', *CARF*, no. 3, October–November 1977, p. 5.

12. ANL, 'Founding statement', leaflet, 1977; for Ernie Robert's support, E. Roberts, *Strike Back* (Orpington: Ernie Roberts, 1994), pp. 251–4.

13. R. Albrecht, 'Symbolkampf in Deutschland 1932. Sergej Tschachotin und der "Symbolkrieg" der drei Pfeile gegen den Nationalsozialismus als Episode im Abwehrkampf der Arbeiterbewegung gegen den Fascismus in Deutschland', *Internationale wissenschaftliche Korrespondenz zur Geschichte der deutschen Arbeiterbewegung*, vol. 22 (1986), pp. 498–533.

14. D. Potter, *Brimstone and Treacle* (London: Eyre Methuen, 1978), p. 33. Many thanks to Ian Birchall for suggesting this reference.

15. 'He taught anti-fascism to anti-racists and anti-racism to anti-fascists', *Searchlight*, July 1981.

16. Anti-Nazi League, *The National Front and the Jews* (London: Anti-Nazi League, 1978); J. Hardy, 'Women and Fascism', *Women's Voice*, August 1978; M. Webster, 'Why I am a Nazi', quoted in *CARF*, no. 3, October–November 1977, p. 4.

17. M. Cottram, 'Keeping in front of the Front: a few ideas on tactics', *IS Bulletin*, September 1976.

18. Anti-Nazi League, *Why You Should Oppose the National Front* (London: Anti-Nazi League, 1978).

19. J. Berry, 'The National Front and . . . football', *Leveller*, March 1978.

20. D. Renton, 'Spurs Against the Nazis', *Fragments*, vol. 2 (2000), pp. 27–30.

21. 'Mitre B are the champs', *Hornsey Journal*, 3 November 1978; 'Spurs spurn Anti-Nazi group', *Weekly Herald*, 16 November 1978.

22. *Socialist Worker*, 16 December 1978; 'Leeds fascists: "violent head cases!"', *ANL Newsletter*, no. 1, spring 1979; '"Big L" hits the wrong target', *Morning Star*, 5 October 1978; C. Nawrat, 'Anti-Nazis cross the great divide', *Morning Star*, 12 May 1979.

23. D. Taylor, 'Anti-Nazi League: perspectives for the coming period (great left headlines we have known, no. 94)', *Leveller*, June 1978.

24. *SKAN*, no. 6, winter 1978, p. 10.

25. B. Pennington, *The Socialist Challenge to Immigration Controls* (London: Socialist Challenge, 1976), p. 3.

26. D. Widgery, 'What is racism?', *Temporary Hoarding*, no. 1; M. Karlin, 'My family suffered from the last upsurge of fascism', *Never Again!* (London: Women Against the Nazis, 1978), pp. 1–2.

27. *Temporary Hoarding*, November–December 1977.

28. *CARF*, no. 4, December 1977–January 1978, p. 11; 'Vegetarians against the Nazis', *ANL Newsletter*, no. 1, spring 1979.

29. *Women's Voice*, September 1977, February 1978, April 1980.

30. *CARF*, no. 2, August–September 1977, p. 10; *CARF*, no. 3, October–November 1977, p. 6; *CARF*, no. 4, p. 15.

31. Later the author of *She Bop: The Definitive History of Women in Rock, Pop, and Soul* (London: Continuum, 1995).

32. 'Against sexism – not sex', *Temporary Hoarding*, summer 1978, 'Bloody furious', *Temporary Hoarding*, March–April 1978; also *Spare Rib*, April 1981; and 'Rock Against Sexism', *Temporary Hoarding*, no. 9.

33. L. Toothpaste, 'Sex vs. fascism', cited in Women and Fascism Study Group, *Breeders for Race* (London: WARF, 1978), pp. 21–2.

34. 'Love sex, hate sexism', *Drastic Measures*, no. 1 (no date).
35. *Drastic Measures*, no. 5, Royal Wedding Special, 1981.
36. J. Watson et al., 'Countering fascism in Bradford', *Peace News*, 20 August 1976.
37. K. Paton, 'How can we relate to it?', *Peace News*, 24 March 1978.
38. G. Jenkins, 'Banning the Nazis or bashing the left?', *Socialist Review*, April–May 1981.
39. W. Frankel, 'How real is the "threat" to Jews in Britain?', *The Times*, 3 November 1978; also D. Leigh, 'Jewish split on NF', *Guardian*, 3 November 1978.
40. 'Out of the gloom and into the summer', *Leveller*, April 1979.
41. 'In defence of the Anti-Nazis', *New Statesman*, 6 October 1978.

Chapter 6   The United Front

1. *Bulldog*, no. 7, May 1978; J. Tomlinson, *Left—Right: The March of Political Extremism in Britain* (London: John Calder, 1981), p. 24.
2. E. Roberts, *Strike Back* (Orpington: Ernie Roberts, 1994), p. 254.
3. The classic statement of the theory is T. Cliff, *State Capitalism in Russia* (London: Bookmarks, several editions).
4. D. Renton, 'Tony Cliff', *Voice of the Turtle* (http://voiceoftheturtle.org), April 2000.
5. T. Cliff, *A World to Win: Memoirs of a Revolutionary* (London: Bookmarks, 2000), p. 124.
6. For the split, Cliff, *A World to Win*, pp. 134–5; also J. Higgins, *More Years for the Locust* (London: IS Group, 1997), pp. 103–33.
7. I. Goodyer, 'The cultural politics of Rock Against Racism', MA thesis, Sheffield Hallam (2002), p. 13.
8. 'Fascism, racism, Mosley, Jordan, no', *Young Guard*, September 1962; 'Fists against Fascists', *International Socialism*, no. 10 (1962), p. 5; 'Notes', *International Socialism*, no. 11 (1962), p. 26; 'The urgent challenge of fascism', leaflet, May 1968, reprinted in D. Widgery, *The Left in Britain 1956–1968* (Harmondsworth: Penguin, 1968), pp. 410–12; I. H. Birchall, *'The Smallest Mass Party in the World': Building the Socialist Workers Party, 1951–1979* (London: Socialist Workers Party, 1981), p. 15; P. Sedgwick, 'The problem of fascism', *International Socialism*, no. 42 (1970), pp. 30–4.
9. For example, N. Fountain, 'The Front', *New Society*, 3 April 1969; C. Hitchens, 'White socialism', *New Statesman*, 31 May 1974; D. Evans, 'News from the Nazi front', *International Socialism*, July–August 1975; J. Fenton, 'An evening with Robert Relf', *New Statesman*, 9 July 1976.
10. 'New Year Horrors list', *Socialist Worker*, 3 January 1976.
11. 'The right to work under attack', *Socialist Worker*, 27 March 1976.
12. Cliff, *A World to Win*, p. 137. The classic account of this movement is J. Reilly, *Anger on the Road, or How the TUC Learned to Hate the Right to Work March* (London: Bookmarks, 1979).
13. 'That's the way to save jobs', *Socialist Worker*, 24 January 1976; 'A flying picket against unemployment', *Socialist Worker*, 6 March 1976.
14. I. Birchall, 'The house of horrors', *Socialist Review*, June 2002.
15. R. Liddle, 'Britain's great divide: London versus the rest', *Guardian*, 5 June 2002.
16. Socialist Workers Party, *The Fight against Fascism and for Socialism* (London: Socialist Workers Party, 1978).
17. D. Widgery, *Beating Time* (London: Chatto and Windus, 1986), p. 112.

18. A. Gibbons, 'Give us an A!', *Socialist Worker*, 15 July 1978.

19. See J. Kelly and M. Metcalf, *The Anti-Nazi League: A Critical Examination* (London: Colin Roach Centre, 1995); also Revolutionary Communist Group, *The Anti-Nazi League and the Struggle against Racism* (London: Revolutionary Communist Group, 1978).

20. This point is made in lively fashion by another ANL veteran, Ian Birchall, in 'Unpopular fronts?', *What Next*, no. 21 (2002), pp. 24–8.

21. Searchlight, *Facing the Threat: Fascism and the Labour Movement* (London and Newcastle: Searchlight and Tyne and Wear Anti-Fascist Association, 1998), p. 32.

22. B. Dunn, 'No to NF, *Morning Star*, 15 November 1978.

23. *SKAN*, summer 1978.

24. The same year also witnessed the launching of a parallel anti-racist organization, All London Teachers Against Racism and Fascism (ALTARF). For their activity, see All London Teachers Against Racism and Fascism, *Challenging Racism* (London: ALTARF, 1978).

25. ANL leaflet, 'NF = No Future for education', undated.

26. *Merseyside Anti-Nazi League Bulletin*, no. 6, November–December 1979.

27. ANL, 'Emergency Appeal', leaflet, spring 1978.

28. See the leaflets produced by national unions, ASTMS, 'Stop racism at work!' (London: Community Relations Group, 1976); General and Municipal Workers' Union, 'Race relations at work' (London: GMWU, 1976?); Trades Union Congress, *Trade Unions and Race Relations* (London: Trades Union Congress, 1977).

29. F. Wheen, 'The National Front's reptilian aspects', *New Statesman*, 22 September 1978.

30. John Rose, *Solidarity Forever: One Hundred Years of King's Cross ASLEF* (London: King's Cross ASLEF, 1986), pp. 49, 73.

31. *Socialist Worker*, 13 May 1978.

32. *ANL News Letter*, February 1979.

33. C. Rosenberg, 'Labour and the fight against fascism', *International Socialism Journal*, no. 39 (1988), pp. 55–92, 77.

34. *Labour Weekly*, 'The fight for our freedoms', no date, January 1978?

35. Copsey, *History of Anti-Fascism*, pp. 148–9.

36. I. Birchall, 'Only rock and roll? A review of Dave Widgery's *Beating Time*', *International Socialism Journal*, no. 33 (1986), pp. 123–33, 126–7; also D. Widgery, '*Beating Time* – a reply to Ian Birchall', *International Socialism Journal*, no. 35 (1987), pp. 148–57.

37. Birchall, 'Only rock and roll?', pp. 126–7.

Chapter 7   Carnival

1. *RARE*, no. 1, 1978; *Tribune*, 22 September 1978, quoted in A. C. Messina, *Race and Party Competition* (Oxford: Clarendon Press, 1989), p. 120.

2. C. Brazier, 'Rock Against Racism', *Melody Maker*, 5 November 1977.

3. D. Widgery, *Beating Time* (London: Chatto and Windus, 1986), p. 85.

4. *Temporary Carnival*, '1950: start here'.

5. *New Musical Express*, 6 May 1978.

6. M. Walker, 'Huge support for rally surprises even Anti-Nazi League chiefs', *Guardian*, 2 May 1978.

7. Widgery, *Beating Time*, p. 86.

8. C. Salewicz, 'Carnival', *New Musical Express*, 6 May 1978.
9. E. Roberts, *Strike Back* (Orpington: Ernie Roberts, 1994), pp. 251–4; G. Weightman, 'Flogging anti-racism', *New Society*, 11 May 1978.
10. R. Samuel, 'Dave Widgery', *History Workshop Journal*, vol. 35 (1993), pp. 283–5, 283; A. Callinicos, 'When the music stops', *Socialist Review*, June 1978.
11. *Northern Hoarding*, 'Straight at the head of the NF'.
12. 'Magic', *Socialist Worker*, 6 May 1978.
13. *Leveller*, June 1978.
14. D. Widgery, R. Gregory, S. Shelton and R. Huddle, 'Look, get it straight', *Socialist Review*, July–August 1978.
15. P. Alexander, *Racism, Resistance and Revolution* (London: Bookmarks, 1987), p. 155; D. Widgery, *Beating Time* (London: Chatto and Windus, 1986), pp. 43, 112.
16. *Socialist Worker Review*, July–August 1986.
17. Race Today, *The Road Make to Walk on Carnival Day* (London: Race Today, 1977).
18. M. Sherwood, *Claudia Jones: A Life in Exile* (London: Lawrence and Wishart, 1999), p. 160.
19. T. Mehmood, *Hand on the Sun* (London: Penguin, 1983), pp. 92, 126.
20. P. Gilroy, *There Ain't No Black in the Union Jack: The Cultural Politics of Race and Nation* (London: Routledge, 1987), pp. 131–4; the origins of Gilroy's argument can be found in Revolutionary Communist Group, *The Struggle against Racism* (London: Revolutionary Communist Group, 1978).
21. P. Alexander and A. Jouhl, 'Organising Asian workers', *Socialist Worker Review*, April–May 1981.
22. M. Jaggi, 'Why Linton is blowing his top', *Guardian*, 26 April 1999.
23. R. Denselow, *When the Music's Over* (London: Faber, 1989), p. 152.
24. Ibid.
25. Ibid., p. 143.
26. Cited in S. Frith and J. Street, 'Rock Against Racism and Red Wedge: from music to politics, from politics to music', in R. Garofalo (ed.), *Rockin' the Boat: Mass Music and Mass Movements* (Boston: South End Press), pp. 67–81, 71.
27. B. Richardson, 'Roots revolutionary', *Socialist Review*, January 2005.
28. Don Letts, *Dread Meets Punk Rockers Uptown* (London: EMI, 2001).
29. 'Developing a nose for "Socialist Workers"; 'Establishment conspirators and Red mobs fail to stop National Front advance', *Spearhead*, September 1977.
30. 'Why the Communists hate the National Front', *Bulldog* 7, May 1978'; 'The carnival is over', *Bulldog*, no. 10, November 1978; A. Birtley, 'How to infiltrate – and learn from – the left', *Spearhead*, November 1978; National Front, *Lifting the Lid Off the 'Anti-Nazi League'* (London: National Front, 1978).
31. 'Reds stage bogus "racist bombings" to get NF banned', *National Front News*, no. 15, winter 1978.
32. '"Anti-Nazi League" crumbles into squabbling farce', *National Front News*, no. 16, spring 1979; *National Front News*, no. 23, June 1980.
33. 'Punk rock supporters join march', *The Times*, 2 May 1978; D. Cook, *A Knife at the Throat of Us All* (London: Communist Party of Great Britain, 1978), p. 20.
34. D. Widgery, 'Who killed Altab Ali?', *CARF*, no. 6, autumn 1978, p. 8.
35. K. Leech, *Brick Lane 1978: The Events and Their Significance* (Birmingham: AFFOR, 1994 edn), p. 9.
36. 'Sit down, stand up!', *Socialist Worker*, 22 July 1978.

37. *NORMANCAR Bulletin*, no. 6, summer 1978.

38. K. Leech, *Struggle in Babylon: Racism in the Cities and Churches of Brit-ain* (London: Sheldon Press, 1988), p. 89.

39. D. Hann and S. Tilzley, *No Retreat: The Secret War Between Britain's Anti-Fascists and Far Right* (Manchester: MILO Books, 2003), p. 34.

40.Widgery, *Beating Time*, p. 94.

41. 'Still united!', *Socialist Worker*, 20 September 1978.

42. Widgery, *Beating Time*, p. 92.

43. T. Benn, *Conflicts of Interest: Diaries 1977–1980* (London: Hutchinson, 1990), p. 345.

44. M. Steel, *Reasons to be Cheerful* (London: Scribner, 2001), p. 15.

Chapter 8   Southall

1. *NORMANCAR Bulletin*, no. 5, spring 1978.

2. K. Leech, *Brick Lane 1978: The Events and Their Significance* (Birming-ham: AFFOR, 1994 edn), p. 88; National Council for Civil Liberties, *Southall 23 April 1979, Report of the Unofficial Committee of Inquiry* (London: NCCL, 1980) p. 190.

3. *State Research Bulletin*, no. 7, August–September 1978, pp. 126–7; *National Front News*, no. 11, December 1997.

4. *Lancashire Evening Post*, 20 September 1977.

5. T. Bogues, K. Gordon and C. L. R. James, *Black Nationalism and Socialism* (London: Flame and the Socialist Workers Party, 1979), p. 71; *Samaj in Babylon*, August–September 1977, p. 12.

6. *NORMANCAR Bulletin*, no. 8, winter 1978–9.

7. A. Jennings, 'Anderton gets machine guns,' *New Manchester Review*, 23 March–6 April 1978, p. 4; 'Anderton: Super Dick', *CARF*, no. 6, autumn 1978, p. 6.

8. 'Manchester: a personal view', *CARF*, no. 3, winter 1977–8, p. 12.

9. See the barely fictionalized description in J. Coe, *The Rotters' Club* (London: Viking, 2001), p. 263.

10. 'Thousands march against the racists', *Socialist Worker*, 19 June 1976.

11. H. Mahamdallie, 'The day the police murdered Blair Peach', *Socialist Worker*, 24 April 1999.

12. Now Labour MP for Ealing Southall.

13. Cited in S. Singh Grewal, 'Capital of the 1970s?', *Socialist History*, no. 23 (2003), p. 21.

14. NCCL, *Southall*, p. 23.

15. SWP, *Southall: The Fight for our Future* (London: SWP, 1979), p. 2.

16. NCCL, *Southall*, p. 32.

17. Grewal, 'Capital of the 1970s?', p. 16.

18. Mahamdallie, 'The day'.

19. NCCL, *Southall*, p. 38.

20. 'Southall 23 April 1979', in *Blair Peach Primary School, Re-naming Cere-mony* (London: Blair Peach School, 1994), p. 37.

21. S. Silver, 'Remember Blair Peach', *Searchlight*, April 1999.

22. Even before Southall, the NCCL had worked to assist the anti-racist move-ment, producing for example a guide to the 1978 Race Relations Act: J. Wright, *Racism: A Threat to Us All* (London: NCCL, 1978).

23. *Women's Voice*, May 1979; National Council for Civil Liberties, *Southall 23 April 1979*, p. 41.

24. P. Dhillon, 'They're killing us in here', in M. Rowe, *Spare Rib Reader* (London: Penguin, 1982), pp. 461–3.

25. N. Copsey, *Anti-Fascism in Britain* (London: Macmillan, 2000), p. 199.

26. NCCL, *Southall*, p. 73.

27. *Peach* v. *Commissioner of Police of the Metropolis* [1986] 2 All ER 129.

28. C. Searle (ed.), *One for Blair: An Anthology of Poems for Young People* (London: Young World Books, 1999), pp. vii–viii.

29. *Guardian*, 24 September 1979.

30. M. Steel, *Reasons to be Cheerful* (London: Scribner, 2001), p. 45.

31. P. Chippindale and A. Ballantyne, 'Teacher dies in Front clashes', *Guardian*, 24 April 1979.

32. *Hereford Evening News*, 24 April 1979; *Oxford Mail*, 24 April 1979; *Swindon Evening Advertiser*, 24 April 1979; *Nottingham Evening Post*, 25 April 1979.

33. *Oldham Evening Chronicle*, 24 April 1979; *Bradford Telegraph and Argus*, 24 April 1979; *Oxford Mail*, 24 April 1979; *Lancashire Evening Post*, 24 April 1979.

34. Campaign Against Racism and Fascism/Southall Rights, *Southall: The Birth of a Black Community* (London: Institute of Race Relations and Southall Rights, 1981), p. 59; Mahamdallie, 'The day'; D. North, 'Blair Peach', *Socialist Worker*, 28 April 1978; Anti-Nazi League, *Who Killed Blair Peach?* (London: Anti-Nazi League, 1979).

35. Campaign Against Racism and Fascism/Southall Rights, *Southall*, pp. 1–3, 56–7; Rock Against Racism, *Southall Kids Are Innocent* (London: RAR, 1979); the RAR leaflet was based on A. Xerox (D. Widgery), 'Long time, see them a come', *Temporary Hoarding*, no. 9; *Daily Telegraph*, 24 April 1979.

36. Grewal, 'Capital of the 1970s?', p. 17.

37. *Guardian*, 14 June 1979; 25 June 1979.

38. P. Foot, 'London diary', *New Statesman*, 1 June 1979.

39. *R.* v *Hammersmith Coroner, ex parte Peach* [1980] 2 All ER 7.

40. The events of the inquest are discussed in D. Ransom, *The Blair Peach Case: Licence to Kill* (London: Friends of Blair Peach, 1980), p. 46.

41. Ransom, *Blair Peach Case*, pp. 62–71.

42. In late 2004, Patricia Hewitt was the Secretary of State for Trade and Industry and a member of Tony Blair's cabinet.

43. NCCL, *Southall*, p. 17.

44. NCCL, *Southall 23 April 1979*, p. 176.

45. 'The cost of the NF', *CARF*, no. 9, spring 1979, p. 2.

Chapter 9 The Anti-Nazi League: Mark Two

1. '"Anti-Nazi League" crumbles into squabbling farce', *National Front News*, no. 16, spring 1979.

2. N. Copsey, *Anti-Fascism in Britain* (London: Macmillan, 2000), p. 134.

3. *Hornsey Journal*, 29 April 1977; *East Ender*, 11 August 1977; *Leicester Mercury*, 29 April 1977; Labour Party, *Statement by the National Executive Council: Response to the National Front* (London: Labour Party, 1978), p. 3; J. Tyndall, *The Eleventh Hour* (London: Albion Press, 1988) p. 230; N. Copsey, *A History of Anti-Fascism in Twentieth Century Britain* (London: Macmillan, 2000).

4. *Martin Guy Webster and Richard Hugh Verrall (On Behalf of Themselves and the National Front)* v. *Newham London Borough Council* 2 All ER 7 [1980].

5. *Verrall* v. *Great Yarmouth Borough Council* [1980] 1 All ER 839.

6. 'Pogo on a Nazi', *Searchlight*, February 1979.

7. D. Brazil, 'Spittin' hate at the future of rock n' roll', *Leveller*, October 1979.

8. 'Ancient history', at http://www.attilathestockbroker.com/ancient.html.

9. Brazil, 'Spittin' hate'; 'Head-banging for Hitler', *Searchlight*, November 1979.

10. C. Sparks, 'Fascism in Britain', 'Fascism and the working class, part two: the National Front today', *International Socialism Journal* 3 (1978), pp. 17–38, 36.

11. *CARF*, no. 5, summer 1978, front cover.

12. M. Barker, *The New Racism* (London: Pluto, 1980).

13. 'I'm not going to work on Maggie's Farm', in D. Widgery, *Preserving Disorder: Selected Essays 1968–1988* (London: Pluto, 1989), pp. 171–6, 172.

14. P. Hain (ed.), *The Crisis and Future of the Left: The Debate of the Decade* (London: Pluto, 1980), p. 7.

15. 'The Great Moving Right Show' (1978), reprinted in S. Hall, *The Hard Road to Renewal: Thatcherism and the Crisis of the Left* (London: Verso, 1988), pp. 39–56, 40, 42.

16. R. Eddington, *Sent from Coventry: The Chequered Past of Two Tone* (London: Independent Music Press, 2004).

17. J. O'Farrell, *Things Can Only Get Better: Eighteen Miserable Years in the Life of a Labour Supporter* (London: Black Swan, 1998), p. 127.

18. 'NF split: support for opposition grows as Tyndall quits', *Searchlight*, no. 56, February 1980.

19. B. Zephaniah, *City Psalms* (London: Bloodaxe Books, 1992), pp. 41–3.

20. ALCARAF report, West Lewisham Labour Party, 24 April 1980.

21. *Morning Star*, 31 July 1980.

22. The shift was more evident on the streets than in the leaflets. A gloriously crude anti-BM leaflet from the early 1980s portrayed a happy punk with mohican and placard, saying 'No Nazis in South London'. See ANL, 'Why we should smash the Bowel Movement . . . Because you get nothing but shit from them!', leaflet, 1980.

23. 'Anti-Nazi youth get together to fight back', *Socialist Worker*, 7 March 1981.

24. C. Bambery, 'Euro-fascism: the lessons of the past and current tasks', *International Socialism Journal*, no. 60 (1993), pp. 3–77, 67.

25. Hain would be elected as the MP for Neath in 1991.

26. S. McGregor, 'Nazis are humiliated by ANL, *Socialist Worker*, 23 August 1980.

27. *Red Rebel*, summer 1981.

28. 'An interview with Peter Hain', *New Musical Express*, 7 March 1981.

29. 'Coventry fights back', *Socialist Worker*, 27 June 1981; 'We won't be kept down', *Socialist Worker*, 11 July 1981.

30. 'Northern carnival for Leeds', *Socialist Worker*, 30 May 1981.

31. R. Denselow, *When the Music's Over* (London: Faber, 1989), p. 152.

32. 'RAR news', *Temporary Hoarding*, August 1981.

33. 'The truth about Brixton', *Socialist Worker*, 18 April 1981.

34. 'Riot storm shakes Tories', *Socialist Worker*, 11 July 1981.

35. 'The Battle for Chapel Market', *Fighting Talk*, no. 19 (1998), pp. 20–1.

36. M. Walker, 'Hain's home hit as National Front targets "enemies"', *Guardian*, 28 February 1981.

37. This incident is discussed, from the perspective of the defendants, in D. Hann and S. Tilzley, *No Retreat: The Secret War Between Britain's Anti-Fascists and Far Right* (Manchester: MILO Books, 2003), pp. 80–90.

38. M. Steel, *Reasons to be Cheerful* (London: Scribner, 2001), pp. 41–2.

39. The Leeds carnival is described in 'The cathedral', *Temporary Hoarding*, no. 20.

40. Prior to 1982, *Socialist Worker* carried a regular listing of anti-racist events. After 1982, such events continued to be advertised, but on a much more ad hoc basis. The last Anti-Nazi League event to be advertised in *Socialist Worker* was a day of action in south London on 18 November 1981, although Rock Against Racism events continued to be advertised for several months afterwards. 'What's on', *Socialist Worker*, 14 November 1981.

41. R. Thurlow, *Fascism in Britain: A History 1918–1985* (London: Basil Blackwell, 1987), p. 290.

Conclusion

1. I. Goodyer, 'The cultural politics of Rock Against Racism', MA thesis, Sheffield Hallam (2002), p. 3.

2. A. M. Messina, *Race and Party Competition in Britain* (Oxford: Clarendon Press, 1989), p. 118. C. Rosenberg, 'Labour and the fight against fascism', *International Socialism Journal*, no. 39 (1988), pp. 55–92, 81; D. Field, 'Flushing out the Front', *Socialist Review*, May 1978; E. Roberts, *Strike Back* (Orpington: Ernie Roberts, 1994), p. 252; Anti-Nazi League, *Inside the National Front: Sheffield's Nazis Uncovered* (Sheffield: Sheffield ANL, 1979); B. Dunn, 'No to NF', *Morning Star*, 15 November 1978.

3. C. T. Husbands, *Racial Exclusionism and the City* (London: Allen and Unwin, 1983), p. 273; P. Wilkinson, *The New Fascists* (London: Grant McIntyre, 1981), pp. 169–70; D. Hiro, *Black Britain, White Britain: A History of Race Relations in Britain* (London: Paladin, 1970), p. 171; R. Thurlow, *Fascism in Britain: From Oswald Mosley's Blackshirts to the National Front* (London: I. B. Tauris, 1998), pp. 255–7; R. Griffin, 'British fascism: the ugly duckling', in M. Cronin (ed.), *The Failure of British Fascism* (Basingstoke: Macmillan, 1996), p. 162; N. Copsey, *Anti-Fascism in Britain* (Basingstoke: Macmillan, 1996), p. 3.

4. A. Callinicos, 'Making racism respectable', *Socialist Review*, May 1978.

5. M. Steel, *Reasons to be Cheerful* (London: Scribner, 2001), p. 47.

6. The 1984 breakthrough is discussed in D. Renton, *Fascism: Theory and Practice* (London: Pluto, 1999).

7. Rosenberg, 'Labour', p. 87.

8. P. Fysh and J. Wolfreys, *The Politics of Racism in France* (Basingstoke: Macmillan, 1998), pp. 163–9.

9. Its papers have been deposited at the University of Massachusetts in Boston.

10. A. Beck, 'Wie die NPD Ende der 70er Jahre geschlagen wurde'; http://www.sozialismus-von-unten.de/archiv/svu6/rockgegenrechts.htm.

11. 'From Rock against Racism to the corridors of power', *Red Pepper*, August 2004; *Rock Against Racism*, no. 1, winter 2004; 'Punk pioneer mourned', *Mirror*, 24 December 2002.

12. P. Foot, 'Dave Widgery', *New Left Review*, no. 196 (1992), pp. 120–4, 122.

13. Rosenberg, 'Labour', p. 83; D. Widgery, *Beating Time* (London: Chatto and Windus, 1986), p. 111.

Index

History and politics from New Clarion Press

'A PLEASANT CHANGE FROM POLITICS'

MUSIC AND THE BRITISH LABOUR MOVEMENT BETWEEN THE WARS

Duncan Hall

'This is an excellent book from a relatively new publisher, which is itself a workers' co-operative. Many such co-operatives have failed in the past. If New Clarion Press continues to produce books of this quality, then it will deserve not to follow them.' *Contemporary British History*

'an evidently well-researched book . . . most likely to be fascinating to those who are drawn to the linkages between music and politics' *British Music Society Newsletter*

'a thoughtful and well-researched history of a fascinating byway in British musical history' *BBC Music Magazine*

ISBN   187379729X   paperback   £12.95
         1873797303   hardback   £25.00   Published 2001

GENETIC POLITICS

FROM EUGENICS TO GENOME

Anne Kerr and Tom Shakespeare

'a thought-provoking book, laden with information and detailed historical records' *Times Higher Education Supplement*

'a very welcome and timely analysis of "the new genetics" from a disability rights perspective . . . an important text, offering a well-argued and reasoned analysis of current genetic policy' *Disability and Society*

'a superb, historically rooted narrative . . . highly readable' *Health, Risk and Society*

ISBN   1873797257   paperback   £12.95   Published 2002